ACTING EMOTIONS

Acting Emotions
Shaping Emotions on Stage

ELLY A. KONIJN

TRANSLATED BY BARBARA LEACH WITH DAVID CHAMBERS

AMSTERDAM UNIVERSITY PRESS

Original title: *Acteren en Emoties* (Amsterdam/Meppel, Boom, 1997)

The translation of this book from Dutch into English has been made possible by a grant from the Netherlands Organization for Scientific Research (NWO).

Cover illustration: *Bakchanten* (Euripides), directed by Jürgen Gosch,Toneelgroep Amsterdam 1999.
Photo: Serge Ligtenberg
Cover design: Crasborn Grafisch Ontwerpers bno, Valkenburg aan de Geul
Lay-out: Magenta, Amsterdam

ISBN 90 5356 444 6

Contents

Acting Emotions - An American Context

Fog banks of sanctimonious mystification, pyscho-jargon, and charlatanism obscure the craft of acting in both Europe and the US. With *Acting Emotions*, Dr. Elly Konijn, once an actress-in-training, now a research psychologist, intends to burn off the mysteries, misapprehensions, and pseudo-theories that obfuscate the actor's art. Her focus, from a cognitive scientist's viewpoint, is on Diderot's 'actor's paradox': Should the emotions of the actor coincide with the emotions of the character, or should they not? More fundamentally, can they coincide? If not, what then? Currently in its second Dutch printing, *Acting Emotions* brings welcome lucidity, exhaustive research, and a structural paradigm to these and other questions about an art that has been analyzed, for the most part, by self-aggrandizing anecdote (cf. *Actors on Acting*, *The Actor Speaks*, etc.).

This English-language edition of *Acting Emotions* contains previously unpublished on-site research undertaken in the United States, including investigations deep inside the jaws of the lion: The Actor's Studio. While Dr. Konijn's investigations are by no means limited to practitioners of Stanislavskian acting principles, it is inside Stanislavsky's 'system' and later Strasberg's 'Method' that the model of the actor's real and the character's supposed emotions dynamically coinciding is idealized. In mainstream American acting, the enmeshing of actor and character into a unified emotional complex is the primary – all too often the only – goal. It is the extraordinary achievement of Dr. Konijn to prove that for the actor onstage in front of an audience, no such thing as 'character empathy' occurs – many other things *do* occur, but not that. A near-century of misconceptions about acting and associated bad training techniques is here rectified. The foundation for a much-needed new theory of acting is here laid.

But why is a new perspective on acting necessary? Because in America, acting is the only artistic undertaking that has not experienced generational renaissance during the past century. Music, dance, poetry, painting – any art popularly practiced in the US in modern times – has undergone frequent aesthetic renewal, even revolution. Except acting. Acting in America looks pretty much the same as it did in the mid-1930's – no other American artistic practice has remained so pridefully resistant to change. In its inherent conservatism, American acting has held captive much of playwrighting, stage directing, film and television, and the ever-aging, diminishing audiences at live theaters. The talon-like grip of emotionally 'realistic' acting on the American theater (and cinema) urgently needs prying loose.

Some history. As imperiously as Freud, Darwin, Marx, or Mendel stand in their respective fields, Konstantin Stanislavsky looms as the towering progenitor of his. In common with these aforementioned brethren, Stanislavsky's theories grew out of the liberal humanist, rationalist intellectual culture of Europe in the nineteenth and early twentieth centuries. Seeking 'a science of acting' based on 'inner truth,' Stanislavsky set off on a lifetime of evolutionary theorizing and attendant experiments. While his sole objective of seeking 'truth on stage' never varied, Stanislavsky made numerous tactical adjustments in technique as he obsessively pursued his elusive goal. Ultimately he gave up directing plays altogether; his rehearsals became a pretext for exploring the actor's quest for emotional truth. By his final years, as he developed his 'method of physical actions' (1936-38), Stanislavsky was blithely renouncing his former experiments with affective recollection.

But it was indeed his early work, particularly that involving 'emotion memory' that grafted so tenaciously in the United States. The first of Stanislavsky's disciples to arrive in the US, Richard Boleslavsky, emigrated to New York in 1922, saturated in the intensive work on emotional recall that The Master was later to reject and abandon. The following year, the Moscow Art Theater itself arrived in America for a nation-wide barnstorm lasting several months. The repertoire consisted of twenty year-old, emotion-laden productions of Chekov's *The Three Sisters* and *The Cherry Orchard*, followed by Gorky's *The Lower Depths*. In 1924, Stanislavsky's rambling autobiography *My Life in Art* was published in the US; the book is overburdened with the author's self-excoriation for his inability to consistently capture and bottle the elusive vapors of emotional truth onstage.

Cultural temperament played a major role in America's impassioned embrace of these Russian experiments. Stanislavsky's system, in whatever variant (and despite its constant call for collaboration), is finally resolutely focused on *the* American topic: The individual and his/her autonomous will. Moreover, underlying the system and its presumed 'universality' is the premise of democratic essentialism: Yeoman or aristocrat, immigrant or gentry, pale or dark we are all composed of the same immaterial essences, spiritual and emotional. In short, the American narrative of autonomous individualists pressing ever forward in a classless humanist society is reinforced. The added fact that much of Stanislavsky's vocabulary included pseudo-sacred nomenclature such as 'communion' and 'spiritual' helped to sanctify the system in America.

Sitting in Boleslavsky's classes, studying vintage Stanislavsky tenets such as 'inner concentration' and 'memory of emotion,' were Stella Adler, Harold Clurman, and Lee Strasberg, the three prime founders of The Group Theater which self-consciously modeled itself on The Moscow Art Theater. From the outset, Strasberg served as both instructor of acting and principal director of The Group. In both pursuits his singular focus was on 'true emotion': The generation of 'real' (i.e., authentic and personalized) emotions. Once he/she is internally aroused, the actor must passionately 'live through' those emotions that are imagined to be experienced by the character being portrayed. In 1934, Stella Adler returned from a month of intensive meetings with Stanislavsky in Paris. She bore news that The Group was misusing affective memory exercises by overemphasizing personalized emotional circumstances. Strasberg trumped her in a full-company meeting by intimating that, for the American actor, what he – Strasberg – had to teach was preferable to whatever Stanislavsky might now be espousing.

The Group was soon to conflagrate over the Adler/Strasberg clash and other incendiary artistic issues. Many phoenixes – institutions and personal careers – arose from the ashes. The most spectacular and influential of these was Strasberg's Actor's Studio, where his fierce personality and zealous advocacy of personalized emotional memory forged something between an acting technique and a cult of celebrity. A generation of exceptionally talented, libidinal, idiosyncratic actors – Paul Newman, James Dean, Marlon Brando, Joanne Woodward, Geraldine Page, Kim Stanley, to name but a few – passed through The Studio and soon became the stars of their day. Suddenly Method Acting (always capitalized in Studio literature) *was* acting. Everything else was inauthentic and superficial.

But whatever the successes of Strasberg's celebrated pupils, their triumphs were mostly in film, a visual medium where quirky, charismatic personality, short sustained bursts of emotion, inward focus, and no small measure of sexuality play best. Conversely, Strasberg's profoundly misguided and astonishingly self-serving plundering of Stanislavsky's experiments has probably done more damage to the American theater than any other single factor including the arrival of television, censorship, or inflated ticket prices. A narrowly-focused, narcissistic style of acting, all built around 'emotional truth,' has dominated American stages since the 1950's. Privileging inner life over outer form, psychoanalysis over textual analysis, infantile self-absorption over mature observation of human nature and society, the Method has at its hollow core the essentially conundrumic supposition that an actor can form an empathetic, affective transference with a set of glyphs on paper called a character.

We are now several artistic generations past the heyday of the Studio and the Method. In that time, an extraordinary American avant-garde theater movement, born in great measure as a refutation of Studio ideology, has had international impact. Numerous university conservatories have added rigorous physical and vocal training to their acting curriculums. Intercultural theater has increasingly brought non-representational acting strategies onstage. Nonetheless much American theater training retains a dogma of hydraulic causality: Emotion creates action, action creates character, and character creates theater. Ergo, personalized emotional truth remains the inner Holy Grail for the American actor.

However, there is a dirty little secret of the mainstream American acting profession: Even the most talented actors will admit that the kind of emotional coincidence with their characters that they have been taught is the essence of acting never actually happens to them onstage. Emotional things happen, yes. But not emotional identification with character. At least not in performance – briefly in rehearsal, maybe – but not live in front of an audience.

This revelation raises at least four questions:

1. Why is the actor in performance *not* experiencing inner emotional alignments with the character being portrayed?

2. If not character empathy, what actually *is* the actor experiencing?

3. How does what the actor actually experiences convert to performance energy?

4. In the best of cases (e.g., a good performance), how does the actor beguile the audience into a belief that the he/she is truly 'feeling' his/her character?

These are the questions Dr. Konijn has pursued so vigorously and thoroughly. Her research spans years of comprehensive investigations. Using advanced cognitive science techniques, Dr. Konijn developed an intricate survey for actors that posed fundamental questions in numerous disguised elaborations – ultimately the subject's true response to a situation was teased out. The resulting data, be it European or American, overwhelmingly affirmed the abundant presence what Dr. Konijn's classifies as 'task emotions' (emotions related to the 'doing' of acting), and a complete absence of so-called character identification. Fully replacing presumed *character-emotions*, Dr. Konijn identifies equally powerful and authentic *actor-emotions* related to challenge ('positive stress') and the gratification of task-fulfillment. For further validation of her discoveries, Dr. Konijn 'wired' certain actors during performance, including one Dutch actress portraying a metabolically introspective, melancholic character. The result?

> During [her] monologues the heart rate reached extremes of 180 beats per minute. By comparison, a person at rest has an average pulse of 60 beats per minute and a parachute jumper's pulse reaches 140 beats per minute just prior to jumping.

Clearly something other than character identification was occurring for this actress. We are challenged to speculate that the inner life of the onstage actor may be far more allied to bungee-jumping than it is to Stanislavskian character identification.

In *Acting Emotions* we are regularly provoked by such propositions. I expect this book will arouse profound admiration in some quarters, sighs of relief in others, and offended ire elsewhere. It will certainly disturb some far-too-long-held shibboleths about the actor's art. Good. If nothing else, *Acting Emotions* will liberate innumerable actors from the self-punishing sense of 'I must be doing something wrong.' Good again. But, it is even possible that *Acting Emotions* can play a major role in re-vitalizing what has become, for the most part, a deadly art form – the American theater. Let us hope.

Whatever the reactions, whatever the utilitarian consequences, *Acting Emotions* can only help to stimulate a sorely needed conversation in the American theater. We are the beneficiaries of Dr. Elly Konijn's bold and scientific probing into this most public, but profoundly under-examined, area: The onstage life of the actor.

David Chambers
Professor of Acting and Directing
Yale School of Drama

1   Acting Emotions: Introduction

I will be brief.
Do you believe that there is any controversial issue, given equally strong
arguments for and against, which remains unresolved?
DENIS DIDEROT (1980: 45)

1.1   Introduction: Does Dustin Really Cry? What About Meryl?

For centuries actors have tried to make their characters as believable as possible, indeed so convincing that the audience no longer sees the actor, but *believes* that the actor
is the character. In the theater and related studies, how best to achieve this goal has
long been the subject of intense debate. The central question in the controversy is the
relationship between the emotions of the character with those of the actor. Should
these coincide or should they not? The portrayal of emotions is a critical component of
acting, and also seems to be one of the most difficult and complex tasks of the actor. In
ancient Greek texts we read how the actors struggled with the problem of making their
characters seem as real as possible. The renowned Greek actor Polus carried an urn
containing his own son's ashes on stage with him to insure 'real' despair. How does
the actress make the audience believe she is Medea, murderer of her three children?
Should the actor attempt to arouse similar feelings in him- or herself or is it better to
leave that to the audience? Again in ancient texts we read that one audience was so subsumed by the drama that after the performance they lay in wait for the 'villain' to teach
him a lesson. Plutarch (46-120 A.D.) asks himself why we become agitated when we
hear voices which are authentically furious, gloomy or afraid, whereas we are enrap-
tured when we hear actors imitate those same emotions.

At the end of the eighteenth century the French philosopher Denis Diderot wrote
Paradoxe sur le Comédien. Diderot takes an extreme stance in the solution of the actors'
dilemma, claiming that a great actor should feel nothing at all during his performance,
and only then is he or she able to elicit the strongest emotions from the audience.
Diderot put the relationship between the quality of acting and the actor's emotional
sensitivity in these terms: 'Extreme sensitivity makes actors mediocre; average sensitivity makes masses of actors bad; an absolute lack of feeling is the basis for those who
reach the highest level.'[1] Becoming emotional or being moved by a performance appears to be one of the most important criteria an audience uses to gauge a performance; whether or not the actor him- or herself must become emotional is the point of
contention. This debate has continued since the *Paradoxe* appeared: Over time new
voices have joined in on the issue known as 'the emotional paradox'. At the end of the
nineteenth century, Constant Coquelin stood as a staunch defender of Diderot against
the fervent emotionalist William Archer. In our century, Konstantin Stanislavsky

and Bertolt Brecht take diametrically opposed views on the subject of the emotions of actor and character. Indeed, contemporary discussions about acting are consistently related to the paradox. It is therefore the starting point for the dissertation on acting in this book.

Such conflicting statements made today indicate that the problem Diderot posed two centuries ago remains relevant. Contemporary theater reviews, among other sources, make this clear. They contain vivid examples of the dilemma which actors still confront in their profession. Is sensitivity incompatible with great acting as the quotes (in the boxes) would suggest and as Diderot proposes in *Paradoxe sur le Comédien*? Must an actor keep a cool head while the audience expects larger-than-life emotions from him? Are actors too involved in 'managing' their performance to actually be 'deeply touched'? Can actors feel emotions and act them at the same time; can emotion converge with reason? Is this a matter of mystery or the key component of 'trade secrets'? Discussions about the relationship of the emotions of the actor with those of the character go to the heart of the art of acting. They are the subject of this book.

Acting Emotions will set out a theoretical analysis of how emotions are performed and examine this theory in practice. Using a present-day analytical approach I will try to unravel the paradox. Opinions drawn from current acting theories will be combined with contemporary viewpoints about emotions drawn from the field of psychology. This synthetic approach, rarely employed until now, provides new insight into the nature and design of emotions on stage. I questioned about three hundred professional actors and actresses in the Netherlands, Flanders (the Dutch speaking portion of Belgium), and the United States about how they shape their characters. Their answers form the basis for examining assumptions that are derived from acting theory. They show how practicing actors 'get into' their characters.

1.2   Editing *Acting Emotions*

The content of this book *Acting Emotions* is a translation of *Acteren en Emoties* (1997), which was largely based on the first Dutch edition *Acteurs Spelen Emoties* by Elly Konijn, published in 1994. The Netherlands Public Broadcasting based a 55-minute documentary with the same title on this publication (directed by Krijn ter Braak, NPS, August 1995). The second book *Acteren en Emoties* (1997) was written (when the first book sold out) because there was interest in a version using less scholarly language, and because the first book was based solely on the results of a survey among Dutch actors. The most important differences between the first and second book are as follows:

Acting Emotions includes the results of a survey of numerous professional actors in the United States. A central idea developed in the first Dutch edition – task-emotion theory – was developed to a great extent by the results of a survey of Dutch and Flemish actors and actresses. Because acting training in the Netherlands differs greatly from that in the United States, it was necessary to re-test these ideas to see if they were peculiar to a Dutch, or European context. By repeating the study on a large scale and in a comparable manner in the United States, it was possible to gain a broader, more international perspective on the task-emotion theory.

In writing the second edition, I wanted to respond to the demand for an accessible book about acting which would also be suitable for theater schools and acting teachers. *Acting Emotions* has been stripped of much 'scholarly' detail and the writing is considerably simpler. In-depth theoretical explanations, in particular extensive foundations for theoretical presumptions are restricted. With this edition, I have kept the theater professional in mind: One who wishes to learn more about styles of acting and the acting of emotions, not in terms of practical exercises, but in a theoretical context. To this end, I have also consulted theater professionals and acting teachers.

In presenting the results of the survey of professional actors (chapter 7) I have not included tables. In the body of this revised text, the complex results of statistical analyses have been explained in simplified language. These results, based on information on acting styles and emotions given by the professional actors surveyed, are illustrated using basic graphs.

A final important adaptation is that *Acting Emotions* is complemented by illustrative text. The boxes contain quotations or photographs, extra commentary and explanations of textual elements. Significant terms are explicated and examples of questions from actors are given. The boxes also include brief biographical sketches of important figures, such as Stanislavsky, Brecht, Brook, and others. Finally, a glossary has been added with definitions of the most complex terms.

1.3 What This Book is About: Acting and Emotions

As stated above, the most contentious debates about acting can be traced back to Diderot's *Paradoxe sur le Comédien*. Therefore, my theoretical argument begins with an account of what Diderot could have meant by his paradox. To do this it is necessary to position it in the context of the eighteenth century. Next follows a discussion of how current acting methods relate to the paradox, confining myself to main streams. Consequently, the focus is on distinguished methods for character acting and the way each method resolves the actor's dilemma. Acting styles tending toward emotional involvement are generally associated with the Russian director Konstantin Stanislavsky and even more strongly with the American *method acting* of Lee Strasberg and The Actors Studio. The more 'detached' acting styles are generally associated with Bertolt Brecht's epic theater and its predecessor Vsevolod Meyerhold's 'bio-mechanical' acting. A third approach can be called 'self-expression'. Here the expression of the innermost self is key, as in the work of Peter Brook and Jerzy Grotowski.

While examining the literature on the art of acting, in chapters two and three, a problem arises which Diderot initially described as follows: '...in the technical language of the theater there is such a considerable margin, a vagueness which permits reasonable people, with diametrically opposed viewpoints, to believe they have detected the light of self-evidence.'[2] Thus, the influential drama teacher Lee Strasberg can attest that Brecht's intention with his 'alienated' acting was the same as Strasberg's own with *method acting*. Those who fail to see this equivalency, according to Strasberg, have not really understood Brecht: '...both adherents and detractors of Brecht misunderstood him' (1988: 195). Elsewhere we read equally fervent arguments that they were on opposite ends of the spectrum. In still other treatises we are told that their acting styles differ only subtly from one another.

Nevertheless, the American director and performance theorist, Richard Schechner, says that there 'is in plain fact no basic methodology or vocabulary of acting; no means by which scholars, teachers, and practitioners can fruitfully (and with some objectivity) discuss acting'. He sees Stanislavsky's terminology and method as a start. But, he adds, 'the System is not systematic: It is not a psychology of acting or of the actor; it is not a basic set of terms and methods which tells us what acting is, how the actor works, and in what context good acting flourishes' (Schechner 1964: 210).

On similar grounds Constantinidis argues the need for empirical research based on the hypotheses and models developed in the study and practice of theater. He says that such 'empirical research articulates its variables and hypotheses in the context of theatrical practice, but it borrows models, methods and techniques from the social sciences' (Constantinidis 1988: 69). In this book, I employ this methodology by combining theater studies, (emotion) psychology and theater as practiced (empiricism). Chapter three closes with an inventory of several central problems in the acting of emotions which the different acting theories appear to have in common. In this way I can also formulate the most important acting tasks the actor must accomplish when portraying emotions. The insights derived by comparing the different acting theories will then be combined with current academic notions about emotion.

For the purposes of this study, the most comprehensive current emotion theory is the cognitive emotion theory as formulated by the Dutch psychologist Nico Frijda (1986). Different theoretical insights into the complex area of research on emotions are integrated into this theory which will be discussed in chapters four and five. The essence of Frijda's theory distills down to viewing emotions as expressions of the individual which fulfill a central function in reacting to the environment. Surroundings or situations offer opportunities or threats; they pose certain demands for satisfying individual needs, desires or concerns and provoke engagement in relationships. Simultaneously, the situation reveals possibilities or impediments that the individual has within this context. When the elements contributed by the situation combine with their potential meaning for the individual, this combination may create an emotional reaction. An emotional reaction betrays the fact that interests are at stake in the situation. I apply this psychological emotion theory to actors in their professional surroundings on the stage as well as to characters in dramatic situations.

In the context of this book a psychological approach to acting means the following: I take the perspective of the actor at work as someone who does his or her work in a certain way, in specific circumstances, as would a psychologist studying 'normal people'. This approach leads to the conclusion that accepted acting

I have vivid memories of this production (*Avondrood* by Het Werktheater), especially because the actors were not at all ashamed to let themselves coincide with their characters (...). None of the actors in this production had anything to hide or anything to put on. No one attempted to hide behind the mask of an old person. The actors of the company were shamelessly themselves. And we, the audience, felt like a band of frightened peeping Tom's.

(Klaus Sandunski, in *Toneel Theatraal*, no. 7, September 1996)

methods handle emotions in a one-sided manner. These methods do not take into account the emotions actors experience as a result of performing their acting tasks in front of a critical audience, or with the demands arising from the theater situation. I have called these emotions task-emotions and these are related to the actor as professional.[3] I propose that task-emotions play an important part in making character-emotions believable and convincing to an audience.

> We confessed to each other that we would love to figure out the secret of Marlon Brando's primal scream in the film A Streetcar Named Desire: 'Stella!!!'. We guessed our professor's answer ourselves: Marlon Brando's scream starts in his stomach, German actors don't act from the lower part of their body (like Americans do), but from their heads. (...).
>
> (Klaus Sandunski in *Toneel Theatraal*, no. 7, September 1996

Sequentially, problematic notions involved in the portraying of character-emotions are introduced. Topics familiar in actor training like 'involvement with the character', 'identification and empathy', 'believability of emotional expression' and 'dual consciousness' are placed in the perspective of views on emotion in contemporary psychology (chapter 5).

Next, the field study I conducted among professional actors in the Netherlands, Flanders and the United States will be discussed. Various considerations played a role in this process. By permitting professional actors to speak for themselves, support for insights previously developed only in theory could now be based on actual practice. This has rarely occurred systematically and never before on such a large scale. With this empirical analysis I have taken a step toward increasing the understanding of professional skills in acting. Chapter six includes a condensed overview of previous field studies on aspects of acting. I also describe how my field study was set up and conducted, and what questions were asked.

Several hundred professional actors and actresses answered the extensive questionnaire. Their responses were collated and used as a basis for statistical analyses, the results of which are presented in chapter seven. The results reveal, among other things, that most actors seldom actually experience the emotions they are portraying on stage as they perform a character. However, the analysis does determine that actors in performance experience intense emotions of a different order, which I name 'task-emotions'. Further, it appears that the acting style utilized has no bearing on the degree of correspondence between the emotions of actors and characters. In practice, it appears that exercising an emotionally 'involved' acting technique does not yield greater correspondence between the emotions of the actor and the character than exercising a 'detached' style of acting.

Finally, in chapter eight, I attempt to point these findings towards the development of a contemporary acting theory.

1.4   What This Book is Not About: Limiting the Subject

This book is predominantly concerned with professional actors (not amateurs or students) who present emotions in roles they perform for a live theater audience. How these actors work during the rehearsal period is only peripherally touched on, though naturally live performance is not unconnected to the rehearsal process. I have limited myself to stage acting and have left film and television acting out of the picture. Nonetheless, some actors in the American survey answered questions about acting for the camera. Their answers are more or less similar to those of the stage actors, but were too few in number to draw sound conclusions from. At certain points in the book film acting to stage acting are compared.

When I speak of characters I generally mean the most important or leading characters in the performance or text and not the minor roles. On most points the same principles would apply to major and minor roles, but the emotional content of minor roles is normally less than in major roles.

The nature of this study assumes that we are primarily trying to understand some fundamental principles of the emotional process of acting, in particular how emotions are shaped on stage. Consequently, the aim is not an exhaustive examination of varieties of acting styles. Neither will I dissect the nuances of diverse character types, genres, dramatic structures, etc., but instead concentrate on the most common, prototypical characters, their dramatic situations, and their presumed emotions. Since Diderot's *Paradoxe* is the starting point, the frame of reference is mainly (traditional) character acting.

During the last number of years in the West, there has been a visible growth of acting styles in which the representation of real (or realistic) character-emotions have assumed decreasing importance. Ensembles like Maatschappij Discordia (the Netherlands) and STAN (in Belgium) propose that the actors themselves – simply as people – are present on stage. Strongly choreographed 'abstract acting', as with De Keersmaeker, Jan Fabre, or Pina Bausch, makes very different demands on actors. Frequently, so-called experimental theater places scenographic aspects above (the portrayal of) characters or their emotions. Alternatively, I have also seen heightened demonstrations of raw character emotions in recent performances, witness Blanche and Stanley in *A Streetcar Named Desire* by Het Zuidelijk Toneel (Netherlands, 1996). One company member recounted that director Ivo van Hove was focused on making a sort of 'x-ray analysis' of the character's emotions.

Experiments with *acting styles* in the Netherlands seem to have developed further than in surrounding countries, most certainly than in the United States. Note that I emphasize *acting styles*; not experimental theater *forms* of which stunning examples may be seen in America. In the context of this book a thorough discussion of such developments would be too great a digression, but I will return in some measure to this issue in the final chapter. However, it is safe to say that the results of this study align well with developments in contemporary theater.

In conclusion I believe that the analysis of creative processes does not detract from their artistic nature, but can make a meaningful contribution to the nature of the arts. Performance scholar Richard Schechner contends: 'I do not believe that any creative process – in-

...according to the tried and tested Discordia method: Everything that is felt to be artificial is taboo. There is then no decor; once on stage the actors stand stock-still reading their lines, without performing any prescribed actions (tea drinking, sitting down, playing cards, looking at each other). One of the tricks they have used for years is that every player can represent any man or woman, young or old without reflecting age or sex in intonation or posture. It is often guess work as to who is speaking, even if director Jan Joris Lamers sometimes calls out half-audible stage directions.

(newspaper *Het Parool*, February 19, 1997)

cluding acting – is beyond discussion and analysis; nor do I believe that analysis destroys creativity (it is not the actor-at-work who will be doing the analyzing)' (Schechner 1964: 211).

1.5   Acknowledgments

This book has been made possible thanks to the support of many people and organizations. Truly indispensable were the actors and actresses in the Netherlands, Flanders (Belgium), and the United States who took great pains to reveal some of their professional secrets by carefully completing an extensive questionnaire. To gain insight into the craft of the actor it was vital that actors entrusted their experiences and knowledge to me. That many have done this, and in such a personal and complex area as the emotions, is of great value.

The research reported in this book has also been made possible thanks to financial support from the Faculty of Arts of Utrecht University, the Netherlands Organization for Scientific Research (NWO) in The Hague, and the Foundation for Studies in Performing Arts (STiPA) in Amsterdam. The research in the United States would have been impossible had not the American *Actors' Equity* trade union, and specifically Guy Pace and Richard Bruir, been prepared to lend assistance. I am very grateful to *Actors' Equity* for making a policy exception which allowed this research to be conducted.

Research in the Netherlands was additionally supported by the department of Theater, Film and Television Studies at Utrecht University (especially Prof. Dr. Henri Schoenmakers), as well as the Faculty of Psychology of the University of Amsterdam (especially Prof. Dr. Nico Frijda) and the department of Psychological Methodology (especially Prof. Dr. Don Mellenbergh, Dr. Wulfert van den Brink, and Drs. Harrie Vorst). Further, the support and assistance of the trade union De Kunstenbond FNV, Prof. Dr. Ed Tan (department of Word and Image Studies, Vrije Universiteit) and Rein Douze (FNV-Kiem) was vital for conducting research among actors in the Netherlands, Flanders, and the United States. The American study was supported there by the City University of New York (CUNY), especially by Professors William Green, Marvin Carlson (Graduate Center of CUNY) and David Chambers (Yale School of Drama, Yale University, New Haven) who aided with moral support and advice on content.

For advice on editing *Acting Emotions* and the creation of this edition, my thanks go to Peter van Lint (chief editor of *Theater and Education*) and the Theater Academies of the Netherlands. Most especially I thank Henk Havens and Leo Swinkels of the Theater Academy Maastricht, Ben Hurkmans of the Theater School Amsterdam, Wim Meuwissen and Gretha Hengst of the Theater School Utrecht, and Rob van Gaal of the Theater Institute the Netherlands (TIN) for their useful advice in making this edition more readable for students. I am greatly indebted to David Chambers for his editorial advice on editing the translation with a view towards the American theater schools, and to Phillip Zarrilli (University of Surrey, UK) for his insightful comments on the final edition of the translation.

For the second Dutch edition, I am very grateful to Astrid Westerbeek as my co-editor and Karin Konijn for their contributions to a readable writing. Thanks go to Ingrid Deddes of Toneelgroep Amsterdam for making photos available, and also Felix-Jan

Kuypers of the theater group Het Amsterdamse Bos for his emotional demonstrations for the camera. I thank Rocco and Dianne van Loenen for their hospitality and support when the printer in New York fell through. Thanks also to sponsorship by the *Hotel Park Savoy* in Manhattan, and especially to John Pappas, Manny and Mussa – the primary necessities of life were there from you.

NWO is greatly acknowledged for funding the English translation, which Barbara Leach did with great sensitivity and responsibility. I am greatly indebted to her and David Chambers, who did the final editing with great understanding and precision. Lastly, thanks go to my husband, family, and friends for always being there for me.

2   *The Paradox Considered*

> ... as so often happens with a frequently preached opinion, without anyone
> asking why, a system is erected upon this point of view.
> WILHELM MÜSELER (1992: 13)

2.1   Introduction: From Paradox to the Actor's Dilemma

To this day, heated discussions are held concerning the paradoxical relationship between the 'truth' of the actor's emotions and the emotions portrayed by his character.
Diderot's *Paradoxe sur le Comédien* was, and frequently still is, the locus of a debate in
which diametrically opposed views are held. On one side are the so-called emotional-
ists, who believe that the actor himself must experience the emotions he/she expresses
in his/her role. On the other side are the so-called anti-emotionalists, who believe that
the actor must not allow himself to be overwhelmed with his character's emotions.
Diderot himself took an extreme point of view: He proposed, as will be discussed in
section 2.2, that a good actor should feel nothing at all.

To begin to unravel the paradox, it is helpful to understand it in its historical context
(2.3). While the issues at hand were already the subject of intense discourse on the art
of acting in the late eighteenth century, the *Paradoxe* itself was not discussed; the first
printed version in its current form was not made public until 1830. The differences of
opinion in eighteenth-century France were, however, clearly illustrated by the dispute
between the actresses Clairon and Dumesnil. The pre-
dominant acting style of the period was the classical
manner. I will also discuss how emotions were regarded
in the eighteenth century and how these views must
have influenced Diderot's *Paradoxe*. Further, in section
2.4, a few problematical terms involved in interpreting
the paradox will be handled.

There has been a shift in current discussions about
the relationship between the actor's emotions and those
of the character. The issue is no longer about the total
presence or the total *absence* of feeling, but rather *the degree
of similarity* between the emotions of the actor and his
character. This has lead to speaking less in terms of the
paradox of the actor, but rather of 'the dilemma' of the
actor. This dilemma involves the various levels of enactment and emotion which exist simultaneously (2.4.).

> Faridech [her acting coach, EK] taught
> me how to go back in my own life and base a
> scene on that. If you are very concentrated,
> you are right back in that situation, then
> there is a personal connection... Acting is the
> language of the heart; you have to feel every-
> thing you do.
> (Actress Johanna ter Steege in *De
> Filmkrant*, January 1997)

> As an actor, you have to know what you
> want to bring about in a scene... It's all in your
> mind. And the art of acting is to be able to turn
> it out.
> (Actress Renée Fokker in *De Filmkrant*,
> September 1996)

2.2 Diderot's *Paradoxe*

The French philosopher, novelist, and playwright Denis Diderot (1713-1784) is best known for creating the first 'real' *Encyclopedia*, a product of the Enlightenment. Enlisting numerous other philosophers, he worked on it for over twenty years. Diderot wrote philosophical essays on diverse subjects, including drama and acting. His work and the reactions to it reveal Diderot to be a versatile, progressive, and independent thinker, but also a controversial one. In 1749 he was imprisoned for his *Lettres sur les Aveugles*, which questions the existence of God. Much of Diderot's work, including the *Paradoxe*, would only finally appear in the nineteenth century; some would wait until the twentieth. In need of money, Diderot was forced to sell his library to the Russian Czarina, Catherine II, in 1766. After his death in 1784, his complete oeuvre was brought to St. Petersburg, where it was kept in private storage until 1917. In 1773-74, Diderot spent eight months in The Hague, en route to Russia. Here he tried to publish *Paradoxe*. The last written version of *Paradoxe sur le Comédien* also dates from this sojourn.[1] The following is a short summary of its contents.

2.2.1 *Paradoxe sur le Comédien*

A good actor feels nothing at all and can therefore evoke the strongest of feelings in the audience – this was Diderot's proposal in *Paradoxe sur le Comédien*. The actor should act emotions on stage *without feeling*. A sensitive actor could never act the same role twice with the same devotion and with equal success. 'If he were to be himself while acting, how would he then be able to stop?' (Diderot 1985: 52). According to Diderot, only one who had completely mastered himself could possibly take off his mask and put it back on again on command. A performance by actors who act with their feelings would be, he argued, very uneven, fluctuating from strong to weak, flat to sublime. On the other hand, a performance would be constant – reliably strong every time – if the actor's play were deliberate. In such a case, after the performance is completed, the actor would feel nothing other than his own fatigue.

Diderot argued further that there are so many varied and complex situations embodied in a single leading role that it would be impossible to actually feel all of them. Moreover, it would be impossible for an actor to rigorously follow all of the stage directions if completely immersed in the emotions of the role. In considering emotions in daily life, Diderot viewed them as a disruptive interference: One can only express one's self clearly once one is out of harm's way and recovered from distress. Before that, there is only stuttering, stammering, and lack of awareness that others fail to share one's enthusiasm. Additionally, Diderot felt that an extreme sensitivity has a negative influence on acting performances: 'A complete absence of feeling is the foundation for those who achieve the highest level. The actor's tears flow from his brain', since 'the sentimental soul is seized with panic at the slightest unexpected occurrence' (1985: 58-59). Emotional people, he felt, only served as examples for great actors in the conception of a '*modèle idéal*'. According to Diderot in *Paradoxe* the actor used this imagined inner model to play his character during the performance.

Diderot also noted the difference between what he calls 'real' tears and the tears evoked by a moving tale. At the sight of an accident, for example, the object, the sensation and the effect coincide: At once the observer's feelings are aroused and he is instantly moved to tears. With a moving story, on the other hand, tears are summoned gradually. Diderot asserted that a spectator 'does not go to the theater to see tears, but to hear words which will bring him to tears' (1985: 118). Likewise, he maintained that real feelings and performed feelings were completely different. The emotions of an actor must necessarily be fictitious, he contended, otherwise his acting would be dull and overly mundane.

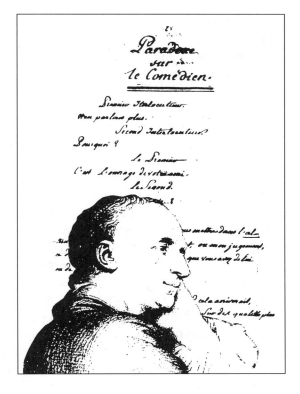

Diderot suggested that authenticity in a scene occurs when actions, words, facial expressions, voice, movement, and gesture all conform to an inner model (modèle idéal) which the playwright has described and which the actor often exaggerates. It is this imagined model that the actor tries to imitate. Therefore, the theater offers the audience heightened caricatures which obey theatrical rules of convention, not reality. If, by contrast, one were to portray oneself, one's acting would be small, timid, reductive. Furthermore, Diderot stated that the talent of a good actor lies in the fact that he can reproduce the external signs of an emotion precisely – and in such good measure – that the spectator will be convinced. 'The actor is, however, not his character; he pretends to be and does this so well that you mistake him for his character. The illusion is yours alone', writes Diderot (1985: 57).

2.2.2 Arguments in *Paradoxe sur le Comédien*

The several reasons Diderot used to support his position in the *Paradoxe* can, according to various scholars, be reduced to two main arguments. First, in Diderot's view, uncontrolled emotion and rational control are mutually exclusive. A controlled emotion is not an emotion, but by definition a pretense. For Diderot, the stage is no place for uncontrolled emotion, it might randomly produce a good effect[2], but in general will simply interfere, making, for instance, actors less intelligible. The actor who plays 'from his heart' would, according to Diderot, never be capable of playing great tragic heroes with any consistency in a series of performances.

It is notable that Diderot made a distinction between acting while performing and while preparing the role. During rehearsals 'the great actor struggles with his feelings, until he has mastered his role' (in Hogendoorn 1985: 26). I would like to look at this extreme premise of the paradox – that actors should feel nothing at all – in this light. What Diderot means by 'having no feelings at all' is that the actor has no feelings in common with his character. This is illustrated by examples such as 'the double scene'

(1985: 67-70), in which an actor and an actress who are in reality husband and wife play two passionate lovers. Meanwhile, they express how much they loathe their marriage with acidic subtexts in, according to Diderot, inaudible stage whispers. This anecdote shows that actors apparently do have feelings, but ones óther than the ones their characters portray. However, in debates stemming from the *Paradoxe* this has not been a point of attention.

The second main argument pointed out by researchers is the fundamental difference between everyday life and that of life as ordered in art, as artifact. This relates to eighteenth-century opinions on classicist aesthetics. Diderot not only remarked that emotions in daily life are of a completely different order than emotions on stage, but also that actors represent the emotions of the character by developing a '*modèle idéal*'. Actors neither imitate reality, nor the emotions in reality, but instead act out a model of their character. Although grafted to reality, the model is larger than life. Through observation and the study of 'common' behavior, the actor uses his imagination to enlarge the most characteristic and general human traits to suit his character. In this manner, the actor's task is to shape a fictitious, yet aptly conceived model of his character. This imagined model subsequently forms the guideline for stage acting, Diderot concluded. In this respect, the actor does not differ from other artists such as the painter, poet, or musician. Diderot also found that stage performances should be repeatable; the quality should not depend on the caprice of the actor's random feelings.

Although other scholars sometimes cite further central propositions in *Paradoxe*, these can generally be covered under one of the two main arguments. But one contention, that of Villiers (1942), does seem to stand apart. For Villiers, Diderot's remark that acting improves with the age of the actor seems to be a separate reason for supporting Diderot's extreme position in the *Paradoxe*. This argument has nothing to do with aging and an increased capacity to feel but instead proposes that an actor 'only masters his art and all its subtleties when he has a great deal of experience, when the fire of passion has subsided ... and [he] has mastered his intellectual faculties' (Diderot 185: 65). Diderot valued professional experience and the acquisition of expert skills to be a good actor. This third argument stands next to the two main arguments above supporting Diderot's thesis.[3]

2.3 A Short History of *Paradoxe sur le Comédien*

The following section will examine how discussion germane to the issue in *Paradoxe*, but prior to its publication, proceeded in the eighteenth century. This section intends only to sketch a brief summary of late eighteenth-century 'enlightened' views about acting and emotions in order to place the paradox within its historical context.

2.3.1 Clairon versus Dumesnil In the period during which Diderot developed his *Paradoxe* the actresses Clairon and Dumesnil were the leading actresses of the Comédie Française. Their styles of acting and their opinions about acting were diametrically opposed and, through extensive correspondence, they were at each other's throats well into their dotage. Dumesnil was described by Diderot as 'the natural, disorganized player, who could occasionally rise to sublime heights'. Her acting, according to

Diderot, was 'only good when she had to display passion and rage'; the basis of her art being 'naturalness', 'pathos', and 'emotional identification' with the role. In contrast, Diderot described Clairon as an 'aware artist, always satisfying, but perhaps never touching the deepest emotional chord' (1985: 53-54). Others also expressed similar thoughts about both actresses: 'The one, an actress completely of study and artifice, the other, an actress completely of temperament.'[4]

In *Réflexions sur l'Art Dramatique*, Clairon abhored the many actors and actresses who thought that it was sufficient to learn the text and leave the rest to 'nature'. An all too common practice, she contended. According to her, the word *nature* was misused (see also 2.4). Clairon emphasized that acting was artificial and went on to develop a quite forward looking method of acting. In this method, the actor needed to study not only the character, but also his historical context and relationships to other characters to be able to understand his role from the character's perspective and express this comprehension correctly. Clairon asserted that differences in the character's age, sex, situation, time, and custom would demand different manners of expression, as opposed to the stereotypical 'character portraits' of the time.[5]

Dumesnil was outraged by Clairon's acting method, remarking that all these things could never have as much influence as the great powers nature exerted on the portrayal of strong emotions. According to her, it was the exceptional gift of a 'natural actress', above all the efforts of art, to forget oneself in an instant, to assume the character and become imbued with the 'great emotions'.[6] For Dumesnil, it was a given that dramatic art was equal to reality, while Clairon would maintain that on the stage, illusion came first: 'In theatrical art, all is convention, all is fiction' (Clairon, in Cole and Chinoy 1970: 177). Given his viewpoint in *Paradoxe sur le Comédien*, it is not surprising that Diderot praised Clairon as the prime example of good acting.

A visit to Paris by the English actor Garrick in 1764-1765 was also an important inspiration for Diderot to write *Paradoxe*. Garrick amazed a salon audience with his lightning fast succession of facial expressions, each expressing a different emotion. Garrick, the 'leading man' from 1741 to 1776, eased the stiff, pompous English acting style and provided much innovation on the English stage. Diderot wrote that Garrick told how he observed people's natural behavior for his models. He further related how Garrick gave a demonstration of his expressive capacities and concluded that a great actor does not

> You try to form a memory: Impressions of youth, a grandmother, a garden shed, certain smells, small details...The better you understand a character, the better you can find the form to play him. Then it becomes less theatrical, less artificial, playing the emotion itself...If I see that moment again, [when he, as Frits van Egters in *De Avonden*, comes out with the truth, EK] I see a completely different person, I really see a completely insane boy standing there. Those are the genuine moments in acting, when an actor loses his own personality and creates another personality. That is magic.
>
> (Actor Thom Hoffman in an interview with Jan Pieter Ekker, *De Filmkrant*, November 1996)

> The other day on television I heard a man from Rwanda say completely calmly: 'We are going to war'. A sentence like this fascinates me. You can already picture the wounded, the sobbing mothers, we all know these images. Not that I copy the images on stage. On stage you have to find other ways. As an actress you can have the image in mind to find the right form for it. If we actually started wailing like those women do, you would think: Cut it out.
>
> (Actress Frieda Pittoors in an interview with Marian Buijs, *de Volkskrant*, January 17, 1997)

become involved in the emotions of the character, but knows precisely how to express these emotions. According to Diderot, a good actor has 'a cool head', as did the actor Lekain, who was considered the French equivalent of Garrick (Diderot 1985: 79). The specific differences in acting styles and opinions, e.g., those of Clairon and Dumesnil, can not be discussed without considering the dominant classical acting style in eighteenth-century France.

2.3.2 Classical Acting Style

In discussions about varying opinions on acting styles in France, it is important to recall that from 1680 until the French Revolution (1789) the Comédie Française was one of the most prominent and influential theater companies. During the first half of the eighteenth century, the Comédie Française had become more and more an 'elitist' company, lacking innovative initiatives. The French classical acting of this period was noted for its very strict adherence to prescribed rules and conventions which originated in a specific and rigorous interpretation of Aristotelian notions of unity of time, place, and action in drama and theater. Classical dramatic texts were written in verse form, the diction being determined by strict 'sing-song' rules of declamation, with the 'natural' characters in the tragedies being kings, princes, and mythological heroes.[7] The classical acting style went into steady decline and fell out of favor in surrounding countries (although, revivals were still held in the nineteenth century).

The foundation of eighteenth-century acting is described by the theater historian Dene Barnett as '...a vocabulary of basic movements, each with its own meaning which is known by all' (1987: 221, 331).[8] The words were always the starting point for the staging: Gestures, movements, mise-en-scène, and postures were always linked to the words (see box on page 24). A dozen basic emotions were expressed using standardized techniques for presentation; all actors used these and all spectators understood them. Barnett describes the same as being true for mise-en-scène and costumes.

With the house lights always burning, the actors could see the audience members clearly. They made themselves fully heard as well, igniting frequent applause, calls to repeat a beautiful phrase or jeers for mean statements (Barnett 1987: 435). The audience consisted mainly of connoisseurs trained in the arts of discourse. The same techniques of classical oratory were applied in salons, the parliament, the law courts, or at ceremonies. Everyone (at least every patrician) understood them. It was equally understood that a good play followed the 'natural' rules of Aristotle, the then accepted interpretation of the '*règles des conditions*'. The theater historian Peter Szondi relates that the classical rules were interpreted as natural rules. 'Natural' in the sense of self-evident and indisputable (not in the Romantic sense of the term).

Liberating acting from the rigors of these rules and making acting 'a likeness of nature' became the goal of the innovators in eighteenth-century drama. Diderot, however, did not share their conclusion that 'natural' emotions or feelings must be paramount on stage. Actors could achieve 'natural quality' in the portrayal of character-emotions, according to Diderot, by observing emotions in daily life. Based on these observations, the actor should create a '*modèle idéal*' of the character-emotions, which he then reproduces as well as possible on stage. Yet, in this epoch, naturalness was still considered a God-given quality, not something that could be created or imitated by men.

The call for naturalism on the stage coincided with the development of 'bourgeois' drama, where the 'rank and file' appeared as characters instead of kings and princes. The bourgeois tragedy made its entrance along with Diderot.[9] His theories about drama also pertained to this 'serious genre' – standard and bourgeois tragedy – but only slightly to comedy. Bourgeois drama was often moralistic and educational, rooted in the hope of improving humanity by providing it with good examples. In *De la Poésie Dramatique*, Diderot advocated writing bourgeois drama in prose because the tragic effect of a drama was in the similarity of social circumstances between the main character and the audience; it is not Clytemnestra's majesty that is moving, it is the expression of ultimate and universal motherly love, Diderot said.[10]

In *Paradoxe*, and other sources, Diderot advocated the ensemble rehearsing together at length to achieve good interaction. In the eighteenth century, rehearsals were highly unusual, but there were already some successful attempts to develop a system for training actors. At the time it was customary for actors to learn their texts quickly and privately, and then rely on the established rules of rhetoric for expression. In short, in the context of eighteenth-century French classical drama, Diderot appears to be an innovator. His desire for change in the theater is also expressed in his *Paradoxe*.

2.3.3 Enlightened Emotions

To understand what Diderot meant by saying that a good actor feels *nothing*, I will try to explain how Diderot presumably thought emotions work. The eighteenth century is known as the century of Enlightenment, noted for, among other things, an emphasis on the importance of human knowledge as directed by reason. Psychology did not yet exist as an independent science. Emotion theories were incorporated into philosophical and medical discourse.[11] The inner life of man, also his emotions, were thought to be controlled by the soul, and the soul in turn driven by God. Diderot rejected these ideas.

The eighteenth-century actor made use of this established 'sign language' with its accompanying declamatory style to transmit the meaning of a sentence (from Barnett 1987)

In as much as emotions were studied (scientifically), they were the object of precise character analyses based on the observation of external (facial) expressions. These were thought to reveal the 'humors' – sanguine, phlegmatic, choleric, and melancholic – as determined by the four body fluids. The doctrine of the humors was originally intended for purely medical purposes; it began to take on a more psychological context in the seventeenth and eighteenth centuries when a connection was made between the bodily fluids and certain personality traits. Diderot disparaged character typologies or the analyses resulting from the doctrine of humors.[12] He felt the character typologies could only describe superficial appearances and had no causal relationship whatsoever with the essence of inner life. The doctrine of humors began to lose ground in the nineteenth century, when the soul became the subject of highly detailed self-analysis and introspection. Diderot died in 1784 before these developments began to exert their influence. At the end of the nineteenth century, psychology gained the recognition as a distinct science. A revival of the debate on *Paradoxe sur le Comédien* also took place at that time with Irving and Coquelin as leading contenders (2.5.1).

Diderot rebelled against the omnipresence of God and against the dominant opinions of Descartes. He rejected not only Descartes' deism, but also his belief that body and soul are divisible. Diderot contended the opposite. Further, Diderot considered movement to be inherent in matter, so that body or soul, thought and emotions could exist *without* presupposing divine intervention. Diderot emphasized the influence of the individual self on his observations and his emotions, at the time a highly unorthodox, even dangerous, notion. In the words of the twentieth-century contemporary philosopher Barzun: 'Diderot was aware that consciousness was not a passive mirror of reality, as his century believed, but individually selective' (Barzun 1986: 21).[13]

Diderot believed that the diaphragm kept emotions and passions under control. The American theater researcher, Joseph Roach (1981) interpreted Diderot's viewpoint: 'Normal' people (and mediocre actors) would not be able to divide body and spirit and thus the spirit would then become clouded by emotion.[14] According to Roach, only a genius possesses the rare capacity to detach himself from his 'bodily machine, to divide himself into two personalities in performance, and so to direct the outward motions of his passions by an inward mental force, itself unmoved, disconnected from the physiological effects it oversees' (Roach 1981: 61). With this interpretation of the paradox, Roach proposed that Diderot meant that this double consciousness was only reserved for an actor of genius.

Roach's reasoning suggests that an actor would most definitely have to feel the emotions he portrays in a character, but the 'genius' actor would not be troubled by them. Through extensive practice, the physical manifestations of the aroused emotions will have become automatic and he can separate these from his mental command of his body. As long as we presume that acted emotions and real emotions, or rather onstage character-emotions and the emotions experienced in daily life, are the same, then this explanation seems reasonable enough. However, Diderot contended that the acted emotions and the real emotions, or rather the onstage character-emotions and the emotions experienced in daily life, were fundamentally different.[15] For Diderot there was no question that an actor, at least not a 'highly gifted' actor in performance, had any emotions in common with his character. There was, according to him, only the illusion of emotion, of perfect expression or portrayal, and not of the actual experience of those portrayed emotions. Using this insight, we need not do damage to Diderot's belief in the unity of body and spirit to maintain his premise that it is exactly the actor who is bereft of emotion who will be able to arouse real emotions in the spectator.

2.4   Problematic Terms

Finally it seems necessary to pursue a few central terms in *Paradoxe*, like *sensibilité* and *nature*, in order to interpret them correctly. This is not intended as an exhaustive discussion – the problem is too complex for that. The difficulty with interpreting specific terms in *Paradoxe* is most evident with the word 'nature'. 'Nature' seems to be the eighteenth century's most ubiquitous word. Ehrard distinguished seven meanings of the word 'nature'.[16] According to Hazard, Diderot used these and many other senses of the term 'nature'. While studying the literature, a specter begins to loom around the eighteenth-century concept of 'nature' as a term that was used for everything that defied explanation: Nature takes its course and nature is created by God. Having emotions would also be part of nature's course.

The Dutch philosopher, Verbeek, pointed out 'the normative aspect which the term "nature" expresses' (1977: 12). We encountered the same normative element earlier (in 2.3.2): Only drama that conformed to the rules of Aristotle was considered 'natural'. This meant that a 'natural' play must obey the rules demanding unity of time, place, and action. With the influence of the natural sciences, the term 'nature' also took on the meaning of an empirically observable reality. Further, Rousseau (Diderot's contemporary) proposed another meaning of the term 'nature', namely the opposite of social convention or artificially acquired behavior.

The related terms *sensibilité*, *sensible*, and *sentiment* also had various meanings. In eighteenth-century French, *sentiment* could indicate an opinion as well as a feeling, which in turn could either mean grand passions or a sense of morals or uprightness. Verbeek pointed out that in the latter part of the eighteenth century, the term *sensibilité* became trendy: 'Sensibility, especially concerning beautiful feelings – the word certainly did not have this meaning in 1769' (1980: 117). Further, according to Diderot, matter could also possess *sensibilité*, sensitivity or susceptibility, the ability to react to stimuli; a stone has the potential to 'feel' the influence of unpredictable processes of movement over the ages.[17] The difficulty with translation is not simply that languages differ, but also that there was a completely different mindset in the eighteenth century. It goes without saying that terms like *génie* and *modèle idéal* can also be interpreted in different ways. In the literature it appears that *modèle idéal* can either mean a figure or an imagined model.[18] If the central terms in *Paradoxe* are seen in this light, we must conclude that it is not possible to accept translations at face value, which can as such lead to paradoxical situations.[19]

The actress Dumesnil was possibly talking about a different sort of nature than Clairon was. Clairon was probably more influenced by the ideas of the Enlightenment philosophers, as she traveled in these circles. The meaning of 'natural' acting, as

Dumesnil used the term, is not unambiguous. Likewise, a 'good, mediocre, or bad actor' means something different to Diderot than to us in the twentieth century. The expression of emotions was not only subject to strict conventions and rules on stage, but also in daily life, as the bourgeoisie were often well trained in the rules of rhetoric. In accordance with the ideas of the Enlightenment philosophers, Diderot stressed the importance of reason for the actor in his *Paradoxe*. Pretense must make way for sincerity, Diderot states. Expression enchained in the iron rules of rhetoric must give way to the expression of emotions modeled on empirical observations of reality. This demanded a sincere study on the part of the actor who, by reproducing a '*modèle idéal*', created the maximum illusion so that the audience would be sincerely moved.

In summary, the precise meaning of the paradox, as Diderot would have meant it, can scarcely be reconstructed. The difficulty is underscored by problems with the interpretation of some of the key terms he used, like *sensibilité*, *nature*, and *génie*. It is therefore not possible to subject the original paradox, as Diderot meant, to empirical tests. It is, however, possible to determine if, and in what terms, the content of *Paradoxe* is discussed today – to see what solutions for the problems posed in *Paradoxe* are offered by various contemporary schools of thought in acting.

2.5   The Actor's Dilemma

Diderot's extreme point of view is recognizable in the form of the actor's dilemma in current discussions about portraying emotions on stage. The actor today faces the dilemma of how far he can go with 'acting from the heart' without losing his head. We will now look at the reason why this dilemma is still such an important issue in discussions about the art of acting. Clearly, there are essential points of difference between the art of acting and other art forms. The fact that the actor is his own instrument, with which he creates a transitory art work, leads to the formulation of different levels of enactment on which actors function (2.6).

2.5.1   The Dilemma The introduction (2.1) already mentioned that Diderot's *Paradoxe* to this day leads to heated discussions about acting. *Tears on Command*, the title of a recent publication of 'theater correspondence' between the drama critic Kester Freriks and theater director Gerardjan Rijnders, brings to mind Diderot's remark that 'the actor's tears flow from his brain'.

Whether stage tears are 'real' or 'unreal', or the question of 'how to balance emotionality and craft' is central to the debate between Freriks and Rijnders. There is a perceptible shift away from the discussions of the *Paradoxe* in its original extreme form, as posed by Diderot. From a total absence of feelings in the actor, the accent has shifted toward what degree of similarity there is (or should be) between the emotions of actor and character.

At the close of the nineteenth century a debate raged around *Paradoxe*, with Constant Coquelin as the staunch defender of Diderot's anti-emotionalist standpoint and Henry Irving as the fervent emotionalist. In 1888, William Archer attempted to quell the dispute between the anti- and pro-emotionalists by conducting a survey among actors and studying (auto)biographical material. Archer concluded that the anti-emotionalists were wrong, but, nevertheless, it was neither common for actors to become totally swept up in the emotions of their characters. He sought an explanation in the 'double consciousness' of the actor fully connecting with the character's emotions, at the same time being in complete control of them. Henceforth, Diderot's *Paradoxe* was frequently cited in conjunction with Archer's study as viewed through the lens of Archer's interpretation. The paradox also lost its extreme form because Diderot's views were placed into the historical context of the development of science.

> Until that point I have showed the audience that this is a woman [Hekabé EK] who has been through many ordeals, but who is strong and who will probably make it. The moment I begin to cry, it is clear she is not going to make it. So the break between being very strong and falling apart totally is a really difficult one. I simply figured out this trick: Just push. Push. Turn my back to the audience and push them out. And: 'De Jong, you've got to do it. Even if you can't. You chose this profession, so just do it.' It works every time.
>
> (Actress Geert de Jong in the documentary *Acteurs spelen emoties* (Actors Act Emotions), based on the book by Elly Konijn, NPS 1995)

The discussions about *Paradoxe* have led to formulating 'the actor's dilemma' as the most essential problem in the art of acting. The dilemma of the actor turns up in many shapes and forms: Should the actor act with 'the head', 'cool calculation', and 'technique', or with 'the heart', 'emotions', and 'involvement'. The concern is, to what degree actors should keep a distance between themselves and the character as opposed to becoming involved in or identifying with the character. The dilemma is also reflected in positioning acting styles in opposition to each other, e.g., the externalists who specialize in technical aspects based on the physique, as opposed to the internalists who claim that acting springs from the soul and the emotions. The alternative phrases used to formulate 'the actor's dilemma' all come down to the relationship between the 'real' emotions of the actor and the emotions to be portrayed in the role.[20] The recurring question where acting is considered remains: 'L'acteur doit-il être ou non ému?' (Villiers 1968: 31). Must the actor truly experience the emotions he portrays on the stage, or must he 'simply' show or demonstrate them, no feelings involved?

In the contemporary 'translation' of the paradox in 'the actor's dilemma' three aspects are generally overlooked. The paradox is, firstly, a statement about 'good' or sublime actors. Diderot himself makes a distinction between the feelings of bad, mediocre, and good actors. Secondly, the paradox is a statement about emotions during the performance and not during rehearsals. Thirdly, the paradox is directed toward having a maximum emotional effect on the audience.

With respect to the first point, as far as 'good' actors are concerned, my study is aimed at professional or career actors and not at beginners or amateurs. I will return to this point in chapter 6. As to the second point, this study focused on the acting of emotions in a public performance, just as in the paradox, and only incidentally on the phase of preparation or rehearsal of a role. At certain points in the following discussion the strict separation between performance and rehearsal becomes difficult. Because this distinction is important, I will indicate which aspect is being discussed. The third aspect, the relation between actor, character, *and* audience, is referred to indirectly at various moments. For example, in contemporary theater, emotional effects on the audience are not necessarily (the only effects) sought after.

Actress Chris Nietvelt as Lulu,
Toneelgroep Amsterdam, 1988

Actress Kitty Courbois as Medea,
Toneelgroep Amsterdam, 1988

2.5.2 Features of Stage Acting Why does 'the actor's dilemma' occupy such a prominent place in discussions about acting? Because it concerns the essence of the actor's art. The American drama teacher, Lee Strasberg, remarked, after a life studying and working with actors, that he originally saw inspiration as the basic problem for actors. Later he maintained that the fundamental problem in the work of the actor is to solve the dilemma: 'How does the actor achieve the right state of emotionality analogous to that of the character to be portrayed?' (Strasberg 1988: 21). Concerning what the 'right state' might be, there are various current opinions, which will be discussed in chapter 3.

The actor's dilemma – to what extent his feelings are the same as his character's – exists because of two closely related features of the art of stage acting. The first feature is the material: 'Because the artist has to use the treacherous, changeable, and mysterious material of himself as his medium' (Brook 1968: 131). The artist and the material he works with are, unlike in other art forms, united in one and the same person: The actor is at the same time the interpreter and the instrument, the pianist and the piano.[21]

The artwork can not be presented without the actor's physical presence; minimizing the physical distance between the artist and the artwork. The second feature is an extension of the first which is also peculiar to the stage actor: The transitory nature of the art. When the actor leaves the stage, the artwork ceases to exist. It is not lasting but ephemeral. Or, to quote Grotowski, 'Acting is a particularly thankless art. It dies with the actor' (1968: 44). The dramatic artwork is reshaped repeatedly in front of an audience. The art of the stage actor is thus situated within a determined lapse of time. The production must take place at the precise moment the actor is confronted by the audience, at a more or less agreed upon time and place, as 'the actor cannot tell the king that he is unable to laugh today' (Diderot 1985: 91). This means that an actor cannot wait for the moment of inspiration or for 'other such factors as talent explosion, the sudden and surprising growth of creative possibilities, etc., ... because unlike the other artistic disciplines, the actor's creation is imperative' (Grotowski 1968: 128). Both of these features in the work of the actor carry a great risk of failure with them. All methods and theories about the art of acting, however different, should take them into account.

2.6 Levels of Enactment and Emotions

Because the artist is his own material, it follows that a number of levels of enactment must exist simultaneously at the moment that the actor portrays emotions in front of an audience. Usually a threesome is used. Bert O. States, for example, distinguishes 'three phenomenal states': 'The actor (I) speaks to the audience (you) about the character (he) he is playing' (States 1983: 360). Michael Quinn also proposes a triad, though with slightly different elements: 'The personal features of the artist; an insubstantial dramatic character residing in the consciousness of the audience; and ... the stage figure, an image of the character which is created by the actor' (Quinn 1990: 155).[22]

Both the actor and the character can each be seen on two levels. This yields four levels of enactment which can be distinguished while acting: (1) The actor as private person; (2) the actor as actor-craftsman; (3) the inner model ('*modèle idéal*') or the idea of how the character will be; and (4) the character as the actor presents him in the performance. The *audience* will in general perceive all four levels of enactment as a single entity. If four levels of enactment are distinguished, this has consequences for distinguishing different kinds of emotions. In the literature on acting these consequences are not usually discussed. However, the existence of different levels of enactment will become important to help unravel the paradox and the actor's dilemma. This classification implies that there can be emotions at each of the levels; respectively 1) the private emotions of the actor as private person; 2) the emotions of the actor as craftsman, which are related to doing his work; 3) the intended emotions following the inner model; and 4) the portrayed emotions of the character in the performance.

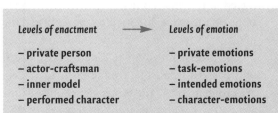

Levels of enactment	$\rightarrow$	Levels of emotion
– private person		– private emotions
– actor-craftsman		– task-emotions
– inner model		– intended emotions
– performed character		– character-emotions

Private emotions are emotions which arise from the personal experiences of the actor as a person in daily life. Emotions on the second level, the actor as craftsman, are connected with executing tasks as an actor onstage. I will call these task-emotions from now on and will elaborate upon in the following chapters. During rehearsals certain arrangements are made and the actor forms an inner model of the character, which guides him through performance, at the third level of enactment. This level concerns the emotions of the character, as the actor would like to, or, depending on the arrangements, will have to portray them. These are the emotions that the actor intends to put across, or the intended emotions.

The emotions of characters as they are presented in the performance, on the fourth level of enactment, are portrayed on the stage as representations of emotions as we know them in daily life. These are not real emotions, but they are intended to create the illusion of real emotions. In other words, character-emotions are formed by the specific behavior of actors, which refers to emotional behavior of characters. Characters as such do not have emotions and can therefore not act in accordance with them. The term character-emotions in this book means the representation of emotions portrayed by the actor.[23]

The designation 'emotions of characters' is often used in reference literature to indicate the *reception* of characters by the audience; the term 'character-emotions' would then refer only to what the audience observes. This interpretation is not used here, because there is an essential difference between the way an actor regards a character-emotion and the way an audience member regards that emotion. The audience can, for example, interpret emotions on the level of the actor-craftsman as belonging to the portrayed character-emotions (3.6; 4.9). In current acting methods it is usually thought that the character in performance (fourth level of enactment) is linked to private emotions the actor may be feeling. In the following chapter I will note that the enactment level of the actor as craftsman has received far too little attention.

2.7 Summary

Denis Diderot developed *Paradoxe sur le Comédien* in eighteenth-century France against the background of the Enlightenment and the primacy of reason. Although, in France, the classical style of acting was still dominant, the call for naturalism on stage was becoming stronger. The dispute between 'reason and emotion', 'head and heart' was illustrated by the strife between the two most prominent actresses of the day, Clairon and Dumesnil. Diderot sided with Clairon and proposed in *Paradoxe* that a good actor feels nothing at all on stage and can therefore arouse the most heightened emotions in the audience. Diderot supported this view with various arguments, which can be reduced to two main ones – First: Reason and feeling are incompatible. Second: Emotions on the stage differ from emotions in daily life. In addition, Diderot argued that a good actor needs to have expert skills developed over time.

The precise meaning of Diderot's paradox is difficult to establish in our time. Not only because it must be seen in its historical context, but also because some key terms are problematical. The terms 'nature', 'sensibilité', and 'modèle idéal' are ambiguous. Subjecting the paradox itself to empirical research is therefore not possible. It can be firmly established that the paradox has had great impact on contemporary acting theory; it is possible to translate the paradox into its current definition as 'the actor's dilemma'. Different opinions about whether actors do or do not feel have shifted in our day to discussions about the degree to which the actor should experience the emotions of the character he is playing. The dilemma of the actor stems from the fact that the actor is his own instrument, and that his artwork is transitory. These features of dramatic art result in a distinction between four levels of enactment, which are coupled with four levels of emotion: The private emotions of the actor as private person, the task-emotions of the actor as craftsman, the intended emotions of the inner model, and the emotions of the character in the realized performance.

Current acting methods are mainly oriented toward the enactment level of the portrayed character and toward its relationship with the private emotions of the actor. From the solutions that different acting styles offer for the dilemma of the actor, it will appear that the enactment level of the actor as craftsman deserves far more consideration (see chapter 3).

3   Acting Styles

Actors – they'll tell you a lot, but they'll never tell you all of it.
RIP TORN (in Kalter 1979: 4)

3.1   Introduction: Different Views on Acting

Opposing viewpoints about the actor and emotions can be recognized today in, for example, the styles of acting advocated by Stanislavsky and Brecht. These styles are diametrically opposed yet they have influenced western acting equally. In contemporary theater we see three general styles which differ from each other relative to the relationship of the emotions of the actor to those of the character. These three acting styles can be classified as 1) the style of involvement, 2) the style of detachment, and 3) the style of self-expression (3.2, 3.3, and 3.4).[1]

These three acting styles implicitly suggest three solutions for 'the dilemma'. These solutions all encounter the problem of the so-called *double consciousness* that the actor should maintain (3.5). Again, I stress that a distinction must be made between dealing with emotions during the rehearsal phase and during live performance: Diderot's paradox concerns the relationship between the emotions of the actor and his character during the *performance*. This distinction is not always simple to make as the methods used in contemporary acting styles apply mainly to the rehearsal phase and only implicitly to the final result in an actual performance.

By comparing disparate views on acting, several common points can be identified which are central to acting emotions (3.6). To portray emotions on stage, the actor forms an inner model which he tries to express as believably and convincingly as possible. While some aspects of the portrayal become 'second nature', the portrayal also contains the illusion of spontaneity. The aspect of task-emotions, which the actor has as a result of doing his work, can be particularly useful in creating the illusion of spontaneity (3.7). Acting emotions not only has an emotional effect on the audience; the audience also has a reciprocal affect on the actor (3.8).

3.2   The Style of Involvement

The style of involvement strives for a presentation of character-emotions so that the illusion of 'truthfulness' or 'reality' is created; the actor himself must not be visible in the portrayal of the character. The style of involvement is also called 'heated acting' and is identified with 'unity of role and acting'.[2] In the style of involvement the emotions portrayed on stage must seem as 'real' as possible. Ideally, this should be achieved by the presence of similar feelings in the actor: '...the best that can happen is that the actor is completely carried away by the piece. He transcends his own will and lives the part, without noticing how he feels himself, without thinking about what he is doing, and everything happens as a matter of course, unconsciously and intuitively' (Stanislavsky 1985).[3] The theater researcher Worthen points out that Stanislavsky in this passage gives the actor an assignment to 'feel spontaneous'. But, by definition, a command to be spontaneous cannot be obeyed.

Director and acting teacher Lee Strasberg based his work on Stanislavsky and developed Stanislavsky's 'system' into the well-known American 'method'. Strasberg said: 'The actor's task is to create that level of belief on stage, so that the actor is capable of experiencing the imaginary events and objects of the play with the full complement of those automatic physiological responses which accompany a real experience' (Strasberg 1988: 132). 'The method' is considered to go even further than Stanislavsky in demanding the immersion of the actor into the emotions of the character. By feeding the character with the actor's personal emotions, the style of involvement believes the

The Russian actor and director Konstantin Sergeyevich Stanislavsky (1863-1938) devoted his entire life to the theater. His father, a wealthy industrialist, and his mother, a descendent of a French actress, were art lovers. Thanks to them he was introduced to ballet, theater and the Italian opera at a young age. At scarcely fourteen years of age, he was being praised for his acting. As he grew more mature, the actor was praised for having exceptional talent and he played many major roles.

In 1888, along with some other Moscow actors, he founded the *Art and Literary Society*. Here, as actor and producer, he began his long search for the true art of acting. Stanislavsky found the acting of his time false, detached, and artificial and desired to replace this acting by – what he terms – lifelike theater.

According to Stanislavsky, in order to make the audience believe in the character, an actor should display authentic emotions. The actor should immerse himself in a role to such an extent that he actually feels the emotions of the character. The actor should achieve this state by delving into the psychology of the character. Tools in this process included the questions about the 'who, what, why, and when' of the character. With this new approach to acting, Stanislavsky introduced a profound change to the theater world. He placed the actor and acting at the center of attention, whereas in his day the text was considered the most crucial part of the performance. Since Stanislavsky, acting, especially the rehearsal process, has undergone a fundamental change.

The American director Lee Strasberg developed Stanislavsky's ideas further with the more extreme *method acting*: more extreme in terms of immersion into, and psychological analysis of, the character. With method acting it is a matter of the actor recalling his or her own personal emotional experiences which fit with the emotions of the character to be played. The actor presents these 'real' and strongly experienced emotions to the audience as if they were those of the character. From 1951 until his death in 1982, Strasberg was artistic director of New York's The *Actors Studio*, which is known as the temple of method acting.

performance will become more believable; the actor's expression will be more convincing and the audience will, in turn, become more involved themselves. This performative process is frequently referred to as 'identification'.

The style of involvement, however, inevitably confronts the problem of 'repeatability'. The actor 'lives the part', according to Stanislavsky and Strasberg, by 'actually experiencing analogous feelings every time the role is recreated' (Stanislavsky 1985: 23). But how can the actor experience fresh emotions time and again, after frequent rehearsals and several performances? In the style of involvement, the actor, assisted by his 'emotional memory', can activate his private emotions in such a way that these correspond with those of the character, 'new, each time'. The dramatic situation of the character is the stimulus for the emotional memory, which the actor puts to work by answering 'who, what, where, and why', the w-questions. Here one can note the influence of Pavlov, who proved that conditioning processes lead to automatic reflexes.[4] Similarly, emotions can also be reproduced, as proponents of the style of involvement contend.

As with Diderot, the primary goal here is to arouse emotions in the audience, (although one must ask whether Diderot meant the same thing by 'arousing emotions' as contemporary advocates of the style of involvement do). According to the style of involvement, moving the audience, creating in them identification or empathy with a character's emotional experiences, demands the presence of similar emotions in the actors of those characters. But this is contrary to Diderot's opinion. Stanislavsky proposes that natural emotions must occur at the same time in the actor in order to arouse emotions in the audience. The style of involvement resolves, or at least obscures, the dilemma of the actor by urging the actor to enter fully into the character, by creating the illusion that the actor actually is the character.[5] This 'solution' presumes a double consciousness on the actor's part. The actor relives the emotions of the character during the performance 'over and over again', but at the same time he keeps them under control. I will discuss to this so-called double consciousness within the several acting styles.

In the style of involvement the emphasis is seemingly placed on the private emotions of the actor, but actually the emphasis is placed on the character-emotions. The actor's private emotions are in the service of the character. The starting point for the emotions in the performance are those of the character, as presented in the dramatic text. The private emotions of the actor are used to shape the inner model, forming the basis for the character in the performance. Shaping the inner model must meet the criteria of 'truthfulness', emotions must be recognizable as they appear in daily life. Therefore the actor fills the model with his own emotional memories and experiences. Moreover, the style of involvement presumes that private emotions will be relived time and again in performance.

Referring back to the four levels of enactment (section 2.6) the level of the actor-craftsman is negligible in the style of involvement, playing a minor part with respect to controlling the acting process. Concentration is required of the actor-craftsman during preparation, but otherwise little mention is made of the actor as a professional with task-related emotions. The actor-craftsman must certainly not be visible to the audience. In the style of involvement emotions are imagined to be completely synchronized and parallel on all four levels of enactment. Moreover the emotions experienced in the audience should also parallel the emotions onstage.

3.3   The Style of Detachment

The style of detachment rejects the principle of identification of the actor with the character during performance: 'A happy character does not need to be played by a happy actor. The same goes for a tragic character' (Boysen 1988c: 11). The style of detachment is most strongly associated with Brecht. The emotions of characters are 'shown' or 'demonstrated' in a reproducible form, referring to emotions as they occur in reality, but not identical to them.[6] Brecht's main goal is to present social situations on the stage as processes which can be altered or reconstructed. The task of the actor is to focus the audience's attention on the socio-political aspects of the situation by presenting the socialized interaction of people, the (social) positions of the characters and the political-economic interests which are at stake. This does not demand the emotional involvement of the actors with their characters.

Brecht's emphatic rejection of the overlap of actor's emotions with character-emotions in performance was a reaction against the central role that emotions play in Stanislavsky's style of involvement. Brecht finds Stanislavsky naive in this respect. With Brecht, actors not only present characters, but also explicitly present 'themselves', their actual beings on stage and have opinions about the characters. By letting go of the demand for identification or involvement and by rejecting the effort to create the illusion of reality on the stage, the style of detachment is clearly parallel to Diderot's standpoint on acting in *Paradoxe*; in 1932 Brecht even wanted to found a Diderot association.[7]

Repeatability is guaranteed in the style of detachment by placing emphasis on technical mastery over the portrayal of emotions, situations, and motives. This style of acting is therefore sometimes referred to as 'calculated'. A question raised by this style is the believability of expression, just as it is with Diderot's 'emotionless' actor: 'While Diderot focused on the "emotion-free" actor of dual consciousness, however, he did not specify *how* the actress could perform *without* appearing unnatural and mannered' (Rovit 1989: 304). For Brecht believability is not only a matter of technical command over emotional portrayal, but also of revealing conflicting aspects in people, e.g., a villain also has a generous side (cf. *Herr Puntilla*). Believability also lies, according to Brecht, in making elements of the situation which lead to emotional reactions visible and by revealing the underlying social interests which are addressed and the social advantages/disadvantages the situation offers the characters.

The acting style directly relates to Brecht's desired effect on the audience. While Brecht wanted critical reflection on the part of the audience, he did not reject emotions outright; indeed at points he spoke of arousing emotions in the audience: 'Is that not precisely why we go to the theatre, to allow such diverse feelings to be aroused in us?' (1967: 393). However, the emotional reactions which occur in the epic theater audience will, according to Brecht, be qualitatively different than those witnessing the theater of involvement. This results from a critical reflection and recognition of the processes being shown. Alongside the 'epic' theater form, the style of detachment can be dis-

cerned in other theatrical forms: Political theater of the sixties and seventies – guerrilla theater, 'agit-prop', etc. – stand as examples. In these forms, the motive was often informational or educational. On the other hand, the physicalized acting of Meyerhold, while directed toward an audience effect, does fall under the style of detachment.[8]

The solution to the actor's dilemma in the style of detachment lies precisely in making the dilemma into a theme. There is no suggestion that the actor is at one with the character, instead both are explicitly shown. Because the epic theater actor also 'shows himself', this raises the question of whether the actor shown on stage is really the same as the actor in private. After all, this 'role' is also included as part of the dramatic action in the course of the performance. The actor does not step out of the performance, the actor steps out of the role of the (one) character and enters in fact into another role: 'Himself'. The question is whether 'the actor who shows himself' is meant to be the actor qua private person, or the actor qua professional. In the first case the actor's private emotions would apparently be relevant, in the second case the emotions of the actor-craftsman. Or, perhaps neither interpretation is correct and 'the actor who shows himself' is part of an extra layer of roles. Nonetheless, the style of detachment does allow space for emotions on the enactment level of the actor-

craftsman (section 2.6). In Brecht's theory, emotions on this level are not rejected or ignored. In this respect the style of detachment is a more complex form of acting than the
style of involvement.

Thus, the style of detachment offers no escape from the actor's dilemma either.
Here as well a double consciousness is presumed, expressed in the Brechtian term 'Ver-
fremdung' which implies the simultaneous presence of both actor and character.
According to the style of detachment, emotions on the level of enactment of the character become clearest by showing the character's situation. This emphasis on presenting
situational/social conditions also determines where the accent must lie in shaping the
inner model of the intended emotions. In addition to shaping an imagined model for
the character, another model is also imagined to express the particular aspects in the
dramatic situation or events that are provoking emotions.

Brecht and Meyerhold only consider the actor's private emotions as far as their function in the style of detachment differs from their function in the style of involvement.
According to the actress Helene Weigel, private emotions did, however, play a role in
rehearsals with Brecht: 'With Brecht we certainly do not work without involvement,
albeit that involvement alone is not enough' (Weigel, in Hoffmeier 1992: 138). 'Empathy' as a technique in rehearsal must be distinguished from the absence of it during the
performance itself. The viewpoint held in the style of detachment is that the actor's
private emotions have no relevance during the performance.[9] In short, this style does
not aim for emotional identification with the characters, neither from the actor nor
from the audience. Here, emotional layers associated with the four levels of enactment
do not parallel each other.

3.4   The Style of Self-Expression

In the style of self-expression, the expression of the actor's own authentic emotions is
key. According to Grotowski (1968: 16): 'Here everything is concentrated on the "ripen-
ing" of the actor which is expressed by a tension towards the extreme, by a complete
stripping down, by the laying bear of one's own intimity – all this without the least
trace of egotism or self-enjoyment. The actor makes a total gift of himself. This is a
technique of the "trance" and of the integration of all the actor's psychic and bodily
powers which emerge from the most intimate layers of his being and his instinct,
springing forth in a sort of "translumination".' The most well-known of the self-expression representatives are Jerzy Grotowski, Peter Brook, Richard Schechner, and Eu-
genio Barba. These directors and authors often replace actor and character with 'performer' and 'role', whereby the distinction between playing roles in the theater and our
roles in social situations becomes 'blurred'.[10]

The emotions characters portray in performance are the emotions of the actors
themselves and must be as spontaneous and true as possible. Improvisation is of paramount importance in these presentations – not as a studio/rehearsal technique as with
Stanislavsky and Strasberg – but as a component of live performance with an audience.
According to Grotowski this is not a question of portraying himself under certain
given circumstances, or of 'living' a part; nor does it entail the distant sort of acting
common to epic theater and based on cold calculation. The important thing is to use

Jerzy Grotowski was born in Poland in 1933 and by age twenty-six, was director of the *Teatr 13 Rzdowin* in Wroclaw, Poland. In this theater – later known as the *Theater Laboratory* – he began by exploring the ideas of Stanislavsky. Grotowski was particularly impressed by Stanislavsky's methods through which actors immerse themselves in the psychology of the character. In 1965 the laboratory was recognized by the state as an official center of research.

Looking for what he believed to be the essence of theater – a direct communication between the audience and the players – Grotowski experimented in his 'laboratory' with two groups: The actors and the audience. By integrating these two, a production gradually emerged. The next step was to see how the

actor could break down all the barriers between himself and the audience. At this point, Grotowski left his mentor Stanislavsky behind and developed his own ideas. Eventually, Grotowski's years of searching led to the creation of the *Poor Theater*. In this form of theater, everything which could possibly be considered superfluous – sets, costumes, make-up, and even the hall – was eliminated. In the seventies his ideas emerged as so-called 'happenings' or 'environmental theater', where the audience joined in the performance. The spectator became an actor. Likewise in these years, theaters were exchanged for schoolrooms, prisons, or factories where experimental performances were given.

Because the Poor Theater only had the actors' presence, without any artificial theatrical elements, Grotowski reasoned that the actor must be in complete control of his physical and mental capacities. Effects which might otherwise be achieved with costume, make-up, lighting, etc. must be theatricalized by the actor himself, for instance with perfect mime skills. Special postures, gestures, and use of voice must further shape the character. To achieve the desired results, the actor is often subjected to strenuous physical training. Grotowski's ideas on theater are compiled in *Towards a Poor Theater* (1968).

the role as a trampolin, an instrument with which to study what is hidden behind our everyday mask – the innermost core of our personality – in order to sacrifice it, expose it' (Grotowski 1968: 37).

In a performance that utilizes the style of self-expression, the actor and the character become one entity to such a great extent that one can properly use the term 'fusion'. Kirby and Hogendoorn go so far as to wonder if the term acting can rightfully be applied to performances in theatrical 'happenings', 'environmental theater', and similar 'performances'.[11] The actor presents himself without pretending to be anything or anyone else.[12] Oddly enough, one finds that the representatives of the seemingly most emotional and active means of expression also demand the tightest discipline and forms of movement. However for Grotowski there was no contradiction between internal technique and artificiality. He contends that 'a personal process which is not supported and expressed by a formal articulation and disciplined structuring of the role is not a release and will collapse in shapelesness'. (1968: 17). The work of other proponents of this acting style also reveals great importance attached to the actor's technique. In the west, ideas are frequently drawn from ritualized eastern theatrical forms and acting traditions such as Noh, Kabuki, and Khatakali, in which precise, strict rules and techniques are foundational (e.g., Zarrilli 1990; 1995).

Grotowski (1968: 121) and Brook (1968: 64) both subscribe to the understanding 'that both spontaneity and discipline, far from weakening each other, mutually reinforce themselves'. In performance the use of voice and kinetic bodies within this acting style verge 'vocally and physically upon acrobatics'. The goal of certain of Grotowski's exercises is, for example, to 'command each facial muscle' so that the actor can consciously isolate and manipulate minute physical areas: 'For example, make the eyebrows quiver very fast while the cheek muscles tremble slowly' (1968: 146). The actor must be able to create masks using all of one's facial muscles.

The importance Brook, Grotowski, and others attach to technical control and discipline of form is not strongly evidenced in much theater practice. In theatrical 'happenings', 'performances', and 'environmental theater', as presented in the seventies, there was a one-sided emphasis on spontaneous 'living', or a full-blown revelation of private emotions. According to Brook, the misapprehensions of this acting style led to the emotional abandon and unhesitating self-exposure, 'the same belief that every detail must be photographically reproduced. ... The result is often soft, flabby, excessive, and unconvincing' (Brook 1968: 132).

As with any style, in self-expressive acting the performance needs to be viewed in relation to the desired effect on the audience. In this case by having actors expose themselves, sometimes literally, and by playing with taboos and provocation: 'The happening shock is there to smash through all the barriers set up by our reason' (Brook 1968: 81, 62) to create a profound emotional response. In this form of acting there is also an educational effect: Audiences learn to analyze themselves, to find themselves by removing their social roles or masks. To achieve or intensify this, the audience is incorporated into the structure of the stage action, leading to an integration of the audience's and the actors' space. Thus, the emotional effect on the audience is radically different from the effects sought by the acting styles of involvement or detachment.

The dilemma is 'resolved' in the style of self-expression by not treating the character as a separate entity. Elements of the characters are used to display the essential personal emotions: '[of] laying oneself bare, of tearing off the mask of daily life, of exteriorizing oneself' (Grotowski 1968: 210). The character serves the actor, an exact reversal of the method of involvement. Therefore the dilemma would apparently appear to be resolved. However, the theater critic Martin Esslin contends that this actor is unable to evade the dilemma. He explains that these actors are unwittingly but centrally preoccupied with showing the audience that they are indeed actors. Reacting to a performance of the *Living Theater* where actors and audience intermingled Esslin writes: 'It became even more essential to make the audience aware of the fact that these were actors; they had to "act" that they were actors pretending to be real people engaging in a conversation. Otherwise they would have been mistaken for just another member of the audience who could be ignored or snubbed' (Esslin 1987: 78). The 'performer' cannot escape making clear in one way or another that he is the actor and is therefore distinct

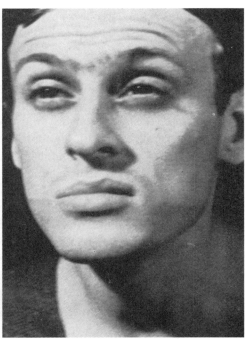

Gestural-ideograms for facial expressions (Grotowski 1968: 71)

from the audience. Theater director Gerardjan Rijnders also maintains that an actor who plays himself onstage is also playing a role.[13] Richard Schechner says: 'Professional actors are aware that they are acting.'[14] The apparent solution of the dilemma in the style of self-expression is then yet another version of double consciousness: An awareness of the presentation for the audience and of 'acting as if the audience is not there' (Barba and Savarese 1991: 242). Self-expressive performances also presume another double awareness: The performance of an artificial form (the role) and the expression of spontaneous, true emotions (the self). Barba talks in this context about the duality of the 'performer': 'Being natural, yet highly artificial' (1991: 148, 242).

By analyzing the style of self-expression in relation to the four levels of enactment, as outlined in section 2.6, the private emotions of the actor as private person form the center point. Private emotions are used in the style of self-expression primarily to express the self, whereas in the style of involvement the actor's private emotions are used to model the emotions of the character. In the style of self-expression, emotions belonging to a character are in the service of the actor's own emotions. The intended emotions (which are on the enactment level of the inner model) are expressed in the style of self-expression with a strict formal discipline, in a 'score'; the character-emotions are noted in this score in such a way that the actor is only free to play 'himself' once he masters the external form completely. If the actor shows 'himself' during the performance one could in principle also include the emotions of the actor-craftsman (on the enactment level of the actor-craftsman), but this is unlikely the intention of the style.

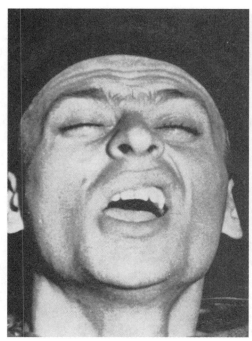

3.5   Solutions for the Dilemma

The three 'solutions' offered for the actor's dilemma in the three styles of acting described above all presume a double consciousness on the part of the actor while portraying emotions in a performance. A double consciousness of 'sincere conviction as well as control, of involvement and control' (the style of involvement), or the dualism of 'not being himself but rather seeming to be another' (the style of detachment) or the 'dual experience of performer as role and actor' (the style of self-expression).[15] The question is then: To what extent does the presumption of double consciousness solve the actor's dilemma? But this seems to be a misleading question, a displacement of the problem, since double consciousness assumes different forms within the different acting styles.[16]

It is noteworthy that as early as 1942 the French researcher Villiers ascertained that there are three different meanings ascribed to 'double consciousness' (*dédoublement*). These can be related to the three acting styles delineated here.[17] First, the style of involvement. The double consciousness of the actor in the style of involvement consists of being swept up completely by emotions, comparable to the character-emotions, while simultaneously controlling them. Villiers describes this as his third definition of '*dédoublement*': 'The actor feels absolutely like the character, but he also reserves the feeling of his own self as an actor' (1942: 203). The involved actor would feel just like the character, but observe himself as well. In this definition of the double consciousness the actor seems to be the character.

In the second distinct acting style, the style of detachment, double consciousness consists of taking actions or 'behaving' like a character and at the same time being visibly present as an actor. This interpretation resembles Villiers' second definition ascribed to '*dédoublement*', in which 'the scenic feeling coincided with a critical attitude' (1942: 202). Villiers proposes that 'this phenomenon is analogous with anyone whose function is to influence a crowd, with all sorts of speakers' (1942: 202). As noted in section 3.3, the role of the actor in the style of detachment can moreover include a double consciousness between who the actor is and who the 'presented actor' is. In other words, the actor is visible as character as well as actor.

In the style of self-expression there is a double consciousness of 'being oneself' and at the same time being aware of 'the artificial nature of the appearance': Becoming immersed in and portraying true emotions versus the unavoidable awareness of being an actor or 'performer', of standing before an audience. This parallels Villiers' first explanation of '*dédoublement*', in which 'the personality of the actor makes place for that of the character' (1942: 202, 203). In this case an actor would not experience discrepancy during the performance, but realizes the distinction once offstage. The comparison with an actor in the style of self-expression does not match completely, because in the style of self-expression the character is 'adjusted' to the personality of the 'self' of the actor. In this sense of '*dédoublement*' the character (the role) is the actor himself.

To solve the paradox by presuming there is a double consciousness in the actor, as something specific to actors and their work, is a spurious solution. Various scholars argue that a reference to the double consciousness can be gleaned from Diderot's *Paradoxe*: 'The requirements of Diderot's ideal actor would use the "split" to become both marionette and marionettist at the same time. In this way the actor exploits his body as

General Approaches to Acting Emotions on Stage
(BASED ON KONIJN 1994)

Acting style	Emotional relationship actor-character	Example of theatrical form or genre	Intended effect on the audience
1 involvement (e.g., Stanislavsky, Strasberg)	actor = character	naturalistic, illusionistic, realistic	involvement, identification, empathy with character
2 detachment (e.g., Meyerhold, Brecht)	actor = not character	'epic', 'lehrstücke', political theater	reflection on situational demands and interests of the character
3 self-expression (e.g., Brook, Grotowski)	character = actor	theater of cruelty, 'happenings', 'living theater'	troubling the 'inner self' and 'unmasking' the audience

an instrument (the puppet) through which he plays roles. It is by means of this "double consciousness" that the actor produces art' (Rovit 1989: 40). Or when Diderot points out that the actress Clairon is 'the soul of a marionette, a doll which surrounds her, in which she has nestled herself firmly through preparation. (...) At such times she is a double: The little Clairon and the great Agrippina'(1985: 54).

Despite the different meanings ascribed to the double consciousness in the different acting styles, a common feature is also clear. By reducing the problem of double consciousness to its more concrete and central constituent problems found in each of the descriptions of acting styles, an inventory can be made of the common acting tasks contained in the actor's work on stage.

3.6   Acting Tasks

However broadly the acting styles discussed differ from one another in their views on acting emotions, in each style there are four central elements. Namely, (1) the 'inner model' of the imagination, (2) believability of expression, (3) repeatability and (4) the problem of spontaneity, inspiration or 'presence'. Using a variety of terminology, the authors discussed above devote concentrated attention to addressing these four elements in their methods. It is an easy task to see these four potentially opposed positions in the phenomenon of the double consciousness. The inner model seems to be at odds with the concept of spontaneity, inspiration and 'presence'. Believability seems to oppose repeatability of the emotions to be portrayed. All four aspects can be found in *Paradoxe sur le Comédien*, and will appear below where these acting tasks are discussed in relation to their importance in the relationship between the emotions of the actor and the character. Each task leads moreover to formulating a skill required to be able to act emotions. In the discussion below, it is assumed that the execution of acting tasks in performance must be prepared during the rehearsal period.

3.6.1   Inner Model

In his imagination or fantasy the actor must form a model of the character he wants to portray on stage. Diderot introduces the '*modèle idéal*' as an internally imagined idea of the character, based on characteristic manifestations of the intended character. He illustrates this with, among others, *The Miser* by Molière, who must be the sum, 'the greatest common denominator of all misers' and not simply 'a' miser we know in daily life. The inner model contains *the* Miser who possesses 'the most general and notable character traits' of all common misers, 'but is not an exact portrait of any' (Diderot 1985: 80). The importance of forming a model in the imagination emerges in the various methods with references to concepts like fantasy, imagination and 'emotional memory'. With Stanislavsky the actor forms an inner model with the help of 'artistic imagination' (1991: 21) to answer the w-questions (who, what, where, why, when).

Strasberg lets the actor relive his personal emotional memories to make the abstract emotions of the character concrete. According to Brecht it is necessary to know and understand the social circumstances and relationships of the people (as characters) to form a model of the most conspicuous features of the emotions. In the method of self-expression, 'the intimacy of the deepest inner emotions' can only be expressed believably by finding universal principles, established in a strict form, a 'score', and also detailed in 'gesture ideograms'.[18] To complete the inner model (of the emotions to be portrayed as the character or the role, the actions and situations) with as much detail and as concretely as possible, knowledge of human interaction and daily emotions is required. During the performance the inner model serves as a guideline. One could say that the style of involvement is directed toward the psychology of the character within the dramatic context; that the style of detachment calls upon the psychology of social relationships; and the style of self-expression is directed toward the psychology of the individual.

3.6.2   **Credibility** The actor must present the imagined model to the audience with credibility and conviction. Because the components of the inner model are different for each method, believability is attached to different aspects of the portrayal of emotions. In the style of involvement, credibility means creating 'the illusion of reality – as in daily life'; the actor is invisible and the audience believes, for a moment, that the actor is the character. With the involved actor, emotional memory recalls personal emotions which are necessary to lend believability to character-emotions. With the style of detachment it is important that the actions, the situations rendered, and the underlying relationships are credible and not so much the emotions as such.

Brecht asks us to believe that the actions and emotions represented find basis in plausible and mutable processes in social reality; the goal is not a temporary belief in a fiction or illusion. Thus acting in the style of detachment incorporates elements which remind the audience of immediate reality, alienation effects, as when actors 'drop' their role to voice a 'personal' opinion of the character they play. The emotions of the characters need not have a detailed illusion of reality, but they must be recognizable to the audience. This can often be achieved with small, symbolic references. Believability in the sense of genuine – not fake – is seen with the style of self-expression when the actor unmasks himself. The audience accepts the role presented as an expression of 'the self' of the actor.

In all three styles credibility requires a well developed 'expressive instrument'. This instrument is the actor himself: Voice, posture, countenance and movement. Grotowski's physical exercises reveal the high standards for these 'expressive instruments' (see 'masks' in box illustrating section 3.4).[19] The believability of Diderot's emotion-free actor lies precisely in his command of technical skills: 'An actor who has achieved technical mastery and a higher self-awareness (...) can most truthfully and gracefully reflect inner conditions through gesture.' (Rovit 1989: 97). The style of detachment in particular raises the question of how to avoid falling into false mannerisms and clichés. With the styles of involvement and self-expression, the question is how to insure control over the emotions and to guarantee the repeatability of 'spontaneous' emotions.

3.6.3   **Repeatability – Second Nature** The expression of the inner model must not only be believable and convincing but must moreover be repeated. Every performance must in great measure resemble the previous one: 'The actor's expression, however, must be unambiguous, ordered, tenacious, and persevering. And it must be repeatable.

And quite during a particular course of action, at the same time, at the same place, in the same situation, and in the same way' (Boysen 1988a: 27). Various scholars have ana-lyzed Diderot's pivotal idea that character behavior can become an automatic process through training the actor: '...train his body to react automatically in portraying already-rehearsed signs of emotion' (Rovit 1989: 98).[20] It is remarkable how these ideas return in contemporary acting theory as one of the fundamental problems in acting.

With the style of involvement, training methods are focused on an automatic pro-gression of intended emotions during every performance: 'If the fantasy is practiced each day systematically referring to the same theme each time, then everything that stands in relation to the imagined situation of the piece will become a habit, a second nature' (Stanislavsky 1991: 38; also 1989: 242; 1985: 23). The style of detachment em-phasizes the technical command of the role and the 'cool' presentation of character-emotions, so that repetition will pose no problem.[21] The difference between the styles of involvement and detachment is aptly described by Emmet: 'If you agree with Con-stant [Coquelin], the rehearsal period is used to learn how to *simulate* emotions. If you agree with Constantin [Stanislavsky], the rehearsal period is used to discover how to *stimulate* emotions (Emmet 1975: 18; italics EK).

In the work of advocates of the style of self-expression, 'second nature' also plays a very important part in the strict discipline of form. As found in eastern theater forms, the expressive actor must make the rigorous patterns of a style so much his own that space will open up therein for personal, creative content (e.g., Zarrilli, 1990). The actor 'must learn to perform all this unconsciously in the culminating phases of his acting' (Grotowski 1968: 36) and 'He must bring into being an unconscious state of which he is completely in charge' (Brook 1968: 143). Frequent rehearsal to make drama texts and actions 'second nature' is necessary so that these will no longer demand the actor's concentration during the actual performance.

In each of the three acting styles a large part of the training is directed toward form-ing 'the instrument', through voice training, text training, posture, gesture, and move-ment, as well as with 'automatic' rendering of specific signals which point to specific character-emotions. The authors discussed agree that the actor needs regular and numerous rehearsals to arrive at 'the seemingly self-evident ease' (Freriks and Rijnders 1992: 57), with which his artwork unfolds for the audience. In short, repeatability requires lengthy training of the general and character-specific features of emotions. 'This "superimposed" form is usually the biggest problem', according to Freriks and Rijnders (1992: 96). How can one make a repeatable, fixed, stylized expression seem 'like new'? The task of making a role 'second nature' seems to be the inverse of making the performance spontaneous, inspired or achieving 'presence'.

3.6.4 Spontaneity – presence

A believable portrayal of emotions seems to require (the illusion of) spontaneous emotions, whereas reproducibility of the inner model requires a more or less fixed form. Interestingly, both aspects – reproducibility and spontaneity – are, according to Grotowski, 'two complementary aspects of the creative process' (1968: 209). The various authors discussed include this idea in the acting methods they describe.

In the style of involvement, spontaneity, in the sense of 'truthfully' presented emotions, purports to be guaranteed by the presumed functioning of emotional memory. However, the portrayal of a chaotic or ugly character must also be designed, controlled and esthetic. The actor must know how to distinguish 'between *what* and *how*, between the theme and the way of performing it' (Chekhov 1953: 15). Stanislavsky points out that habit contributes greatly to spontaneity, in the sense of creativity, and that inspiration can exist thanks to technique.[22] Grotowski (self-expression) shares this view: 'Creativity, ... is boundless sincerity, yet disciplined: i.e. articulated through signs' (1968: 261). Emmet also states: 'Inspiration in performance, as so many actors have pointed out, is more likely to descend from heaven the more painstakingly the role has been prepared' (1975: 18). Brook compares the need for a rigid form to express spontaneous emotions with the basic training of a pianist.[23] According to Brook, an actor can only experience how much freedom there can be within the strictest discipline when he commands his technique. Grotowski too demands discipline for self-expression in acting: 'We find that artificial composition not only does not limit the spiritual but actually leads to it. ... The form is like a baited trap, to which the spiritual process responds spontaneously and against which it struggles' (1968: 17).

From these statements one can deduce that spontaneity, creativity, and inspiration point to 'something' in the presented emotions which makes the authenticity, liveliness, or immediate nature of the portrayal visible and tangible. 'Something' that shows the here and now, the actuality of the performance, to the audience: 'There is only one element of which film and television cannot rob the theater: The closeness of the living organism' (Grotowski 1968: 41). 'Something' which moreover prevents a mechanical portrayal of 'cold' emotional expressions or hollow tricks. 'The study of what exactly this means opens a rich field. It compels us to see what living action means, ..., what is partially alive, what is completely artificial – until slowly we can begin to define what the actual factors are that make the act of representation so difficult' (Brook 1968: 155).

This 'something' points toward a slightly different use of the term 'spontaneity' in the acting methods described, e.g., the spontaneous, inspired acting or the actor's 'presence' where presence connotes more than merely the opposite of absence. Stanislavsky calls it 'a state of being' or 'having charisma' or 'beaming radiance'.[24] Josef Kelera says in Grotowski's book: 'The actor radiates a sort of psychic light. I can not find another way to put it. At the high point of the role everything that is technical by nature is illuminated from within' (in Grotowski 1968: 109).[25] With Barba, presence is the central point around which the rest of the actor's performance revolves. As a result of anthropological studies on acting, Barba comes to the conclusion that an actor's energy and inner tension give him presence and that this is one of the universal principles of acting. As with Brook: 'The energy that fed the months of work that eventually illuminated all the structure of sub-plot' (1968: 91). With Barba we find, moreover, that being able to create presence is part of the actor's task description, and relates to his capacity to make an impression on the audience – preferably an unforgettable one.

It is a requirement of the gifted actor to 'have' or to create 'something', with which he forges a memorable impression on the audience.[26] In anticipation of the following chapters, I suggest here that 'having presence' is a crucial part of creating the illusion of 'spontaneous' character-emotions: It is the active agent which renders the illusion 'real'.

3.7 Emotions of the Actor-Craftsman

In the acting methods discussed above, there is a notable absence of interest in the emotions of the actor himself; that is to say, emotions which result from the level of enactment of the actor as a professional craftsman – the emotions connected to executing acting tasks on stage before an audience. I have already named this category of emotions *task-emotions*. The tasks assigned to the actor, as distilled from the above, can be placed into a temporary, general task description. I propose that during a performance it is the actor's task to give expression to an inner model with as much conviction and believability as possible. In this process, some aspects of the portrayal have, on the one hand, become second nature (repeatable) and, on the other hand, the portrayal of the character has the illusion or the element of spontaneously aroused emotions.

Task-emotions can arise from the conflict between the inner model, 'as the actor imagined the character would be', and his actual rendition of the character, but also from the effect that the audience has on the actor. Brecht pays great attention to the fact

Peter Brook was born in 1925 in London to Russian parents. His first productions were performed during World War II and soon after the war he was engaged by the *Royal Shakespeare Company*. The director caused a furor with, among others, his production of *Titus Andronicus* (1955), with Lawrence Olivier in the leading role. In the sixties, Brook was drawn to the self-expressive acting of Antonin Artaud and the detached acting of Bertolt Brecht. These conflicting acting styles influenced him greatly and by combining these two extremes, Brook created an acting style which became the hallmark of the *Royal Shakespeare Company*.

In 1970 Brook established an international center for theater research in Paris, where he brought together actors, musicians, mimes, and acrobats from many countries. With this group he aimed to transcend the boundaries of nations, cultures, and disciplines. Brook won international celebrity by moving into desolate villages in the Sahara with his theater group to explore the border between life and death. These experiences formed the essence for his later theater productions. Brook's most acclaimed and daunting achievement was his production of *The Mahabharata* (1985); a nine-hour epic centered around Indian religious mythology.

that an actor is not only present on stage as the character but also as an actor, a professional, but he then fails to draw the conclusion that the actor would necessarily also bring his own emotions with him and not only those concerning the character. With Brecht and in general, views about acting seem singularly concerned with the preparation of tasks to be performed, the rehearsal process.

The acting theories described give only minimal consideration to two sorts of task-emotions: Concentration and 'stage fright'. Concentration is cited, especially by Stanislavsky and Michael Chekhov, as an important and necessary condition for the actor to complete his task in performance. According to Stanislavsky, the actor can only become involved in the character by concentrating on the details of the dramatic situation. In this book, I will consider concentration not only as a means to attain empathetic involvement, but also as an important task-emotion (4.6). Stage fright is usually referred to as something which can be disastrous for acting and which must be eradicated immediately (although opinions differ on this matter inside the profession). According to conventional wisdom stage fright has a paralyzing effect.[27] Strasberg bluntly calls stage fright 'the most vulgar preoccupation of all' (1988: 57). The actor must solve this by 'simply concentrating', concludes Strasberg (1988: 102).

Strictly speaking, stage fright does not happen during the performance, but just before. According to Villiers 'le trac' is not part of the role interpretation but 'a sort of impatient anxiety which precedes the role interpretation, and usually disappears quickly' (1942: 148-150). Villiers seems to be indicating general task-related tensions in the actor, not so much related to the specific emotions of the specific character, but attached to the actor's work itself.

In an earlier study, I also demonstrated that high degrees of tension or stress occur during actual performance and that these levels must be distinguished from stage fright (4.8). Actors' tension and energy during a performance are central concerns in the work of Barba and Savarese. They discuss it as an important component of stage presence. They find strong parallels between successful performances in different acting styles in Western and Eastern theater traditions. I suspect that task-emotions play a major function in achieving presence, radiance and power in the presentation.

My hypothesis is that in portraying character-emotions on stage, the actor will use or apply task-emotions. The actor is present on stage as a professional and uses the emotions which are related to this level of enactment to complete his task. He uses the emotions as an actor-craftsman to lend the illusion of spontaneity and believability to the reproducible form which has become second nature, based on the inner model. Seen in this way, it is striking that so little attention has been paid to task-emotions in the various acting methods.

Without meaning to do so, Strasberg does provide a lead for using task-emotions: 'The important thing is ... not that what the actor deals with is an exact parallel to the play or the character, but that when the character thinks, the actor really thinks; when the character experiences, the actor really experiences – *something*' (Strasberg 1988: 67, 68; italics EK). And further: '...it does not matter so much what the actor thinks, but the fact that he is really thinking something that is real to him at that particular moment' (1988: 110). In the next two chapters I will expound step by step, using a psychological theory of emotion, that it is mainly the task situation which is 'real' for the actor 'at that particular moment'.

3.8   Actor and Audience

An important aspect which has bearing on task-emotions is the presence of an audience: 'The very fact of performance creates tension for the actor' (Strasberg 1988: 125). Brook notes that the public assists: 'The audience assists the actor, and at the same time for the audience itself assistance comes back from the stage' (1968: 156). Analogous to the tension in the actor, caused by the audience, runs the tension (suspense) or interest of the audience in the performance. Regardless of the desired effect, the actor's performance requires that the audience will at least become interested, and at best develop a certain degree of concern, attention, fascination, admiration, etc. An important aspect of stage acting is therefore to direct the audience's attention; in this context one also speaks of 'manipulating the audience'.[28]

According to Kirby, the actor's task is to effect or impact the audience with the intention to do so. One tool for achieving this is a believable, repeatable portrayal of an inner model of character-emotions, as noted in the discussion of acting styles. The desired effects can be of an emotional, reflexive or aesthetic nature (see box on page 42). Despite the aim of contemporary drama to evoke other effects than purely emotional ones, it seems that moving the audience is consistently the main issue, as the following quote indicates: 'The very great actors, who arouse the most emotion in the audience...' (Freriks and Rijnders 1992: 57). Similarly Diderot writes: 'The actor is tired, but you are dejected; that is because he has exerted himself without feeling anything, and you have experienced feelings without exerting yourself. If it were otherwise, the profession of acting would be the most miserable on earth; he is not actually his character, he plays the role and does it so well that you mistake him for the character: The illusion is yours alone, he knows himself that it is not real' (Diderot 1985: 57). Moreover, the audience seems to value a performance the more their emotions have been aroused.[29]

Esslin pointed out that the audience comes not only to witness events full of suspense, emotion and interesting trials and tribulations which appear as 'real' as possible, but also to enjoy the skill with which the illusion is produced in the art.[30] After the most 'lifelike' and compelling performance, the audience member praises the acting as 'splendidly natural' or that it was 'so real'. The audience member moreover has expectations as to the 'correct' degree of involvement by actors (and audience) in different genres of theater and acting styles: 'If self-involvement at each level of role-enactment appears too little or too much for each type of theater they know, spectators may judge role-enactment as unconvincing or displeasing' (Constantinidis 1988: 75).[31]

In previous sections we saw that all specific theater forms create specific expectations. The audience observing a theatrical work employing an involvement style of acting is expected to believe (temporarily) in the 'reality' of the character-emotions: The actor 'is' the character. In theater pieces utilizing a style of detachment, the audience is expected to reflect critically on the

> Observation of what the spectator sees and what I experience as an actress, is completely different. Moreover, who sees those tears? Only the people in the first four rows.
>
> (Actress Elsie de Brauw in the documentary *Acteurs Spelen Emoties*, NPS 1995)

dialectical relationship of the actor to his character; and concurrently believes in the possibility of truth in the emotions presented. The audience for theater events in a style of self-expression is expected to believe the emotions on stage are indisputably those of the actors themselves. Then, the character is only the vehicle. Indeed, it is probable that audience members base their choice to attend a certain performance on these expectations. Audience expectation and the willingness of the audience to 'go along with it' will also have an effect on the credibility or persuasiveness of the character-emotions displayed (4.6).

In conclusion, I note again here that the actor functions on all four levels of enactment – as private person, actor-craftsman, inner model, and character – simultaneously during the performance, with different accents depending on different acting styles. The audience, in principle, observes all four levels simultaneously, and usually implicitly. The perception of the audience will usually be directed toward interpreting the observed behavior as belonging to the character.[32] The audience member will moreover have his own idea about each of the levels of enactment; what the character 'should' look like (that is to say the inner model of the spectator) or whether the degree to which the emotions of the actor-craftsman may be visible. It is emphasized that there is a difference in the perception of the performance among the participants, e.g., the actors, and for the audience.[33] In a recent study by the researcher Johan Hoorn and me, the perspective of the spectator on perceiving and experiencing fictional characters is elaborated.[34] In this book I place focus on the perspective of the actor.

3.9   Summary

The question as to what extent the emotions of the actor himself must coincide with those of his character was addressed by Diderot in the eighteenth century. His attempt to respond is found in his *Paradoxe*. In contemporary views on acting emotions, we recognize Diderot's paradox as the dilemma of the actor. Three general styles of acting – involvement, detachment and self-expression – have been distinguished on the basis of the variable 'correspondence between emotions of actor and character'. The three styles pose different views on the relationship between the actor's emotions and the emotions portrayed as the character.

One solution for the actor's dilemma found in all three styles is the notion of a 'double consciousness' of the actor. This appears to be a spurious solution, resulting in three different forms which this double consciousness can assume, all of which merely displace the problem. The concept of double consciousness can be translated into a few central aspects, which can be found as common elements in all the acting styles. These can be reformulated into the actor's tasks when portraying character-emotions on stage: The inner model of the character in the imagination, the believability of expression, the repeatability of the role as second nature, and the need to achieve spontaneity, inspiration, or presence.

A closer look at these four acting tasks leads to the formulation of at least four task-requirements for performing emotions, respectively: Knowledge of human behavior and how emotions function in daily life; a well-developed expressive instrument; training of stage actions and emotional signals so they become second nature; and applying and controlling task-emotions. The emotions connected to executing acting tasks, which were called task-emotions, are underexposed in the documented acting methods. They seem however to fulfill an efficacious function in shaping emotions on stage. For a professional, these task-emotions can contribute to the conviction and believability of character-emotions as perceived by the spectator. The mutual influence of the actor and the audience member is perceptible in the tension a critical audience causes the actor to feel, while the actor directs or manipulates the attention or interest of the audience.

The suggested approach to the actor's work also reveals the psychological nature of acting emotions. The psychological nature of the double consciousness, the four acting tasks and the task-emotions leads us directly to look more closely at what emotions actually are and how they function in daily life. What is now needed to continue this line of reasoning is a model of the emotion process which we can apply to the actor in a live theater situation. The following chapter will therefore describe a contemporary theory of emotions from the field of psychology. From this psychological perspective I will focus on the emotions of the actor as a professional craftsman.

4   *Emotions and Acting*

> Well, lending the illusion of truth to that which is not
> and sir, without cause, as a game...
> Is it not your profession to give life
> to fantasized characters on stage?
> LUIGI PIRANDELLO (1990 [1921]: 144)

4.1   Introduction: General Human Emotions

In the last chapter I suggested that task-emotions can play a central part in portraying character-emotions on stage. They would seem to be useful for acting with conviction, but are not discussed in any of the accepted acting theories. This is perhaps because most acting theory is limited to the description of a practice-oriented method with which the actor can reach an optimal job performance relating to his role. Opinions differ as to exactly what an optimal job performance is, as well as on how to achieve it. In this book, the accent lies on the acting process and related emotions in the actual performance. It is plausible that the emotions in performance are different from those in rehearsals. The presence of an expectant audience is an important factor here. The effect of the audience on the actor is only broached in most acting theories in terms of the widely feared idea of stage fright. In this chapter it will become clear that this approach to the actors' task-emotions is too limited.

With the help of current psychological insight into emotions, it will further be shown that the 'real' emotions in performance are a variety of task-emotions of the actor. The cognitive emotion theory of Nico Frijda will serve here as a framework. He bases his theory mainly on important theoretical insights in emotions of Jean-Paul Sartre, Magda Arnold, and Richard Lazarus. The most important aspects of Frijda's theory on the nature of emotions and the emotion process of general human emotions will be outlined briefly in the next section (4.2), after which the process of emotion during acting can be described. This psychological emotion theory will be explained and elaborated further while applying it to the situation of the actor on stage.

4.2   Sadness is Contained in the Situation

Nearly a century ago it was thought that emotion stemmed from certain physical sensations. This reasoning formed the basis for the then generally accepted theory of emotion. This school is referred to as the 'I shake, therefore I am afraid theory'; the James-Lange-theory (1884). Jean-Paul Sartre (1905-1980) opened the way to a cognitive and functional approach to emotions. He no longer views emotions as 'subjective states of mind roaming in the individual detached from an objective world' (1971: 83), but as having a function in relating to the world around us. Sartre: 'The emotion is a certain way to understand the world' (1971: 84). Following Sartre, among others, Frijda's theory views emotions as functional expressions of the individual in response to his environment. Emotions are no longer exclusively physical, internal disturbances, but serve the personal motives, needs or concerns relating to pleasure and pain, attraction and aversion. Emotions betray the notion that there are individual interests at stake. These can be more or less universal and one need not always be conscious of them.

The emotional perception is formed initially through the perception of the situation. Where one person sees a situation as threatening, another might see it as inevitable or challenging. The situation itself does not give rise to emotions. The meaning which someone gives to a situation makes this person afraid or irritated or provokes a specific action. Emotions are the convergence of the (im)possibilities offered by the surroundings or situation with the (im)possibilities the individual has with respect to satisfying his concerns. Both the threat as well as the hope of satisfying concerns set the emotion process in motion. Emotions arise in 'the interaction of the situational meanings and concerns' (Frijda 1988: 352).

The emotion process passes through different stages but is completed in a fraction of a second. After an event or a situation (in the surroundings or in thought, fantasy or imagination) has taken on meaning for a person, it is judged according to its relevance for satisfying concerns. This assessment (relevance evaluation) determines whether or not there will be emotion. Next, the person appraises whether he can cope with the situation and what the best course of action is (context evaluation). These possibilities for action determine which emotion will arise, if any do arise. The urgency, gravity, and difficulty of the situation ultimately determine the intensity the specific emotion will have (urgency evaluation).[1]

Together the evaluations form a proposal for action, or indicate a tendency (an urge) to do something: An action tendency. Frijda defines emotions as changes in action readiness with a quantitative aspect of 'activation' and a qualitative aspect of 'action tendency'. This is the urge to act, to refrain from action, or to suppress the action. Frijda proposes that each emotion is paired with an action tendency, with an urge or impulse to change the relationship between the person and the environment. Such an impulse can result in three possible outcomes of the process, or three expressions of an emotion: (1) Emotional perception, also including plans for goal-oriented behavior or fantasy; (2) noticeable behavioral expression such as verbal and non-verbal behavior and facial expression; and (3) physiological change, for example arousal, accelerated heartbeat, changes in blood pressure and hormone levels.

In the emotion process every phase has outputs, which are input for the following phase and lead to feedback loops. 'Every phase in the core process is subject to regulatory intervention by mechanisms, outcome-controlled processes, or voluntary self-control' (Frijda 1986: 456). Regulatory intervention has an effect on the results of the emotion process: The output. Regulation influences the often disturbing or uncomfortable side effects of emotions, but regulation has limitations. It will be explained in section 4.9 how regulation processes can benefit acting. Regulation processes are constantly active; for example in the 'social roles' we perform. We often mask our 'true' nature or our 'real' feelings by other signs, for example a polite smile instead of a jealous glance. Now that Frijda's model has been sketched, this model can be used to describe the emotion process in acting. Gradually, the 'deeper layers' of the emotion process will be explained.

4.3 The Emotions of Characters

We will apply Frijda's model quite literally to describe the emotion process of an imaginary actor who portrays the emotions of a character, for example the revenge of *Medea*. In the first phase, it becomes clear immediately that the situation for the actor has a different meaning than for the character. Concerning the situation of the actor, there is an actual context in which the confrontation with an actual audience takes place. In this context, specific tasks must be executed which involves, among other things, rendering character-emotions. For the character, there is a dramatic context in which, for example, the character Medea is betrayed and abandoned by Jason, after she left her country and family for him and has sacrificed much. The essence of her womanhood has been offended.

The actor's emotions relate to the actual context, which is called here the *task situation*. For the actor, the character-emotions relate to the fictional context, which, in this study, is called the character situation or the *dramatic situation*. These two 'worlds' are connected to the various levels of enactment of the actor. The actor's private emotions and task-emotions each concern the actual context: Respectively the actor acting as private person and the actor acting as professional. The intended emotions and the character-emotions each concern the dramatic world (a fictional world for the actor): Respectively the enactment levels of the character as inner model and the character as actually portrayed in the performance.

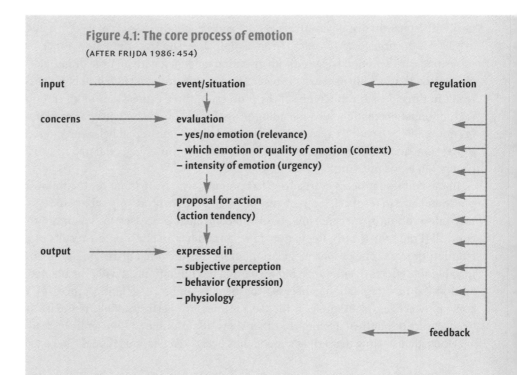

Figure 4.1: The core process of emotion
(AFTER FRIJDA 1986: 454)

input ⟶ event/situation   ⟵⟶ regulation

concerns ⟶ evaluation
- yes/no emotion (relevance)
- which emotion or quality of emotion (context)
- intensity of emotion (urgency)

proposal for action
(action tendency)

output ⟶ expressed in
- subjective perception
- behavior (expression)
- physiology

feedback

Terms in Emotion Theory

Concerns, interests: Desires, needs, passions, or personality traits. The emotion process revolves around, as it were, looking after concerns.

Relevance evaluation: The situation or event is appraised in order to determine whether concerns are at stake. This appraisal determines whether or not an emotion will arise.

Context evaluation: The situation or event is evaluated in order to judge whether the person can cope with the situation and, subsequently, what action he can best take. This judgment signals the main contextual components and determines which emotion will arise.

Urgency evaluation: The intensity of the emotion is determined as a result of the urgency, gravity, and difficulty of the situation. The more serious the situation, the more intense the emotion.

Action tendency: Urge or impulse to execute a specific action, or to suppress one.

Regulation: Corrections (restraints) on the different phases and the output of the emotion process. Social codes of behavior or uncertainty can be strong regulators.

The actor's private emotions fall into the category of general human emotions, as we know them in daily life and which are the subject of psychological emotion theories. The task-emotions of the actor are a specific sub-set of these. The question is to what extent it is possible to consider the intended emotions and character-emotions as subsets of general human emotions. I presume that they are of a fundamentally different nature than the emotions we encounter in daily life. The intended emotions exist in the fantasy of the actor: A mental image of how he is going to portray the emotions of his character on stage. The realization of this inner model on the stage leads to specific behavior by the actor which is intended to be seen by the audience as the behavior of the character (which perhaps indicates emotion). Because the character-emotions are a realization of the intended emotions, their nature and kind will be comparable to each other, but they are not the same as emotions in daily life. This will be further explained below.

4.3.1 Character-Emotions Most drama or theater performances represent human interaction and human conflict. In principle all the emotions of daily life can be touched in a theater piece. Dramatic action is usually characterized by a great diversity and high concentration of emotions, varying in quality and intensity. The dramatist Baker even proposed that 'the accurate portrayal of emotions is the basis of good drama'.[2] The diversity and intensity of the emotions which an actress has to parade in the short span of time in which she plays Medea, Elektra, or Andromaché, for example, would not be possible in daily life. The capacity of people to 'play act' offers possibilities to 'conjure up worlds which do not exist, and to do so in such a convincing way that the audience easily exchanges these conjured worlds for a real world, as though a pretend emotion were a real emotion' (Schoenmakers 1989: 38). Emotions of characters are then not the same as the general emotions in daily life: 'Things are not as they seem.'

Because we see 'real people' who portray character-emotions, and moreover use the same term *emotion* for general human emotions as well as for the emotions of characters, the interchange is understandable. This is partially explained by the habit of giving the same name to the observation of behavior (which seems to suggest an emotion) as to the emotion itself. This impression has sometimes also been created by the research on emotion (see chapter 5). In these cases, emotions have been attributed to fellow men, having been deduced from or reduced to a behavioral expression. In theory this is understandable because these expressions of emotion are the part of an emotion which can be observed in others. In this book, the hyphenated term character-emotions or the combined use of 'portrayed emotions' will always be used to indicate the represented behavior of characters meant to suggest the character's 'emotion'.

The character-emotions are therefore, in this book, only understood as the behavior an actor exhibits on stage which, in the eyes of the audience, appears to be an expression of a real emotion: '…the living characters who the actors are on stage are measured with the same standards with which we judge people in daily life.'[3] A character-emotion is a representation of an apparently real emotion. In 2.4 a character-emotion was defined as a construction of signs, formed after a model of a general human emotion, to create a believable and convincing illusion of the emotion as we know it in daily life. The desirability in some acting styles, namely the styles of involvement and self-expression, of arousing the same emotions in the actor will be discussed further in chapter 5. We are all familiar with how acting out or watching someone else acting out emotions can give rise to 'real' emotions. For now, this chapter will consider character-emotions and character-situations as constructions of behavior which represent emotional behavior, apart from how their portrayal is achieved. First, the emotion process of the actor will be discussed.

4.3.2 Task-Emotions of the Actor

A psychological consideration of acting leads to the presumption that the *real* emotional experiences of the actor on stage are aroused by the task situation as its primary source. The actor's task-emotions concern the core of stage acting. As seen in the previous section, the specific meaning a situation has for a person is the root of an emotion. This meaning is determined by the individual concerns at stake combined with the results of the evaluation of the situation's relevance, context, and urgency (figure 4.1). Thus, in order to describe the task-emotions one must identify the relevant concerns involved in executing acting tasks and the most important characteristics of the context at hand.

Because the focus in this study is on character-acting, only limited aspects of the actor's tasks are dealt with. Particularly the acting tasks concerned with giving shape to character-emotions; the actor has to do this in a way that an audience will recognize them as (represented) emotions and, preferably, the audience will be moved by them. This is perhaps the most difficult among the tasks of acting. The specific interpretation of tasks may vary according to acting style or genre, but on a more general level the task situation is more or less the same for all professional actors impersonating characters in a live performance. The actor's tasks include, among other things, creating a model of the character in the imagination and giving expression to this model as convincingly and believably as possible. On the one hand, aspects of the portrayal are put in a repeatable form and, on the other hand, the portrayal is given the illusion of spontaneously generated emotion (3.6). The audience is seduced into interpreting the representations as 'real emotions', especially in traditional stage acting and Hollywood films.

The remainder of this chapter will describe how the task situation gives rise to an emotion process during a performance for a live audience, and further how these task-emotions can be functional to acting.

4.4   Task-Emotions and Task Concerns

Whether the elements of the functional core of an emotion process are present, must be checked by finding which of the actor's concerns, if any, are put at stake by the task situation. As Frijda says: If there is no concern, there is also no emotion (1986: 334). Concerns motivate emotional behavior. Frijda distinguishes source concerns from surface concerns. Source concerns refer to general concerns and motivations related to desirable situations and goals (for example safety or competence), while surface concerns refer to specific interests which relate to specific goals, people, or objects (for example a sense of security with mother). Thus, in the case of the actor, source concerns can become surface concerns in executing the acting tasks. The name task concerns is given to the concerns which are involved in executing acting tasks. The task concerns of the actor are probably related to the actor's desire to give a successful performance, to preserve one's good reputation, or not to blunder.

4.4.1   Competence Acting has to do with the source concern 'competence', as a first task concern. It is in the interest of the actor to exhibit his competence and talent in his own way in the presentation. Competence regards the importance of acquiring skills and techniques needed to relate with the environment as well as with one's own desires and emotions. Feeling competent contributes to feeling good, to a sense of well-being and refers at the same time to the source concern 'self-esteem'. Competence also involves learning, self-development, growth, and the growth of autonomy. When the actor is proficient, the source concern of competence becomes concrete. This source concern, incidentally, can be unraveled into many surface concerns. In part these are the task requirements of the profession, such as an expressive capacity to portray various characters and be able to repeat the portrayal. In part these are related to insights into the

> My whole body tingles. Cold sweat. Stomach cramps. Dizzy, lightheaded. I have to hold on to something. After fifteen years in television I still have the same symptoms – five minutes before taping. At that moment you see Henny Huisman as the scared boxer who has to enter the ring... 'You can still leave' says Frits [his coach, EK] sometimes. 'Go ahead, I'll tell the audience that you are sick.' 'NO, NO', I yell then, 'of course not.' At that moment he's caught me. This is my trade, my life. I am one of the top three [hosts]: André, Ron, and Henny. And if I lose my edge and the will to fight for that rank, I am lost. After a year no one will remember Henny Huisman. Then I won't exist anymore. To be noticed, *seen* – that has always been a part of me.
>
> (Television host Henny Huisman in an interview with Pieter Webeling, *De Volkskrant*, April 19, 1997)

emotions (and how they function) and the skills to transmit information and emotions to an audience.

The difficulty and urgency of the task situation contribute to the potential threat to the competency concern, as will be seen later in this chapter. This is primarily a matter of the subjective feeling of proficiency and the belief in one's own competence, especially the belief and self-confidence in one's own capability as an actor. For example, in a study by the psychologist Suzanne Piët, the belief in one's own ability to cope with risky situations was shown to be an important motivational factor for stunt men and racing drivers. The importance of the source concern competence for the actor is underscored because the execution of complex tasks in front of an audience demands a high degree of skills.[4] The competence of the actor is tested in direct confrontation with the audience; there is nowhere for an actor to hide an evident lack of skills.

4.4.2　**Self-Image** Closely related to the concern of competence, is the importance of self-image: The general need for approval and recognition, the care taken to make a good impression or to avoid loss of face. The actor sees himself confronted with a critical and expectant audience. It is important for the actor to meet their expectations and to make a good impression on the audience. He is not only judged as a character, but also as an actor, a professional, and a person. His reputation as an actor is at stake, as is the preservation of his (social) self-esteem and self-respect. The sociologist, Goffman, speaks of *impression management* and *presentation of self* as the central motive behind the behavior of people in social situations, where they want to make a good impression on others.

The social psychologist, Snyder, speaks of *self-monitoring* in this respect. Self-image is an essential concern, which can be threatened in social situations resulting in intensely felt emotions like shame or embarrassment. When a good appearance has to be made in full view of others, this specific concern is addressed: At the very least try not to look like a fool. The risk to self-image is considerably greater in the acting situation than in most daily social situations; perhaps the risk is even greater during an unaccompanied soliloquy than when the actor is on stage with fellow performers.

4.4.3　**Need for Sensation** Capturing and holding the interest of an audience, to captivate them in other words, is a minimum requirement for the actor. Studies show that presenting oneself to spectators is one of the most stressful activities that can be experienced. Subjects in an experiment indicated that they found speaking in public to be the most stressful out of a selection of ten types of activity. The high level of stress involved in a public presentation (like a theater performance) also appears in other experiments. Telling a subject that they will be observed from behind a one-way mirror appeared to be enough to arouse a considerable amount of stress. According to the emotion psychologist Martin, 'public speaking' is one of the most successful methods of arousing emotions in a research situation.

It has been established that a strong build-up of emotions in the actor is repeated during every performance with an audience (see chapter 6). It therefore seems justified to presume that the source concern of sensation-seeking is relevant to the task situation of the actor (see also 4.6.1). Seeking sensation involves the need for tension and excitement or the willingness to seek out activities which involve (physical or social) risks. Zuckerman, a psychological researcher, considers the conscious search for tension and risky situations, and deriving pleasure from it, to be a stable character trait. According to Zuckerman, sensation-seeking is even a genetic trait. Risky activities are probably undertaken because you think you can handle them.[5] In short, the need for excitement or sensation seems to be a relevant source concern for professional actors, because they regularly subject themselves to the stressful situation of a stage performance. Most of them choose to make it their profession.

4.4.4 Esthetic Concerns Finally, I suggest that the need 'to make something beautiful', to be creative and original, is an important motivation for the stage artist. A feeling for style, color, and form touch on esthetic needs and concerns. Wang discusses the idea that actors are highly motivated by esthetic concerns: 'Emotional development in performing artists is motivated by the strong urge and affinity for beauty' (Wang 1984). The esthetic concerns or the need for beauty are mainly expressed in what is called esthetic emotions. Esthetic aspirations of the professional actor can be either greatly satisfied or seriously squelched during performance. The artistic design of emotions, myriad beautiful phrases, and flowing interactions satisfy the need for beauty in the actor (and hopefully in the audience as well), but the need is threatened when the director asks the actor to perform something he finds distasteful. Esthetic concerns will always have to do with features of the product itself, as artifact: The talent of the actors, the colorful decor, the lucid mise-en-scène, the wonderful music, and the poetic texts.

The esthetic concerns do not have much to do with the characters as such (or at the most only as an indirect derivative). This is also true of the esthetic concerns of the actor. For example, an actor may take pleasure in believing that he has acted the impotent rage of his character beautifully. In this case, the actor's craft is the object of emotion derived from a beautiful portrayal of anger, and not his possible sympathy with the character. In this context one must distinguish esthetic emotions from empathetic emotions. Empathetic emotions relate to one or another form of empathizing or sympathizing with the characters, but not to the 'beauty' of the art of acting as such or to its esthetic concerns. This is not to say that empathetic emotions are not relevant to the actor. Empathetic emotions relate to the concerns of 'proximity and coherence' or 'familiarity and orientation', which probably belong to the more subordinate concerns in this situation of live performance.[6] Examples of the esthetic emotions are: Being moved, being affected by something, excitement, poignancy, pride, satisfaction, pleasure, and admiration. This type of emotion, incidentally, also touches on competence as a source concern, for example, the pleasure in being competent enough to act so artfully or convincingly.

All in all, the task situation of the professional actor is clearly a potentially emotional situation, on theoretical grounds, because source concerns are at stake when the actor takes the stage to 'show off his art'. As described, the task situation offers the promise of satisfaction or the risk of damaging at least four source concerns: Competence, self-image, sensation-seeking, and esthetic concerns. Because relevant concerns are at stake in the acting situation, emotions arise. Which emotions these will be depend on the specific features of the situation or event (4.2). The presence of certain features or components in the situation is a second condition for the arousal of an emotion.

4.5   Components in the Task Situation

The meaning an actor gives to the situation in which he portrays a character for an audience is composed of a number of specific features, which Frijda calls components. These are divided, by Frijda, into core components and context components. This section addresses firstly the question of whether the situation holds core components, secondly what the context components are.

Core components are part of the relevance evaluation and are jointly responsible for the presence or absence of an emotion. 'Core components are those that make (or do not make) the situation an emotional one. They pertain to emotional relevance and constitute emotional experience per se.' (Frijda 1986: 204). Without core components it is impossible for an emotion to arise; they affect the concerns of the person. During the relevance evaluation the relevant features of the situation meet the relevant concerns. It is clear from the previous section that the actor's concerns with respect to the actual, real context of a live performance, are quite definitely at stake. Desired goals can be realized or threatened. Informing, captivating, and arousing the audience is the actor's task. This is difficult and the situation is urgent. The most important core components in the situation during acting are therefore, in Frijda's terms: *Objectivity, reality, valence, demand character, difficulty,* and *urgency.*[7] These will be explained below.

> ### Core Components:
>
> Core components determine whether the essence of a situation is potentially favorable or damaging to an individual's concerns. Of the many different features contained in a situation, only a few have significance for one or more concerns. Only when a situation contains some of this type of significant features, can one say that the situation has core components. Or rather, if a situation has no core components for a person, then the situation does not affect the person's concerns. 'Screening' a situation for possible core components happens during the relevance evaluation (figure 4.1).
>
> For the actor in the acting situation there are six important core components: Objectivity, reality, valence, demand character, difficulty and urgency.

> ### Context Components:
>
> Context components are features of a situation which determine what sort of emotion will arise. Complementary to the core components, the context components help to judge whether it is possible to act in the given context and how difficult that will be. This action will be directed toward satisfying concerns. 'Screening' a situation for possible context components happens during the context-evaluation.
>
> In the task situation of the actor on stage there are two important context components: (Un)controllability and (un)familiarity.

Context components are linked with the context evaluation (figure 4.1) and relate to the type of emotion. They are mainly dependent upon the person's abilities to cope or not to cope with the situation.[8] Thus, the coincidence of certain context components in the situation determines which emotion will come into play. The fact that an audience is waiting to be entertained is, for example, an essential feature of the actor's task situation. For the actor, the context evaluation is an appraisal of his command of the task requirements, of his clarity of understanding and of the risk of failure, of his expectations about the audience and his preparedness for reactions from the audience and co-actors. Of the context components named by Frijda, *controllability* and *strangeness-familiarity* are the two most important ones in the actor's task situation. Thus, together with the six core components, there are a total of eight components which are the most characteristic of the acting situation and which define the situational meaning structure to the actor.

4.5.1 Objectivity and Reality

The *objectivity* of the situation in which the actor is face to face with the audience, and with eventual co-actors, is immense. Objectivity is the feeling that the situation is imposing itself on you, inevitably addressing specific concerns: 'The sense of being overcome by the event as well as by one's own response...' (Frijda 1986: 205). Objectivity gives the situation the feeling of being immediate, here and now, overwhelming and certain. In other words, a real emotion stems from a situation which seems inevitable, something which you can not escape from. In the relevance evaluation, the core component of objectivity can be seen as indispensable for the presence of a real emotion. Objectivity is closely tied to the belief that concerns are actually being affected as well as to the reality level of the situation.

Reality level is also an indispensable core component for the presence of emotion: 'A situation may in principle be relevant, but be only play, or a fantasy, or an abstraction; ... Emotional involvement varies correspondingly' (Frijda 1986: 206). For the arousal of a 'real' emotion, the situation must be judged as 'real', having a high reality level, and the concerns must actually be addressed (compare with section 5.5). The reality level for the actor performing for an audience will be very high. Coughing, laughing, or tense silence, for example, will persistently remind the actor that all eyes are upon him; a scene change will remind him as well of the reality of the task situation in the performance.

4.5.2 Difficulty and Urgency

The demands placed on the actor are high as far as the task itself is concerned (3.6). In addition it is a difficult situation for the actor in terms of satisfying his concerns. Executing a complex task, like acting emotions in a dramatic performance, with one or more persons observing, generally leads to stress or tension and often impairs task performance (4.4.3; 4.6). Within the limited time span of the performance the actor must exhibit all the detailed nuances of his skills, while 'they're all out there checking him out'. He cannot relax for a single moment, which is a common feature of most other work situations. In addition, the audience wants to see a performance *now*. The actor's task situation, in other words, has a high level of urgency. It is imperative to act immediately; later will be too late. 'Difficulty and urgency are the situational meaning components corresponding to emotional upset, to emotion in the excited sense of the word' (Frijda 1986: 206). The *difficulty* and *urgency* of the task situation demand a high degree of command or control over the task requirements and the task situation.

4.5.3 Controllability and Valence

Controllability relates to the actor's capacity to undertake the demands of the situation. Precisely because the actor functions simultaneously on different levels of enactment and must represent a recognizable and believable character to the audience, a great degree of control is demanded. Even if the characters are out of control, and even if the actor lets himself be completely swept away by the emotions portrayed in the performance of the character, even then, the professional actor will nonetheless have to control his acting to let the performance proceed as planned. 'As an actor, you the artist have to perform on the most difficult instrument to master, that is, your own self – your physical being and your emotional being. That, I believe, is where all the confusion of the different schools of acting stems from' (Brynner in Chekhov 1953: x). Moreover the behavior of the actor on stage, as character, must also match certain esthetic or artistic standards, which are to some extent dependent on current conventions. Likewise, controlling and directing the audience's attention is part of the actor's task as a professional. By maximizing command of the required stage action, the actor will be capable of controlling unexpected events.

In acting, control coupled with the expectation that source concerns will be satisfied, alongside the opportunity for acclaim and success, make the component *valence* – Frijda's term for emotional value – positive, at least for the professional actor who is secure in his profession. At the same time, the risk of failure must not be underestimated. The concerns at stake can be seriously jeopardized or greatly advanced. In this respect the task situation is extreme – failure is serious failure and source concerns are consequently seriously damaged. The actor could lose face because his reputation is at stake when he undergoes critical judgment. One the other hand, a moment of success is almost immediately rewarded, sometimes with an unanticipated curtain call (we are speaking here of professional actors in leading roles.)

Characteristic of the acting situation is that in the case of either success or failure the respective experience is felt to the hilt; a bit of success or a bit of failure is almost an impossibility. The reason being that 'all those people are out there watching you'. It is characteristic of the acting situation, and for similar risky task situations – live musicians, athletes, and stunt men – that a subjective belief in one's chances of success reduces the threat of failure. A proficient actor develops the necessary skills and believes he truly can act. When the actor knows how to transform the risk of failure into success, the situation assumes a positive valence.

4.5.4 Familiarity and Demand Character

Strangeness-familiarity is a twofold component in the actor's task situation, as is the aforementioned component of valence. The professional actor is familiar with the play, with what he must do, with co-actors and so forth. Depending on his level of experience he is more or less familiar with confronting an audience. At the same time, there is always a great element of *unfamiliarity* with respect to this specific audience, this stage, the course of this particular show and the levels of alertness of oneself, co-actors, technicians, etc. The actor will always face the struggle with the unpredictability of the surroundings, the audience who changes nightly, and with his own unpredictability – will he be able to react adequately to the situation? This unfamiliarity or unpredictability will prompt a screening of the situation and probably prompt selective attention for all that appears unfamiliar. Ability to cope with the situation will have to be incorporated into the acting, for example when another actor does not appear on the requisite cue. Strangeness stimulates cognitive activity, while familiarity is an important component for feelings of security and recognition.

The demand for attention through addressing concerns or otherwise due to the importance of an event, person, or situation, is called *demand character* by Frijda.[9] This is the component corresponding to interest, wonder or curiosity, but also to concentration and challenge. The task situation of the actor is interesting and demands attention because, for one thing, the unfamiliar elements in the situation increase that risk of failure. Estimating possible risks on the basis of unfamiliar aspects in the situation will not be too difficult for professionals. An all too familiar situation, however, can become boring and thereby clash with the need for sensation. Thus the unfamiliar aspects of the situation can become a source of inspiration, providing they can be controlled with professional expertise. The unfamiliarity will then transform the situation into a challenge.

In sum, the situational meaning structure of the task situation for the actor portraying a character on stage before an audience, contains eight relevant components. As Frijda states, the combination of these core and context components determines what sort of emotion comes into play. The coincidence of risk and control with a positive valence denotes the meaning structure of challenge, which will be elaborated in the next section.

4.6   A Precarious Balance

The emotion challenge is linked with positive or pleasant feelings like fun (in playing), courage, spunk or nerve, being primed for the task, pleasant excitement, concentration, eagerness, and feeling strong and confident. When control fails, as for example when the rehearsal period has not been successful, the valence will become negative and the situation will be judged as threatening. Threat is linked to emotions such as fear, insecurity, or shame. The action situation calls on the actor's skills to tackle the situation. Especially during preparations, the actor will practice controlling the skills and demands necessitated by his role. The right balance between the risky aspects of the situation and the skills to control them can result in a positive feeling. A threatening, negative emotion is thereby rendered positive. Controllability is the component which gives danger the appearance of challenge rather than threat; it turns a negative emotion into a positive one.[10] Challenge seems to come to the fore as the most prominent task emotion, provided the rehearsal period has been successful.[11]

In the last section, arguments were presented to show that positive emotional value, or positive valence, is dependent on being able to cope with the (im)possibilities of the situation. An essentially risky or threatening situation can only take on a positive character if the individual can manage or control the situation. The risky, possibly threatening situation of giving a public presentation, like acting, can be transformed into a positive situation of challenge by maximizing the feeling of control or command. This can mainly be achieved through training in specific skills which are necessary to meet the demands of the situation. Also, aspects of the situation can be more or less emphasized to a greater or lesser degree or brought into focus in such a way that the situation, within the given circumstances, will appear as favorable as possible. Conversely, when a specific situation takes on a negative meaning, it will be seen as threatening. Studies show that the potential judgment of a situation as being challenging also depends on certain personality traits. Moreover, challenge is linked to attaining higher achievements.

4.6.1 Personality, Accomplishment, and Challenge

Judging a situation as challenging – as noted in a study with pilots – is related to positive thinking and to good performance. On the other hand, judging a situation as threatening is associated with negative thinking and poor performance.[12] According to Larsson and Hayward, good performance in pilots is synonymous with seeing the situation as being a challenge and with functional self-control, while poor performance is associated with threat and with judging the situation as irrelevant. Irion and Blanchard-Fields also found that goal-oriented strategies were more often used in challenging situations, while strategies for alleviating discomfort are more often applied in threatening situations.

The positive relationships discovered between challenge and good performance, as well as between threat and poor performance, support the presumed relevance of the need for competence in the acting situation discussed in section 4.4. Pleasure in handling potentially risky situations, characteristic to challenge, is mainly found in individuals who have a strong tendency toward sensation-seeking.[13] Moreover, the 'sensation seeker' seems to have similarities with the strong personality. A person with a strong personality has a strong commitment to what he does, a great sense of self-control, and the ability to regard unexpected changes or possible threats in life as positive challenges.[14] Presumably, having self-confidence, or a belief in one's own capacities as an actor, also contributes to viewing acting as a challenge.

A challenging situation is a precarious situation in which a delicate balance must be maintained between the amount of risk and the amount of control one has over required skills. For creative professionals, guarding this delicate balance is part of a day's work.[15] The ability to alternate between risk and challenge and the belief in being able to handle both offers the possibility of creating the experience of 'flow'.

4.6.2 The Right Balance: 'Flow'

The right balance between risk and control results in the sensation as if tasks are being performed by themselves in one fluid movement. A balanced relationship between challenging, exciting or risky elements in a situation and the necessary skills to encounter them, will result in the sensation of optimal experience or 'flow', according to research psychologist Mihalyi Csikszentmihalyi. Flow is an experience often reported by artists, top athletes, and members of creative professions where a high level of performance is expected.[16] A high degree of control over the task requirements also affords one the freedom to launch into momentary, unexpected turns in the situation while performing the task. This is a conclusion which seems to concur with statements made mainly by Grotowski and Brook, to the effect that command of technical skills and discipline are necessary for creativity and inspiration.

Too much experience or practice may however jeopardize the sensation of flow in an optimally challenging situation by endangering the balance. The combination of great competence and great familiarity with a situation can result in an actor 'going through the motions'. The acting can become so routine that the character portrayal may become cold and mechanical. This problem is a primary fear of the advocates of the style of involvement. The optimal balance can also be threatened by becoming too accustomed to satisfaction or success. To maintain an optimal level of challenge, ever more complex situations will be sought out, or other aspects of the situation will be highlighted to create new challenges to skills and to extend existing boundaries.[17] To maintain the optimal balance in performance, a proficient actor may seek out new challenges in variations in audiences, in theater venues, or in the moods of himself and colleagues. He might change nuances in his acting, or play different roles.

When an actor overestimates his skills, overconfidence can result in too much daring or 'spunk'; one might call the actor a daredevil or show-off. Such 'hubris' can also lead an actor to underestimate actual risks or hazards. Overestimating one's own capacity can initially lead to pleasurable or possibly euphoric feelings, such as excitement, eagerness, concentration, flow, strength, and confidence. When control of the necessary skills falls short, the balance will shift to the negative because risks are in fact greater than anticipated, or because unanticipated obstacles or hurdles arise. The situation then becomes threatening and results in unpleasant feelings such as fear, anxiety, or shame, which could possibly negate the desire to take action.

In short, the realization that once the right balance is achieved, it must be carefully guarded because it could be lost at any moment, guarantees maximum commitment to the situation and to accomplishing the task. The precarious nature of the situation demands the actor's full attention and results in an optimal level of concentration (compare the component demand character). With an optimal level of challenge, a level the individual can just manage and which leads to the sensation of flow, concentration is 'automatically' sharpened. One could also argue that challenge results in concentration, because of the risky or threatening elements in the challenging situation. To get an idea of what flow is,

> It's just like driving a car. You can take a nice ride or a bad trip. You take a bad trip if other actors don't go along with you or if you miss the accelerator by accident, and when you can't use the mechanical features of the car correctly. If you drive well and nothing happens along the way and you drive by pretty trees and no one else on the road bothers you, then it can feel like a really nice ride.
>
> (Actor Porgy Franssen in the documentary Acteurs spelen emoties, NPS 1995)

> There is a sort of hyper-reality [on stage] which makes you forget everything. You put yourself on another plane of consciousness. Once I was playing a scene and stepped on an enormous nail. I just kept playing with terrible pain. But when I walked off stage, I immediately fainted.
>
> (Actress Linda van Dijk in Psychologie, October 1996)

we can recall some of the seemingly effortless peak performances delivered by top athletes. If these performances are translated to the art of the actor, will a link be found with the actor's radiance, power of persuasion, or presence? Perhaps we can think of flow as a bundling of the most positive task-emotions. It seems to me that the apparent ease in the execution of acting tasks along with the positive emotions ensuing from performance are conditions for achieving presence. By playing with the balance along the narrow path of the flow experience, the actor can also play on the audience's attention.

4.6.3 Acting and Manipulating

While Tan (1996: 93) speaks of the 'Challenge that Everyone can Meet', in reference to the viewer of a traditional film, it became clear in section 4.4.3 above that not everyone can handle the situation of being an actor on stage. When we, observers, watch someone doing something we know is difficult and perhaps risky, and then perceive that he cannot quite handle the situation or has lost his nerve, we are immediately 'gripped'. We watch anxiously for the outcome of the task to be accomplished – 'will he make it or not?' The involvement and interest of the spectator in such a case is as optimal as the measure of challenge and concentration in the actor. The audience challenges the actor with 'show me that you are Hamlet', while the actor challenges the audience with 'who says I'm not Hamlet'. Success will depend in part on the model that the audience has formed of 'his' Hamlet and on the conviction with which the actor plays his Hamlet.

For the actor, this condition has at least two implications. One, that the actor's task situation in itself has elements which engage the audience's attention; they speculate (for example) how this particular actor will produce the difficult scene of Hamlet's 'to be or not to be'. Along with the persuasiveness of his acting, certain choices in direction, as well as all sorts of scenic and technical tools can also aid the actor. When audience emotions are aroused in this manner, they are esthetic emotions or artifact emotions.[18] Two, the actor or director can exploit this fact and increase the involvement of the audience by enlarging the risks or hazards of the situation, either artificially or directly. The actor can, for example, create an initial impression that he possibly lacks the skills to meet the challenge of the role. Then, by gradually 'letting loose', he 'ropes in' the audience. Imagine an actor, at first seemingly nervous, but ultimately delivering his role passionately – our admiration for him becomes even greater. These are, of course, speculative assertions, deserving further research.

All in all, it is assumed that a good acting performance, or a positive appraisal of the quality of acting, requires that an actor judge the task situation a challenge rather than a threat. When the actor feels challenged by the situation of a live performance, which appeals to his relevant concerns, the situation will insist on changes in action readiness.[19] A change in action readiness is a defining feature of an emotion and creates the impulse to do something or avoid doing something: The action tendency.

4.7 Impulses and Control Precedence

An 'emotion' is, according to Frijda, not truly an emotion without a change in action readiness: A tendency, an urge or an impulse to act or to refrain from acting. An emotion is not only characterized by its specific situational meaning structure, but also by a specific action tendency.[20] An action tendency is directed toward changing the individual's relationship with others or with the surroundings, in order to obtain a specific satisfaction. A situation with features related to the emotion 'challenge' will demand a confrontation with a possible threat. When one thinks that the situation can be dealt with (by judging one's own skills positively) and victory seems possible, the challenge will evoke the impulse to approach.[21] Comparable action tendencies with challenge are: The urge or impulse to 'overcome difficulties', 'go for it', and the urge to 'do something, sing, jump, or dance'. If contrarily a situation is judged to be threatening, it then evokes the action tendency of avoidance, like the impulse 'to flee', the impulse 'to avoid' the threat, or 'to sink into the ground'. In general, task emotions will be paired with action tendencies directed toward the desire to give expression to the character, and to convince the audience of the authenticity of the portrayal.

Once aroused, an emotion brings forth an action tendency which dominates the control of the execution and actions. In other words, one can not put up resistance to the impulse to 'attack' or to 'flee'. Frijda calls this the claim for *control precedence* by emotions: The feelings, thoughts, impulses, actions, or activation going along with the aroused emotion take precedence over other planned or half executed thoughts, feelings, impulses, etc. The degree of dominance and inevitability is also dependent on the influence of regulation processes, which will be discussed in section 4.9. Without control precedence there is no emotion, then one can only speak of a feeling. Control precedence can manifest itself by sudden interruption of behavior, changes in behavior or by persistence of behavior.[22]

At the moment the performance begins, one would expect that the control precedence of challenge will take the form of behavior changes, from non-challenge to challenge, and then to persistence. Just before it begins, the actor may be apprehensive about the performance, he is nervous or listless or reluctant. As soon as the performance starts, however, he will let himself be driven by performing the show, even possibly experiencing 'flow'. He will not allow any distractions and will desire to complete the (sequence of) performance in an unbroken succession of actions. This concurs with the 'law of enclosure' of emotions, in which Frijda postulates that once an emotion is aroused its development is more or less irresistible.[23] The control precedence of challenge then provokes persistence in the behavior; this continues until success is achieved, or in less favorable cases, until failure must be accepted. Normally this continues until the curtain falls at the end of the performance.

The feature of control precedence makes challenge a 'real' emotion. It leads to focusing all attention on winning over the audience, on captivating them, on being a master of the tension, on displaying and expanding skills, etc. Challenge brings a highly intense concentration with it, in concurrence with the component 'demand character'. Concentration with control precedence is also a true emotion and possesses the feature of 'taking over' behavior. When an actor is concentrating intensely, he will refuse to let himself be distracted by rustling noises in the audience; more likely he will not even notice them. Instead, all of his attention, action, and impulses are directed toward accomplishing the task of playing the role with as much conviction as possible. When concentration develops as an emotion, the 'feeling' of concentration gains the upper hand over the other emotions and thoughts, which had previously come into play. The actor himself feels fulfilled with challenge and concentration; a feeling which was described above as the optimal sensation of 'flow'.

Control precedence is strengthened by the intensity of the emotion, which is dictated by the evaluation of the components 'difficulty' and 'urgency'. As seen in section 4.5, the difficulty of the task situation plus urgency contributes to the intensity of task emotions. The more intense the aroused emotions are, the stronger the control precedence will be and the more difficult the action tendency (the urge to take action) will be to suppress, after Frijda. The control precedence of challenge will exert unbearable pressure to execute the action tendency, in other words activation and behavior corresponding with this emotion. This can cause problems for the actor in portraying his character: As audience members we come primarily to see characters like Hamlet and Medea. Only secondarily are we there to see 'how he does it' (3.8). Even if it is the other way around, it is doubtful that we are there to see the expression of the task-emotions of the actor themselves. I presume that spectators in general want to see the portrayal of character-emotions and not what task-emotions look like. They are often even prepared to believe that these character-emotions are a direct reflection of the emotions the actor himself has. I will now try to make a reasonable case for the idea that the expression of task-emotions is, or at least could be, directed at the expression of character-emotions.

> I always tell: The actor Pierrre Bokma is not of interest to me, neither does Richard III. But, the actor Pierre Bokma putting Richard III on stage – that's interesting, that is what interests me. That makes me thinking. Actually Bokma says to me: 'You think I'm Pierre Bokma, don't you? That's not true, I'm Richard III. But if you think I'm Richard III, you're wrong – I'm Pierre Bokma.' And that's what I find so fascinating of theater, of stage acting. And I think thus, that the students should learn thát, that they should develop themselves to enjoy that kind of game.
>
> (Teacher at the Theater Academy in Maastricht, the Netherlands, 1997)

4.8   Expressions of Task-Emotions

An action tendency insists on expressing an emotion through the following channels: Behavioral expression, physiological changes, and subjective perception (4.2). These three channels for emotions as they apply to the actor's task-emotions will be discussed.

4.8.1   Behavioral Expression   In the behavioral expression of emotions, the actor and the character are one and the same. The actor's behavior on stage in the form of character-appropriate behavior is what the audience sees. The actor's repertoire of possible actions is bound by the repertoire of possible actions which the playwright and director or theater maker have proscribed in agreements made during rehearsal.[24] The task-emotions and accompanying action tendencies of the actor must therefore be shaped so that their expression will create the illusion, for the audience, that the behavior observed is an expression of the character's action tendencies and emotions (at least in traditional character acting). Then, action tendencies and task-emotions reveal themselves in the display of behavior that fits the intended emotions of the characters, and agrees with the inner model thereof. Behavioral expression as an output of the emotion process concerns visual behavior, like posture, movement, and facial expression, as well as phonetic features, like words, sound, and pitch. They are all the visible and audible manifestations by which the audience derives conclusions about the character's state of mind. The audience will also try to deduce this from, for example, the content of the text, the set, the lights, and the context of the dramatic situation in which the action takes place (5.6).

Task-emotions have no clearly recognizable manifestations, in the way that, for example, anger does; we recognize anger by 'the way it looks'. Experiments by Paul Ekman, for one, show that a number of basic emotions can be recognized universally (5.6).[25] The observable phenomena of task-emotions, such as challenge, are more like signals which indicate persisting in a certain behavior, directing attention exclusively to a certain task, being alert, driven, and goal-oriented. The perceivable expression of challenge is in the first instance, task oriented behavior. One of the main tasks of the actor is precisely to display behavior that fits with the portrayal of the character (and his emotions). In this sense, the behavioral expression of task-emotions of the actor in performance is the same as the behavioral expression of the character (-emotions).

It is the non-specific expression of challenge that makes it possible for it to take on the countenance of other types of emotions, in other words, clothing challenge in another form. The expression of task emotions in general, and of challenge and concentration in particular, is in principle mainly observable in the alertness of the individual, as a state of optimal action readiness. This optimal state of alertness provides a sort of basic tension which is useful for portraying all sorts of intense character-emotions. It might be said that the emotions of the character to be portrayed have already been given an 'undercoat primer', and need 'only' the finishing touch of the emotion-specific color. I suspect that this optimal state of alertness, which accompanies a state of 'flow', lends the illusion of spontaneity to the portrayal of character-emotions and at the same time denotes what is known as 'presence'. The next chapter will explain that there are more reasons to suspect this process, especially in the discussion of believability and effects of imitating emotional expression in sections 5.6 and 5.7 respectively.

When the possible expression of the task-emotions themselves is not in accordance with the character-emotions to be portrayed, the actor will mask them and where possible transform them, this being necessary to achieve a believable and convincing portrayal of character-emotions. In general, audiences will respond negatively to an acting performance in which they think they have seen the actor's task-emotions, especially overt nervousness. A possible exception occurs when an actor inadvertently gets the giggles or 'cracks up', but here too, the (traditional) dramatic action is disturbed. The actor will therefore shape the output of the emotion process, in the task situation, in such a way that the observable phenomena of his task-emotions look like character-emotions (4.9). For the sake of completeness, the physiological phenomena, which accompany task-emotions, and subjective perception as output of the emotion process during acting will be discussed first.

4.8.2   Physiological Phenomena Research on the physiological aspects of challenge has scarcely been conducted, but there is some connection with research in the general category of 'stress'. Researchers like Lazarus, Dienstbier, and others point out that the generally negative connotations related to 'stress' are not applicable to challenge; instead challenge leads to positive stress. It has been discovered that mental exertion, as a form of stress, leads to physiological activation. The general conclusion of such research is that stress situations lead to high levels of physiological activation, like 'autonomous arousal', accelerated heartbeat, changes in breathing, hormonal secretion, sweating, and blushing. I draw the analogous conclusion that challenge is likewise accompanied by high levels of physiological activation. It must be noted that the physiological research conducted to date is not specific enough to determine whether the reported physiological activation is linked with the threatening or with the challenging aspects of the situation. However, Dienstbier does conclude that challenge is linked to positive physiological activation and with a positive effect on performance (4.6).

Some empirical tests with (professional) actors show that the physiological changes are more likely related to the actor's work than with the portrayed character-emotions. Villiers concluded this as early as 1942, for example, on the basis of measuring pulse rate and blood pressure in actors. He tested professional actors in Paris at various moments when they were back stage. Recent psychophysiological studies on actors, with more modern instruments and a more systematic approach show comparable results. Weisweiler and myself, separately, have found strongly increased levels of physiological activation ('arousal') in actors during performance as compared with (dress) rehearsals.

Figure 4.2: Heartbeat of an actress

Below is a graphic representation of the heartbeat of an actress. The lighter, upper portion indicates the rate of the heartbeat during a so-called run through (a final rehearsal during which the entire piece is rehearsed). The darker shaded area shows the heartbeat during a performance. During a monologue the heartbeat reaches a rate of 180 beats per minute (this is the lowest point in the figure).

A: Director announces
   the start of the
   rehearsal/performance
B: Performance begins
C: Monologue
D: End of rehearsal – I
E: End of performance – I

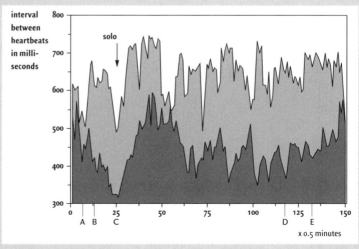

Explanation: **A smaller interval in milliseconds indicates a faster heartbeat and vice versa.**

There is no reason to assume that the cause of heightened activation must lie in the character related emotions. The findings point toward task-emotions as being the cause: The highs and lows measured in activation levels correspond to being on or off stage, respectively to whether the actor is on the stage or in the wings. Further, the highest peaks were found during monologues, even though the most intense character-emotions were not necessarily being portrayed then. Neither was there more physical exertion during monologues than during other comparable moments of the performance.[26] I ascertained moreover that the appraisal of the quality of the individual performances was more favorable during performances with high tension levels than during rehearsals with low tension levels. This corroborates the findings of earlier studies on challenge.

4.8.3 The Subjective Perception

In general, Frijda proposes that subjective emotional perception is the experience of having one's concerns addressed by an event or a situation, and of the impulse to react to this. As stated above, challenge will in general be accompanied by positively shaded or pleasant feelings and of feeling tensed. The subjective perception of the 'feeling' of the task-emotion challenge will probably be termed by the actor as tension, enthusiasm, excitement, concentration, courage, nerve, and perhaps the experience of 'flow'. When the person involved does not have enough control over the situation, he will then judge it negatively and experience the action tendency 'to avoid'. The accompanying perception will be termed by the person concerned as threatening, fearful, uncertain, ashamed, guilty, or listless.

It is clearly unlikely that a professional and proficient actor would wish, or in fact be able, to choose avoidance. Because of the negative connotations associated with terms like stage fright and because of some empirical results concerning 'public speaking'[27], I have nevertheless chosen to also include negative designations for emotions in the questionnaire (6.6). I believe that a professional actor will be able to transform the more negative emotions – as well as positive ones – to support the portrayal of the character, providing that control precedence and the intensity of the emotion do not become 'uncontrollable'. In addition, I presume – given the aspects that factor into the output of the emotion process (during acting in a performance) – that the professional actor consciously applies and uses task-emotions to give the character portrayal the 'warmth and persuasiveness' it needs.

As a result of their study of actors, Jackson and Latané state the following: 'It is widely believed among professionals that there is a mysterious process by which a skilled performer can transmute the nervous tension of stage fright into stage presence and project this energy back to the audience in the form of vivacity, depth, or intensity' (1981: 84).

4.9 Regulation by Design

Regulation of general human emotions in daily life, in Frijda's theory, mainly involves suppressing or masking emotions, which are felt to be negative, unsuitable or disturbing. This pattern happens more or less subconsciously. Conversely, transforming or shaping emotions in the acting process engages a more conscious and, if possible, a more intense use of aspects of task-emotions in order to support the portrayal of the character. This process is positive; it turns possibly disturbing or unpleasant aspects of task-emotions into useful and therefore pleasant aspects. The transformation, design or shaping of activation, action tendencies and (behavioral) expression linked to task-emotions can be compared with the 'regulation' of general human emotions. According to Frijda the 'regulation of emotion is not always voluntary; it mostly is not' (1986: 402). Something we are not always aware of in daily life seems to be very important for the actor.

The task situation of the actor is a special one when it comes to studying regulation; a specific form of regulation probably plays an explicit part and even a necessary part in being able to accomplish tasks successfully. With emotions in daily life, regulation is much more implicitly woven into the emotion process. In order to make a distinction between the process found in acting and the general process of emotion regulation, the terms 'transformation' or 'shaping of emotions' will be used. The process of transformation or shaping which influences the emotion process during acting does show some similarities with the way regulation functions. Therefore the features of regulation will be discussed which I believe to be applicable to transformation in the emotion process during acting.

4.9.1 **Shaping Expressions of Task-Emotions** The output of the emotion process during acting undergoes 'transformation', whereas the expression of emotion in the process of general human emotions undergoes 'regulation', in the terminology of this study. Regulation of the expression of emotions is usually more successful than regulation in an earlier stage of the emotion process. A good example of social regulation is being a good loser: 'In our culture, we are expected to act like a good loser, meaning that we do not appear too distressed nor blame anyone, but express positive regard for the winner and equanimity at the loss' (Lazarus 1985: 52). This indicates the possibility of influencing behavioral expression by masking or transforming it. Similarly, regulation, in the sense of transforming or designing expressions of behavior is vital for the actor because he communicates with the audience using this behavioral expression. The parts of the emotions which eventually become visible are these behavioral expressions. It is mainly through this behavioral aspect of emotion that character-emotions can be represented.

Regulation, in the sense of design, can moreover be one of the ways in which the actor can take pleasure in acting 'negative emotions'. A successful portrayal of Medea's revenge and sorrow can in this way give the actress intense satisfaction, because, for one thing, she is succeeding in accomplishing her task. She can also partake in esthetic pleasures, the enjoyment of beautiful acting or the experience of 'flow'. She can experience these feelings, while simultaneously giving expression to the behavior which suits the negative and unpleasant character-emotions.

4.9.2 **Shaping Physiological Phenomena** The intensity of the task-emotions, in any case, causes physiological activation. The high level of arousal observed in actors during performance, which has been interpreted as indicating a high level of task tension, does not need to be transformed in itself. Transformation, in the form of amplification, can be desirable when the level of task tension is too low. It is precisely the physiological activation that can, I presume, lend support to the portrayal of a character. The audience member will pick up signals that there is a high level of alertness, activation, readiness, and emotionality. He will then be disposed to interpret these signals as expressions of character-emotions, because he has no reason not to do so. In the eyes of the audience, the character will be given more 'liveliness and warmth'. It is difficult to say precisely how we, as audience members, observe physiological phenomena and what part of these we observe. An example is perhaps the blush of tension in an actor, which the audience may interpret as the character being in love. But, how character-emotions should look like to appear real to an audience will be discussed in the following chapter.

The physiological phenomena of what I call task-emotions can be used in the portrayal of character-emotions. Different aspects of the task-emotions can contribute to

ntaneity increases and contributes to
part of the physiological phenomena
ess and goal-orientation in the behav-
of an observable state of alertness as
to an actor (3.6.4). This is probably
hen they speak of energy and tension
ers to as the shining or radiance of an
e of task-emotions supports the per-
rpretation are probably involved. Re-
na, which are seen as a 'talisman' for
in section 5.6.

ctice of theater, I have, in this chapter,
mer has strategies at hand to direct his
a craftsman). He can also use his task-
t and design the portrayal of a charac-
ter. The actor's work seems then, in part, to consist of maximizing the task-emotions and shaping these into behavior which can be construed as the expression of emotions in the character. This is done in such a way that the form in which these task-emotions are expressed becomes identical to the portrayal of character-emotions. To describe the emotion process during acting a theoretical psychological framework after Frijda's model of the emotion process was provided. Frijda proposes that emotions have a function in satisfying an individual's concerns, and to maintain or change relationships with his surroundings. Relational action tendencies are then, according to him, the core of the emotion process.

The actor's emotions on stage fulfill the functionality criterion of the cognitive approach when the emotions stem from the nature of the acting task. The task situation offers the professional actor the possibility to satisfy primary concerns, like being competent, preserving self-image, seeking sensation, and esthetic satisfaction. Relevance-evaluation for the actor is characterized by the coincidence of risk with control, evoking challenge as a central emotion, which is in turn linked with pleasant or positive feelings. Under optimal conditions challenge leads to the experience of 'flow'. Because the task is difficult and has a high level of urgency, and because the assessment of the task situation results in maximum strengths of the components of objectivity and reality, these result in action tendencies with control precedence.

Challenge will generally evoke impulses or action tendencies 'to approach' or 'to overcome difficulties', because one thinks they can indeed be overcome. I presume that the actor shapes the emotional phenomena, which are related to the task-emotions in the acting situation, for the benefit of the portrayal of the character. In the behavioral expression the actor and the character come together, and that is what the audience sees and hears. Behavioral expression connected to the task-emotions assumes a form which suits the portrayal of the character. Physiological phenomena which have been observed in studies with actors suggest that they have intense task related emotions and that these can serve a twofold purpose: a) They lend the portrayal of character-emotions 'the illusion of spontaneity' and b) they contribute to the presence of the actor. In this respect task-emotions are functional and therefore fit within a contemporary interpretation of the functionality of emotions.

Working with comparable theoretical psychological conceptions as well as the results of psychological research, I will attempt in the next chapter to make a connection with the general idea, stemming from involvement theories, that the actor must have emotions which are similar to those of the character. This idea persists stubbornly, as the researchers Hammond and Edelman (1991) still attest, despite the obvious fact that everyone knows that the actor is not the character. We must therefore ask ourselves how the imagination of emotions relates to the impersonation of emotions.

Andromaché, Toneelgroep Amsterdam, directed by Gerardjan Rijnders 1990-1991. The acting style was based on the 18th C. Classicistic performance style in France.

5   *Imagination and Impersonation*

> ...either in tragedy, or in farce,
> the actor immersed in its spirits,
> stands outside his role,
> while seeming to believe utterly in its reality.
> JOHN L. STYAN (1975)

5.1   Introduction: Character Representation

Acting is traditionally, among other things, directed toward portraying a character's emotional world as believably and convincingly as possible. Such characters are perceived as experiencing emotions that correspond to those that people have in real life. However, the emotion characters experience are not emotions in the true sense, as was shown in subsection 4.3.1. This chapter will concentrate on the impersonation of character-emotions, as well as the relationship between the impersonation of a character-emotion and the actor's own feelings.

As stated, character-emotions are representations of emotions, not the emotions themselves. In the foregoing chapter various important aspects of the emotion process and their relevance for the *actor* were discussed. In section 5.2 ingredients of the emotion process for portraying a *character* will be discussed. There are elements in the representation which create the impression that we are dealing with emotions.

According to the acting theories which advocate involvement it is necessary for the actor to experience the character-emotions himself. The imagining of emotions will be linked to the concepts of empathy and identification such as these are used in psychologically oriented research (5.3). The significance of the stage situation for the actor will then be compared with that of the dramatic situation for the character. It will be revealed that a high degree of involvement is liable to push aside task-emotions and the accomplishment of acting tasks (5.4). The 'emotions' an actor invokes through involvement or imagination, which are similar to those of the character, differ fundamentally in a number of respects from 'spontaneously' aroused emotions (5.5).

Although the involvement theory is perhaps based on the idea that expressions of 'real' emotions will be more believable and appealing to audiences than feigned emotions, psychological research reveals that this is not necessarily so. Although, imitating emotional expression can indeed lead to feelings which the actor might imagine to be his own emotional experience (5.7). By bringing a number of important aspects of the emotion process during acting into conjunction with insights from psychological research, we will understand why an actor is thought to have a 'double consciousness'. In chapter three, this notion came up as a potential solution for the actor's dilemma. Psychological research on double or plural states of consciousness reveals that specific experiences, for example disassociating feeling from behavior, are characteristic features of double consciousness. I will discuss how this applies to acting in section 5.8.

5.2 Acting Character-Emotions

Character-emotions are not real emotions (4.3.1). They are representations of behavior suggesting emotion, used to create the illusion of the real emotion we know in daily life in a convincing and believable way. To quote Dennet (1987): 'Characters are observed as real people'. The most common dramatic situations are about death, danger, large sums of money, and lost or not yet captured loves, where temptation, jealousy, revenge, and such come into play. The essence of drama is conflict, which indicates that concerns are at stake. Polti suggests that a maximum of 36 dramatic conflict situations can be constructed, based on his estimate that there is a maximum of 36 (basic) emotions (1990: 9). The most typical character-emotions are connected with conflict situations, like despair, anger, revenge, hatred, fear, jealousy, disgust, but also with love, eroticism, tenderness, pleasure, and happiness. The emotions characteristic for dramatic roles are comparable to what are known in psychological literature as basic emotions or prototypical emotions.[1]

To make it possible for audiences to interpret certain behavior of actors as behavior that indicates emotions, audience members must at minimum be able to recognize behavior as appropriate to the emotions of the character. Subsequently audiences may let themselves become involved in the emotion. This raises the question as to what character-emotions should look like in order to seem real or be perceived as emotions. The character-emotions are suggested on stage by providing the audience with information on aspects relevant to the dramatic situation. Further, character-emotions are suggested by imitating behavior, especially by making presumably appropriate action tendencies or impulses visible. I will describe some of the most relevant concerns and features for characters in dramatic situations.

It seems plausible that a process takes place in audience members, which is the reverse of the emotion process Frijda describes (figure 4.1). Audiences will deduce the character's emotions, concerns, and situational meaning from the behavior exhibited and from information given about the context. The direction the impersonated character-impulse takes – either avoidance or approach – will help the audience interpret the 'emotional behavior' so that they will be able to understand the character's actions. In this way it becomes possible to sympathize with the character. Information from other sources like the dramatic course of action and the spoken text can also help. The portrayal of character-emotions must necessarily point to defining features of real emotions; to concerns in combination with situational components, which can arouse impulses with control precedence.

5.2.1 Characters and Concerns

The main theme of dramatic action is usually determined by the concerns of the characters, as well as by their goals, plans, motivations, and desires. In principle any imaginable concern could be suitable as a concern of a stage character. However, a great majority of dramatic literature and theater practice, seems to show preference for a certain category of emotions and to address certain types of concerns. This is especially true of 'lead' characters (to which this study is limited). For example, Medea's source concerns such as self-esteem, survival, restitution, and justice, are threatened when she hears that Jason will marry the princess. These concerns lead her to plot her own departure; they generate allusions to the cruelest of revenge scenarios: Destroying Jason by murdering their children. The most treasured renditions on stage are those of the 'big' emotions, those which refer to universal source concerns. These involve survival, love, self-esteem, power, freedom, etc. Because fundamental interests are at stake, characters are often entangled in violent conflicts and passionate affairs; they are confronted with seemingly insurmountable difficulties, suffer intensely and undergo unbridled passions.[2] It seems easier to act out, and to put across the audience, a story line with concrete surface concerns than with general and abstract source concerns. The source concerns of characters are therefore usually expressed by employing the more concrete surface concerns. Referring to source concerns by using surface concerns is a practical strategy (for actor and audience), because concrete matters in the here and now make a stronger appeal to emotions than abstract issues.[3] The idea that audience concerns will be addressed through events in the fictional world of characters is found most clearly in Brecht's texts on theater.[4] Brecht places great emphasis on showing the audience recognizable concerns of the characters and specific features of the dramatic situation (3.3). With Stanislavsky one recognizes the need to know and portray character's concerns in formulating the character's 'highest aspirations' in order to shape the inner model and arrive at 'identification'. In the acting method of self-expression, with Grotowski for example, we recognize an appeal to concerns when the Polish director speaks of revealing the 'deepest self' (with actor and audience) (3.4).

Values can also become concerns and are therefore an important source of intense emotion. Values are connected with social rules, what 'should and should not be'. 'People may become enraged about offenses against values to a degree that would likely be exceptional for them in personal matters' (Frijda 1986: 354). Grotowski and Brook endeavored to touch audiences deeply by challenging taboos. Many concerns which are rendered in dramatic works involve these types of values that are turned into vested interests, thus emotionally touching the interests of the audience and move them. Classical dramatic texts in particular appeal to morals or tend to be moralistic.[5] Values transformed to vested interests are generally not the most prominent interests of the dramatic characters; characters are more often representatives of these values. Sympathy for the character often ceases the moment his deeds go too far: When they offend the audience's own vested interest values.[6] To make the interests of characters clear, relevant components of the event or situation are crucial to a representative reflection of emotions.

5.2.2 **Components in Dramatic Situations** Character-emotions can only be recognized by the audience as reflections of real emotions when the characters' situations include references to the components objectivity and reality. These core components are, ultimately, all indispensable for arousing and experiencing real emotions (4.3). As mentioned earlier, any possible emotion or concern could be conceivable for characters, and the same holds for any conceivable situation. Some of the most relevant components which appear frequently in dramatic situations will be described below. These are concerns and components which can be presumed to be characteristic for character-emotions in leading characters. I shall now discuss the importance of the components for the *characters*, and not their possible relevance for the actor. The two will be compared in section 5.4.

The impersonated character-emotions will be plausible for the audience if they refer to realistic concerns and features in a dramatic situation and if there are realistic occasions. This is the core component *reality*. Brecht sought conviction in character-emotions not inside the reality of the portrayed emotion in itself (e.g., where both the advocates of the styles of self-expression and involvement look for 'reality'), but by showing plausible motives for character-emotions (3.3). The component *reality* also has another function in dramatic work. The boundary between fiction and truth, between seeming and being, is a favorite theme of modern playwrights (cf. *Six Characters in Search of an Author*, Pirandello 1921; *Waiting for Godot*, Beckett 1953; *Liefhebber*, Rijnders 1992). These authors create situations where characters, and sometimes audiences, seem to be in a state of uncertainty about how profoundly their interests are concerned. Likewise, toying with *objectivity* seems to be an important ingredient for creating tension and drama in fictional situations; the events on stage overtake the character and the character's interests are instantly in the balance. Countless examples of dramatic literature and performance reveal that objectivity and reality are critical components of dramatic situations.

The core component which is probably most typical for character situations is *difficulty*; problems must be overcome, battles fought, lovers won and lost, in-laws and families convinced they are wrong, etc. Goals, plans, interests, and desires are usually difficult for characters to fulfill in the given situation and various obstacles and hurdles must be overcome. The component of *urgency* also plays a major part in dramatic situations, as when 'deadlines' are set. In *Hamlet* there are many moments when the urgency factor is being exploited: The murder of Hamlet's father must be avenged *now*; to rescue Ophelia from her madness (and death) Hamlet has to unmask himself *now* (later proves to be too late – Ophelia dies); in the final duel scene Hamlet must strike Laertes *now*. In performance, urgency is most likely translated partially into 'timing'. For the audience, the urgency component takes effect when the show becomes exciting and suspenseful. The components of urgency and difficulty determine how intense the character-emotions will be.

The continual struggle with a seemingly uncontrollable event, object or opponent (the component *controllability*) is another source of intense character-emotions. Juliet's passionate, albeit doomed, desire for Romeo would not be nearly so 'dramatic' were she to have more control over the situation. We sympathize, as spectators, so much more with Medea because her misery has been wrought by others, in particular by Jason; she has no ability to control the inflicted distress. Characters usually find themselves in situations where they try to avoid or change their relationship with their surroundings and fellow characters so that the negative aspects will be removed. In other words, the *valence* of the dramatic situation is usually negative. Thus, the situation for

Andromaché (Racine 1667) is negative throughout the play. She is confronted with an impossible choice to free her imprisoned son and finally decides to die. When characters do reach coveted goals, as in romances and comedies, it is usually not until the end of the play.

Lastly, I mention the core components *strangeness-familiarity* and *demand character*. Dramatic situations are unfamiliar for the character, who never knows what is about to happen, and have a high demand character. For example, Hamlet is completely fixated on the idea of avenging his father's murder. However, he does not know for certain who the murderer is.

5.2.3 'Action Tendencies' and Behavior in Characters
To make character-emotions seem like 'real' emotions, actors will impersonate action tendencies or impulses which coincide with these 'emotions'. Because these are not real action tendencies, like those paired with real emotions (characters cannot really feel), these will be called *character-tendencies*. The actor can only make character-tendencies visible by exhibiting behavior, through facial expression, movement or voice, and in so doing set the tone for the character-emotions. Thus avoidance behavior is a representation of the impulse to avoid associated with negative emotions because aspects of the situation are threatening to the concerns of the character. When, for example, Medea's context evaluation consists of an evaluation of her options for punishing Jason, the pain to be suffered and abandonment of her country, her presumed character-tendencies will be a combination of the impulses 'to flee', 'to avoid', 'to attack', and perhaps the tendency 'to burst into tears', or 'to scream'. Such impulses are compatible with a combination of grief and fury.[7] Similarly, approach behavior expresses the impulse to approach, which is compatible with positive emotions, because the situation is probably favorable to the satisfaction of one's interests.

Control precedence of character-tendencies becomes visible in the form of obsession. The situation is so urgent for the character that other activities no longer take priority. The characters are driven and seemingly only controlled by impulses pertaining to the aroused emotions; their behavior appears to express only these character-tendencies. In the world of the character, seen from an audience perspective, it seems like nothing exists other than the object of the emotion or the realization of the coveted goal. It is precisely this demand precedence that we recognize in the impersonation of impassioned characters.

In performance, a character-emotion is nothing more than the behavior an actor exhibits, normally interpreted by the audience as part of the character. Moreover, the behavioral expression of character-emotions diverges from everyday behavioral expression because it is based on an imaginary model (3.6.1). When imitating the behavior which suits the intended emotions, the actor is one with the character. The behavior which suits the characters-emotions is identical to the behavior of the actor as character. This behavior is what the audience sees (and hears); it is what they deduce character-emotions from (along with other information). The three ways in which an emotion can be expressed are limited to behavior only when it comes to expressing character-emotions. The other channels of expression (subjective perception and physiological reactions; 4.8) can only exist for character-emotions in the minds of the audience through their interpretation of behavior. In this sense character-emotions are 'empty' behavior. That this behavior can also be 'filled' with outputs from the actor's own emotion process is a different matter, as was discussed in chapter four. As such, these outputs are not part of the character-emotion itself, in a strict sense. The impersonation of character-emotions is largely prescribed, in a script or during a rehearsal process, and must meet the demands a director (or other theater maker) makes on such portrayals, including, among other things, being recognizable, believable, convincing, and somehow appealing.

> Once, during a try out, I sat on a chair that was painted just before. While I was seated, I realized it was still wet. I knew that, when I would get up, everybody could see the paint on me. Afterwards, a colleague asked me why I blushed so much, with such a red face: 'Was it so hot in there?' The audience thought I got excited by the way I was ill treated by Hermioné (the character) in the play. My mind was only occupied by thinking how to get rid of the paint and how my dress would stick to the chair. Sure, I had to pay attention to my part as well, but that was something different. And so, each night has its own things to cope with, something from outside influencing your play. For example, one night 'it' is there, the other night 'it' is not there, but ... what is 'it'?
> (Actress Oda Spelbos in the documentary *Acteurs Spelen Emoties*, NPS 1995, based on Konijn 1994).

To sum up, it is clear that dramatic texts, performances and scripts include a number of ingredients which bear resemblance to features of everyday emotions in order to appear like real emotions. For the actor these features (components in Frijda's terms) will be relevant for shaping an inner model of the character-emotions. But, in impersonating character-emotions, how do they relate to the actor's own feeling? In general, the prevailing acting theories do not acknowledge what I call task-emotions as discussed in chapter three. The acting style of *detachment* seems to be the only one to recognize a distinction between various levels of enactment. Detachment acting does not however suggest that the actor uses or shows his task-emotions per se; the emotions of the actor qua actor are, as it were, ignored.

The advocates of the style of *self-expression* urge the actor to present his own (private) emotions. In this style there is no illusion of 'real' characters intended, but of 'real' people – the actors present themselves. The style of *involvement* is the most problematic in light of Diderot's paradoxical standpoint. The view held by advocates of the style of involvement on the question raised in *Paradoxe* is the opposite of Diderot's anti-emotionalist opinion. According to the style of involvement the actor has emotions during an acting performance which correspond to those of the character. Moreover, the style of involvement, or variants thereof, seems to be the most accepted method in contemporary theater and film practice (e.g., Hornby 1992). The work of Stanislavsky and his successors (mostly an Americanized interpretation) is the most popular method in drama schools. This was revealed in the 1993 BBC documentary, *The Drama Centre*. But how can we understand what involvement means?

5.3   Involving Oneself in Character-Emotions

To gain insight into the process of 'immersing oneself' into a character emotion, I will try to make a connection with some psychological research on involvement. Psychological research uses the terms empathy and identification for processes which in acting theory and practice usually are called 'involvement' or 'projecting into'.[8] Rather than a complete theoretical discussion of these terms, I will suffice with a discussion of the aspects of empathy and identification which are connected with the emotion process during acting.

5.3.1 Empathy and Identification

Empathy and identification are not emotions in themselves, but processes by which individuals experience similar emotions. The terms involvement, empathy, and identification are usually used interchangeably. Research on empathy and identification is important to understand the 'involvement' of the actor in character-emotions. A common feature of empathy and identification is that the fate of another, the observed or the object of emotion, becomes part of the emotional experience of the observer. *Empathy* refers to the source concern of 'caring for the well-being of loved ones' or of 'proximity and coherence' and 'intimacy', or of a sympathy concern.[9] In part, these concerns stem from specific sensitivity to pain or need in others, which evokes caring behavior. Empathetic emotions include pity, compassion, malign pleasure, sympathy, wonder, and fascination.

The main distinction between empathy and identification is found in the separation or lack of separation between oneself and the other.[10] The drama scholar Schoenmakers defines identification as a process through which the spectator begins to experience emotions similar to those of the other: 'Those processes by which the subject places him- or herself in the situation of an object, and accordingly experiences the same emotions as he or she thinks the object experiences' (Schoenmakers 1988: 142). According to Frijda, identification is distinct from empathy because with identification there is a *self-object-dissolution*, in which the sense is lost that events are taking place outside of ourselves; this feels like 'being one' with the world. This can also mean 'being one' with another person or character. This seems to correspond with the trance-like experience of the actor which Brook and Constantinidis, among others, describe, and which occurs in certain rituals, primarily in non-Western cultures. Perhaps this state of being is also comparable with that of an actor who 'identifies completely' with his character. Identification does not result in feelings of sympathy for another, but in having feelings similar to the emotions the character presumably has.

Identification thus leads to emotions *similar* to those of the character and empathy leads to emotions *different* from those of the character. With empathy, the emotions, components, and concerns of the actor and character are not comparable (such as the actress feeling pity for Electra's distress). The concerns underlying empathetic emotions are of another order (namely 'sympathy' or 'proximity and coherence') than that of the character's. Moreover, the object of the empathetic emotions is actually the other person, and not a direct result of a situation or event in which 'I find myself' (in thought). Conversely, with identification, a similar concern is shared by two individuals, possibly in the imagination or in a fantasy: The concerns of the character are 'like my own'. Likewise, the other is not the object and not a meaningful part of the process, but rather the other is 'like myself'; there is a merging with the subject.

Research on empathy and identification, as far as theater studies are concerned, usually concerns the relationship between spectators and characters and seldom concerns the relationship between actors and characters. Moreover, the characters studied are usually film characters.[11] To be able to empathize or identify, the actor will in a sense have to be an observer for the character, even though he will be a different type of viewer than an audience member. According to Tan's (1996) psychological studies in film, empathetic emotions in viewers are 'eye witness emotions'. Empathy in actors seems to be of a different nature; an actor imagines how it would feel to be like the character and also how the audience will see him as the character. The actor can certainly have empathy for the character, but the task situation does not allow for pausing to consider the fate of the character in the sense of empathy. In the foregoing chapter a plausible case was made for the notion that the task situation demands the actor's full attention. If an actor empathizes during a performance, this will more likely be prompted by a task concern than because the actor feels the need to care. The need for caring is a source concern and one of the important underlying sources of empathetic emotions.[12]

Understanding and 'immersing oneself' in the character will probably be more important for the actor during the *rehearsal period*. Delving into the emotion provides information about the relevant concerns and situational components in order to create a model in the imagination. In addition, it provides insight into the information that the actor will transmit to the audience. However, even advocates of the style of involvement, like method acting, may not lose sight of the aspects of control over the acting process and the consciousness of the task situation. That is why one can not expect a total overlap in the various phases of the emotion process between actor and character (5.4.1).

Thus, when drama theoreticians speak of involvement with a character, namely in the context of the actor's dilemma and acting in a performance, they seem to mean identification. After all, through involvement the actor would have emotions similar to those of his character.[13] Similarity of emotions is based on the presumption that the meaning of the situation for the character has some congruence with the situational meaning from the actor's point of view. In this case there would be comparable concerns at stake (for instance, anxiety about self-preservation that the actress shares with Medea). Nevertheless, involvement during the rehearsal process can just as easily point at empathy. Which strategies can the actor use to involve himself with the character, in the sense of identification, to arrive at similar emotions or attaining a similar state of mind?

5.3.2   **Strategies for Involvement** Because the character's dramatic situation is not the same as the actual situation in which the actor finds himself, it is germane to discuss some research in which emotions are aroused without the confrontation with the actual emotional stimulus. In psychological research on emotions, various procedures are used on test subjects to arouse emotions, since the actual test situation itself does not contain direct provocation. In this sort of research, three strategies to arouse emotions through involvement can be discerned: (a) By using film, (b) by using specific instructions, and (c) through mimicry. Often the various procedures are combined.

Koriat's research used film segments showing accidents in a sawmill. The subjects were instructed in advance to either a) involve themselves in the film, or to b) distance themselves from it. This strategy yielded particularly interesting results in reference to the acting process. To involve themselves in the situation, most subjects tried to imagine that they were the accident victim. To distance themselves they generally convinced themselves that what they were seeing was not real and concentrated on the technical aspects of the film.[14] The subjects' involvement strategy can be seen as an attempt to make the situation concrete. By placing themselves in the role of the character they rendered the situation concrete. Concretization makes emotions stronger, while abstraction weakens them. The 'here and now' has a much stronger, more direct reality value than the 'there and then' (5.2). To involve oneself it is therefore important that the imagined situation is brought closer to the 'here and now' than the actual context which the subject (or actor) is in. The actor can understand the concerns and the components of the character better and involve himself better by imagining himself in the position of the character. To design an inner model it is important that one forms an image of the most relevant concerns, goals, and motivations of a character and of the most important features of the dramatic situation.

The researcher Lang and his colleagues used different instructions to evoke an emotional image or vision. One group of test subjects was offered descriptions in which their attention was completely focused on stimulation features of the situation. For example: 'You notice an insect'. The other group focused attention mainly on behavioral and physiological responses to the stimulus, for example 'you hear the buzzing of an insect' (Lang et al. 1980: 183).[15] The results show that the latter reaction-directed instructions evoked the strongest and liveliest images. My interpretation is that, with reaction-directed instructions the person himself is directly involved and therefore focuses more on the 'here' than the 'there'. According to an overview survey by Martin (1990) it appears rather difficult to arouse intense emotions 'in imagine' in research situations. Diderot already pointed to the difference between emotional feelings brought on by a sensitive reading of an event and the emotion during the event itself, in which the object, feeling, and effect coincide (1985: 58).

A third line of research involves mimicry. Here the basic assumption is that we more or less unconsciously try to imitate the emotions we observe in others. Thus Zajonc says: 'Reproducing the expression of another may well produce in the onlooker a similar emotional state. Of course the feeling is not experienced equally. But this might be so only because the movements are *not faithfully* reproduced' (Zajonc 1985: 19, italics EK). Applied to actors this would mean that emotions similar to the portrayed character's will arise because actors imitate emotional expressions. This theoretical assumption is in line with notions like 'emotional infection' during acting.[16]

In short, the above shows that 'involving oneself in emotions' principally concerns involving oneself in potentially emotional *situations*. By imagining the situation in the most concrete way, reactions can be evoked which are like the phenomena of spontaneously aroused emotions. Impersonating or imitating the related behavioral expression may possibly also contribute to arousing sensations. To what extent imagining or imitating emotional expressions can lead to 'real' emotions is still an unresolved problem, to which I will return in section 5.5. Yet, the theoretical analysis so far does not provide any reason to suppose that the actor must identify with the character. Why then is this idea so persistent? What could be the *function* of becoming involved with character-emotions, or the actor imagining himself as having the character's emotions? Involvement supposedly assists the recognition and believability of the portrayal which subsequently makes the impersonation more convincing. The question to what extent identification is necessary for a recognizable and believable impersonation of character-emotions on stage will be answered in section 5.6. However, when an actor imagines the character-emotions or the emotional situations in which characters find themselves, identification is intended. Then, the imagined situation or 'emotion' will have to correspond in one way or another with the actor's task situation.

5.4   Opposing Concerns, Components, and Impulses?

Suppose that an actor involves himself in the situation of a character. How do the concerns, components, and action tendencies of character-emotions relate to the actor's task-emotions? The types of character-emotions the actor might possibly immerse himself in were discussed in section 5.2. The degree to which typical character-emotions, in terms of concerns and situational components are in opposition to or in agreement with the most relevant task concerns and situational components in the acting situation will be explored in this section.

5.4.1   **Concerns in the Drama and in the Task** The actor's task concerns (competence, self-image, sensation seeking, and esthetic concerns; discussed in section 4.4), are seldom the most relevant concerns of central characters (5.2.1). They might even be in opposition to one another during a performance. The struggle for 'restitution' or 'survival', for example, cannot easily be equated with the actor's image concern. Therefore it becomes difficult to imagine how involving oneself in the character's concerns can serve to accomplish the most relevant task concerns of the actor (in his profession). His interests in the 'here and now' in the acting situation of a live performance will affect the professional actor more directly than the concerns he has imagined to resemble the character's concerns. It is therefore not likely that specific emotions conjured up by the actor to resemble the character-emotions will override the actual task emotions. Nor will an emotion evoked through involvement during a performance fulfill the functional core of emotions, because it does not serve the interests of the actor in the acting situation. After all, emotions function to serve actual interests.

5.4.2   **Partially Comparable Components** When an actor has the sensation that he experiences the character's emotions, there has to be at least a modicum of similarity in the situational components of the task emotions and character-emotions. In the last chapter, various important aspects of the emotion process and its significance for the *actor* were discussed (4.5). In section 5.2, the significance of these aspects for the *character* was described. Below, I will discuss the components in the emotion process – objectivity, reality, urgency, difficulty, controllability, valence, strangeness-familiarity, and demand character – for the situation of the actor *in comparison to* those of the character.

Characters in dramatic situations are inevitably entangled in seemingly realistic conflicts. We saw that the *reality* and *objectivity* levels for them are high. The high degrees of *reality* and *objectivity* in the actual task situation in acting were also mentioned in subsection 4.5.1. When the actor involves himself with the character, it is not likely that he will be able to trade the objectivity and reality of the task situation for these same components in the dramatic situation through involvement. That would seem to be impossible as long as there is an audience present and as long as the actor is not deluded or in a 'trance'. Perhaps he can use 'the feeling' of objectivity and reality in the task situation, in the sense of transforming these sensations, to assist his sense of involvement (compare with 4.9).

The components called *urgency* and *difficulty* score high for both the character and the dramatic situation. As already seen, these components cause the emotions to be very intense (4.5.2). The imagined situation into which the actor projects himself can at that moment not be urgent for the actor; certainly no more urgent than the actual task situation which puts him face to face with an audience. The dramatic situation of the character may be difficult to depict, but for the actor, the character situation will not be difficult as a part of his own emotional experience. Thanks to many rehearsals, (usually), he knows the dramatic situation very well. The difficulty and urgency of the task situation felt by an actor who adheres to a style of involvement may possibly contribute to the 'feeling of having the character's emotions'.

Characters often have very low or even no *control* over a particular situation; characters are often just pawns of the dramatic events, as Medea is at the mercy of her fate. The threat emanating from the lack of control makes the component *valence* in most dramatic situations negative for the character. The task emotions of the actor, on the other hand, have a positive base as argued in the last chapter. The task demands and the command of skills will be balanced to the extent that possible risks will provoke the emotion challenge. The values of the components called *controllability* and *valence* seem to be opposite for character and actor. Therefore the task situation will, in this respect, not contribute to possible feelings of involvement. When the actor involves himself with his character the 'emotions' he calls forth will be relatively easier to control than his task emotions. Moreover, he will not be imagining the dramatic situation for the first time in performance.

The situations that characters discover themselves in are *unknown* to them; likewise, that will be the impression created for the audience. Being unfamiliar with difficult situations heightens the sense of uncontrollability and demands attention. However, when an actor involves himself into a character, the dramatic situation is completely *familiar*. He needs to know the situation to be able to imagine it. Situations of central characters generally have a high *demand character*, because, for them, they concern major events and important persons demanding the character's attention. Demand character for the actor in the task situation is also high. During every performance there will be unexpected aspects in the acting situation which require attention to be handled successfully. The demand character of the situation in the imagination is negligible compared to the actual task situation; it does not lay the same claim on the capacity to concentrate as the task situation does.

Thus, the comparison of some important components in the task situation with equivalent components in most typical dramatic situations shows, on the one hand, that corresponding levels of a few components can contribute to giving an actor who involves himself with the role the 'feeling' that he too is experiencing the character-emotions. On the other hand, the comparison shows that the differences are so fundamental that they provide *no* ground for similarity between the emotions of the actor and the character. Only if the actor involves himself to the extent that he *forgets* the task situation and the imagined situation actually takes over, can this imagined situation have an impact on the actor that is similar to the dramatic situation. But, I think that even if the recalled (private) emotions are strongly present, the task situation will dominate during the performance. The memory of a sad experience can revive the 'feeling' of sadness again and again. This may even be a very intense feeling, yet, it is not the same experience as when the emotion first arose during the original occurrence of the sad event. It is also possible that the private emotion still persists and that recollection strengthens its intensity; the components called urgency and gravity then become actual or heightened. Furthermore, frequent rehearsals put the character-emotions into another light for the actor. Note again that we are discussing involvement during a live performance; involvement during rehearsals can be helpful indeed.

5.4.3 **Transforming Impulses** Action tendencies or impulses which are related to the task situation and have the same orientation as the character impulses to be impersonated, can also contribute to the actor's sense of experiencing the character-emotions himself. However, the direction of the impulses of actor and character seem, at first glance, to be incompatible. Characters always want something, they have clear goals, desires, and plans that they want to see accomplished. They head for these goals like heroic 'fighting dragons', even if, in a similar situation in daily life, our impulse would be 'to flee'. Unlike daily life, negative or unpleasant character-emotions in dramatic conflicts seldom lead to avoidance behavior (of the character). That would, after all, put an end to the drama and bring down the final curtain. Dramatic conflict usually stems from the fact that a character wants or needs something which is not always actually attainable (and if so, seldom easy).

The impulses associated with task emotions are generally oriented toward approach. 'To go for it' and 'overcome difficulties' are characteristic action tendencies associated with challenge (4.7). There appears, finally, a substantial degree of overlap possible in the struggles and the impulses of actor and character; action tendencies of task-emotions and the character-tendencies generally point in the same direction. The actor can transform, apply, and use the action tendencies or impulses of task-emotions to give the character gestalt. Recalling subsection 4.3.1, the emotions of characters are not really emotions, but only reflections of behavior which (for an audience) resemble behavior that we recognize or know as expressing an emotion. In the process of playing a character before an audience, impulses or action tendencies related to the task-emotions can be reversed and used to fill in the character. Likewise, it is not difficult to imagine how control precedence of the actor's task emotions (4.8) can take on the appearance of 'obsession' in the character. The drive of the actor to keep the audience in his grip can easily resemble Hamlet's fixation on the revenge of his father's murder.

The 'empty' portrayal of character-emotions (5.2.3) can thus be 'filled in' with the action tendencies of the actor's task-emotions. The actress playing Medea obviously cannot actually murder the players opposite her. However, an urge (for example) to 'overcome difficulties', to 'go for it', or to 'do something' will arise automatically, as it were, from her task situation; she can give these urges the semblance of Medea 'wanting to murder'. There is no competition for control precedence: Those of actor and character are in line of each other. The action impulses and control precedence of the actor will be deployed or shaped as an illusion of the impersonated action tendency of the character. To clarify this, figure 5.1 shows an adapted version of figure 4.1 concerning the emotion process during acting.

The action tendencies linked to task-emotions which steer toward behavior, can in general not be shown to audiences as observable behavior *without* transformation or shaping them. It is possible for the actor to give these impulses a different expression. He can for instance use the impulse to support fright in a character, or to embrace his character's lover passionately (now alone at last). Because a 'reflection of a character's action tendency' is partially sustained by a 'real action tendency in the actor', the impersonation of the character tendencies will seem more authentic. The conviction of the acting will be enhanced.

The professional actor will have to mask or reshape the impulses and urges which *do not* fit into the character impersonation. The urge, for example, to shout that a colleague has forgotten his wig cannot be expressed right away on stage. Neither may an

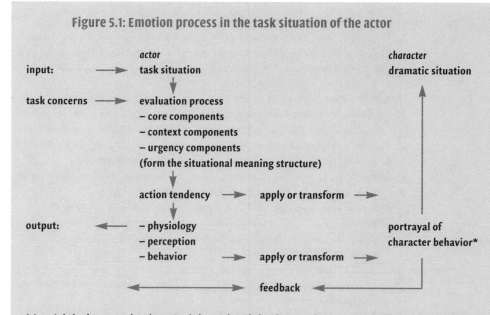

Figure 5.1: Emotion process in the task situation of the actor

	actor	character
input: →	task situation	dramatic situation
task concerns →	evaluation process	
	– core components	
	– context components	
	– urgency components	
	(form the situational meaning structure)	
	action tendency → apply or transform →	
output: ←	– physiology	portrayal of
	– perception	character behavior*
	– behavior → apply or transform →	
←	feedback ←	

* Actor's behavior expression shown (and observed) as 'belonging' to a character-emotion, in which the audience member deduces presumptions about character-concerns and the meaning of the dramatic situation in which the character finds himself.

actor burst out laughing unless his character is particularly jolly at that precise moment. Happy or positive emotions as central character-emotions seem to appear relatively less frequently than negative character-emotions (5.2). Perhaps impersonations of positive character-emotions are more easily paired with the generally positive task-emotions, which are associated with approach impulses. Listlessness, apathy, boredom, or other 'non-energy' emotions only occur to a limited extent in the portrayal of important characters. When these do occur the actor will have to switch to a more radical reshaping or even suppression of task tendencies. Nonetheless, impersonations of apathy, boredom and such, when they do occur in leading roles, need to have an underlying tension and cannot come across as 'dull'. Here as well, reshaping task-tendencies is in line with the character-tendencies.

If the actor involves himself in negative or unpleasant character-emotions, there is a risk that the possible positive effect of the similarity in the impulses of the character and the task could be negated. The 'emotion' evoked through involvement could then seem too much like an everyday emotion. For a great number of emotions, especially negative ones, this in turn leads to avoidance tendencies. If the actor were really to involve himself to such an extent that he actually experiences the negative emotions himself, he might have the impulse to run away. If the actor involves himself to an overwhelming extent, achieving complete identification with the character, there is also another danger: Losing track of the working situation. 'Losing track' of the task situation naturally has negative consequences, not only because the actor is neglecting the task situation but also, for example, because this will probably irritate angered colleagues – thus their self-image is also at stake.

Q: 'What do actors feel on stage then?

A: Hopefully an actor feels what anybody would feel when he is on stage. A battery of lights in his face; one, two, eight-hundred people staring at him and expecting something from him. Or that his clothes itch, his make-up is running, maybe that he's nervous. He does not feel his nerves, unless they are infected.

Q: But doesn't he feel great feelings or...?

A: Maybe. If he's just had a big argument with his colleague or partner. Or someone in the second row is yawning or browsing through his program out of boredom. Otherwise, there are undoubtedly a whole series of bigger and smaller feelings playing in his brain, not unlike a surgeon during an operation for instance. Or a dental technician watching television.

Q: But if he has to act like he's terribly in love or mad as hell or has to die later?

A: Then he has to use all his concentration to make the audience see, to let them feel if you like, that he is very much in love or angry or jealous or scared or uncertain. ...

Q: But how does the audience feel everything the character the actor is playing feels?

A: Partly from the text, partly from what the actor does or doesn't do. Usually that is agreed and rehearsed. An actor has all sorts of techniques to manipulate. ... You learn these techniques in school and/or in practice. Acting is a profession.

Q: But don't some actors really cry on stage?

A: What is really? Some can produce tears on command. I even know an actress who can cry at a comma if you asked her. But how 'real' is 'really' crying? ...

Q: Are actors who can't 'really' cry worse actors?

A: Not necessarily. Maybe they can do other tricks better.'

(Director G.J. Rijnders responding to theater critic K. Freriks, in Freriks and Rijnders 1992: 12)

In conclusion, the chance that the actor in performance will actually be touched (during the performance) by the essence of an emotion evoked through imagination is very slight. This is simply because the task concerns in the acting situation have more reality, objectivity, and urgency for the professional actor than the dramatic situation does. Being threatened with a prop knife does not arouse real emotion because the physical well-being of the actor is not truly being threatened; his personal concerns are not really at stake. The essence of a real emotion is that a sensed action impulse takes control precedence. On stage this process is absent, no matter to what degree the actor has involved himself. Consequently, the overriding need to behave in verisimilitude with the 'emotion' evoked through involvement is also missing. As will be seen later, there are a number of important differences between spontaneously aroused emotions and 'emotions' evoked through imagination.

5.5   Spontaneous and Imagined Emotions

Sensations aroused through imagination have no bearing on the actual context (of stage acting) for the actor, but relate to a fantasized, dramatic context. Nevertheless, as Frijda indicates, a fantasy or an imagined event can also function as an input in the emotion process. I will show that the distinction between emotions in daily life (that is to say, spontaneously aroused or real emotions) and imagined emotions on stage, is not a matter of all or nothing. By 'imagined emotions' I mean the experiences evoked in the imagination which resemble emotions: The imagining of oneself in emotional situations similar to those of the character. I again emphasize that I am talking about emotions imagined while acting in a live performance, where the acting situation is dominant. When the actual situation does not insist that action be taken, it will be easier to lose oneself in the imagination and (temporarily) forget that one is pretending, fantasizing, or remembering.

5.5.1   **Five Differences** It appears from the above that spontaneously aroused emotions can be distinguished from emotions evoked through involvement (during the acting situation in performance). I will outline the differences in five aspects of the emotion process: (1) The 'objective' and 'real' addressing of concerns; (2) control precedence; (3) consequences of the emotional experience; (4) arousal, duration, and subsidence, and (5) expression of the emotion.

1. By imagining a situation, it is true that concerns are addressed, although not inevitably and not actually; 'only' in the imagination. The actor will always know that he will not actually be stabbed to death: *Objectivity* and *reality* are low. Likewise, the actress does not forget the moment when she felt just like Medea, Electra, or Antigone (maybe in a rehearsal), but as soon as she realizes she does not have a *reason*, the feeling will simply vanish.[17] Involvement can in principle lead to intense feelings, but for real emotions to occur it is necessary that concerns be addressed in a real and unavoidable way. Depending on the strength of the illusion that one is 'present' in the character's world, the sense of objectivity and reality might be great to very great, even conceivably approaching 'trance' or 'self-object-dissolution' (5.3). But in fact the actor will have little opportunity to forget the actual situation. Aspects of the actor's task situation will

repeatedly remind him that there is work to be done; that he has to disappear into the wings on cue between scenes, interact, apply corrections, etc.

2. 'Emotions' evoked in the imagination do not take *control precedence* over possible action tendencies. If an impulse to take action arises, this will not readily take priority over behavior motors. This implies that the control over an imagined emotion is relatively greater than over a spontaneous emotion. One can easily escape an imagined emotion by, for example, walking off stage or 'dropping' lines. An emotion evoked in the imagination can, however, result in behavior. For instance, remembering a funny experience sometimes results in a grin. Likewise, physiological activation resulting from imagined emotions has been measured although it is not clear precisely what caused these results (the evoked emotion or the effort of invoking the emotion; see 5.7).

3. Spontaneous emotions have *consequences* for 'who you are', one's identity and social roles in daily life, and one's 'social intention'. On the other hand, an impersonated emotion does not have direct consequences for a social role in daily life or for who you are; it is, after all, 'only make believe' (assuming both parties acknowledge that it's a game!). Medea's descent for example, will not affect the actress personally (not her identity). On the contrary, if she interprets the role brilliantly, she will gain esteem. It is not the emotion the actress has (perhaps) become immersed in and the behavior depicting it (which was in the script to begin with) that have consequences for the reputation of the actress, but the acting itself – how well she performs. A more recent example is actor Nicholas Cage, who won acclaim for his role as the degenerate alcoholic in the film *Leaving Las Vegas* (1996). Such critical recognition of craftsmanship is of a different order and refers to task concerns on the level of enactment of the actor-craftsman. As Goffman says: '... unlike ordinary life, nothing real or actual can happen to the performed characters – although at another level of course, something real and actual can happen to the reputation of performers qua professionals whose everyday job it is to put on theatrical performances' (1959: 246).

4. There is also a difference with the *arousal (onset)*, *duration (offset)*, and *subsidence (dynamics)* of each sort of emotion: Through involvement, an 'emotion' is slowly evoked, while a spontaneous emotion usually catches us off guard or overcomes us suddenly.[18] The activity of imagining an emotion can be postponed or timed; there can be a more or less agreed upon, or self-imposed, beginning and end. An imagined emotion does not usually continue into an after-impression. This abrupt duration is usually betrayed in the expression: 'A fast ending suggests conscious activity or suppression of response' (Frijda 1986: 43; Hess and Kleck 1990). Think of the polite smile which disappears from your face before you have even turned around, versus a genuine smile. The duration of emotions has a positive correlation with their intensity.[19]

5. When an imagined emotion is *expressed* as a character on stage, it has been preconceived from a model in the imagination. An imagined emotion has a greater degree of stylization and conformity to rules of expression than spontaneous expressions of emotions, although the latter generally conform to culturally rooted rules of expression as well. An example is the professional mourners, who shed 'real' tears.[20] The expression of 'imagined emotions' diverging from rules of expression is often cause for praise in the theater. In real life, however, nonconformity to the rules of expression is usually

'punished' or at least provokes puzzled responses. If in real life a person were to laugh out loud during a funeral this would be judged as unsuitable or rude. If the same were to happen on stage, we would try to find a deeper meaning.

5.5.2 Real and Pretended Emotions

The distinction between real emotions and simulated emotions is subtle and diffuse, although pretense does not per se also presume involvement! Emotions in real life also contain a certain degree of pretense, regulation, or theatricality. According to the emotion psychologist Lazarus, we underestimate the degree to which real life emotions are continually regulated. On

> There are incidentally fake emotions which are only behavior. If I get a present that only half interests me, I might give the impression of being so extremely joyful that I clasp my hands and skip and dance. I might even let myself get a bit carried away with it and then it would not be completely true to say that I am not happy. And still, this joy is not real, I will discard it, I will cast it far from me as soon as the visitor has left. Let us agree that this will be called an untrue joy and remember that the untruth is not a logical feature of a certain judgment, but an existential condition. In this way I can also have untrue fear or unreal sadness. These unreal states are nevertheless distinct from those in acting. The actor makes the gestures of someone who is joyful, or sad, but he is not joyful or sad, as these gestures are directed toward a fictional world. He imitates behavior, but he does not behave. ... Spontaneous emotion is something altogether different: It is accompanied by belief. The qualities intended for the objects are perceived as realities.
>
> (J.P. Sartre, 1971 [1939]: 99 – 100)

stage an inverted interrelation can occur with simulated emotions (character-emotions impersonated without using involvement) and real life emotions, including task-emotions as well as private emotions. The passage from Sartre's *Magic and Emotion* (see box) makes clear how complex the relationship is between different degrees of truth, involvement and pretense.

The issue is not so much about the distinction between real and unreal emotions, but more about a distinction in the degree of sincerity – sincerity in the sense of accord between external behavior and the underlying, inner feeling which as yet can scarcely be measured. Different gradations in the degree of sincerity are described by words like real, trance, played, staged, or faked, which connote an increasing degree of disparity between expression and the underlying 'truthful feeling'. The greater the disparity, the 'phonier' the expression.

In conclusion, I have proposed that the task situation impedes complete identification between actor and character and therefore prevents 'real' emotions from arising which are like those of the character. Experiences or feelings which are evoked through imagining an emotion can indeed seem a great deal like the experiences of having a real emotion. But these are still not the same thing, at least not when we speak of a professional actor in performance in front of an audience. No matter how much an actor involves himself in his role, the essential elements of a real emotion are missing.[21] 'Having an emotion in the imagination' differs from having a similar emotion oneself. However, this still fails to answer the critical question: Is it necessary or important for the actor in performance to experience similar emotions in order for his character to be believable and convincing?

5.6   Believability of Emotional Expressions

With the exception of contemporary 'abstract' and experimental acting, most acting styles consider the believable and convincing portrayal of emotions as one of the central tasks of the actor (3.6). Is it necessary for an emotional expression to be real for it to be believable? For an expression of emotion to be believable, it is important, first off, that the audience recognizes this expression as indicating a certain emotion.[22] We will see, however, that context-information is an important source for the audience to determine which emotion comes into play. Research on this subject is usually limited to facial expressions.

5.6.1   Recognizing Spontaneous and Posed Expressions

The current body of research on the recognition of emotion through facial expression shows evidence that facial expression often yields sufficient information for recognition of the intended emotion and that people generally do this well.[23] This is especially true for a number of basic emotions like anger, sorrow, joy, fear, surprise, and disgust. Such prototypical emotions are also often characteristic for dramatic characters. Being able to name an emotion correctly does have some limitations. People appear to be better at recognizing intentionally posed emotions than spontaneous expressions, especially when static images or photographs are used. If, however, the expression was made visible on film throughout its entire course, the measure of recognition increased significantly. Frijda remarks: 'One need not distinguish much of the expressions to recognize them, as long as the behavioral part is visible' (1958: 91). In other words, recognition of an emotion is the recognition of the accompanying action tendency or impulse, as the most essential feature of the 'sort' of emotion. In conjunction with knowledge of the situation and the relevant components in the situation, an *interpretation* follows that the observed behavior is emotional. When context-information is missing, as is the case with still photographs, the percentage of correct readings of emotion decreases considerably. According to the researcher Wallbott, 'expressive' actors are better able to convey emotions without context information than 'non-expressive' actors.

The correct recognition of emotions, based on facial expression, is also considerably poorer if random photographs are used, whereby test subjects are free to choose a suitable emotion word (which is also the case for theater audiences). That is because different emotions can have similar action tendencies and these provoke similar expressions, according to Frijda.[24] In subsection 5.4.3 it was suggested that impersonating character-tendencies is important for conveying intended emotions to an audience. Providing information about the relevant concerns and the meaning of the situation, the context-information, is equally important.[25]

5.6.2   Indications in Expressions for Authenticity

It is generally assumed that emotion cannot be kept completely concealed by a totally calm facial expression or calm voice. Because these uncontrollable manifestations can show through a 'mask' of pretense, it becomes possible to detect lies or deception. For this reason, facial expressions and features of the voice are often used to determine the authenticity of an emo-

a   b

Spontaneous (a) facial expression and posed (b) expression of disgust/revulsion.

tion. Subtle differences are shown mainly in the muscle activity around the eyes, which can separate a real smile from a misleading or false smile. However, 'When these differences of type of smiling were ignored and smiling was treated as a unitary phenomenon, there was *no difference between truthful and deceptive* behavior' (Ekman et al. 1988: 414, italics EK: 1990).

According to the emotion psychologists Rinn and Zajonc, there are different structures in the nervous system for non-emotional facial expressions and for spontaneous emotional expressions, which are moreover specific to each emotion. The researchers Hess and Kleck found that deliberate posed expressions contain more irregularities than spontaneous expressions, but that there was no difference in their duration. The posed expressions followed after the instruction: 'To pose expressions of happiness or disgust "as well as possible", but not to feel it'. The spontaneous expressions were registered during the viewing of a short film or after an instruction to relive an emotional experience. If the request was to specially express a different emotion than the one felt (which was elicited by viewing a film), these subsided more quickly than spontaneous emotions (see also 5.5.1).

The differences between posed and spontaneous (facial) expressions of emotions are, however, so minimal that they would scarcely be perceptible in a theater. Whether an emotional expression is supported by a real emotion cannot be judged by a spectator solely on the basis of observation. At most, one can interpret the behavior or *presume* a corresponding inner emotion. Frijda suggests: 'It is difficult or impossible, to recognize pretense on the basis of the expressive image itself, or to know what is happening under the controlled surface; one possibly sees only the controlling tension' (1958: 84). Thus, according to him, it is also impossible to distinguish between expressions of someone who gets water thrown in his face, or is afraid, or is tensed in concentration.[26]

Recent research on (the recognition of) various differences between posed and spontaneous emotional facial expressions confirm that spectators cannot make distinctions between them.[27] According to Hess and Kleck, people are incapable of making a correct distinction between spontaneous and deliberately posed emotional expressions of happiness and disgust because they do not pay attention to the right cues or signals.

Attempting to detect the 'authenticity' of an emotion seems, for an audience then, to be a futile activity. It can sufficiently be concluded that there is indeed a difference between spontaneous and simulated emotional expressions but that the audience will usually not be able to tell which is which. The possible authenticity of an emotional expression can therefore not be crucial to judging its believability. This disregards the question of whether actors are capable of such complete control of the (facial) muscles, that they can achieve expressions so real that 'you can't see the difference'. A few researchers have studied the command of emotional expressions in actors on stage.[28] These studies also fail to assert that authenticity of emotional expression is necessary for a believable portrayal.

It seems to me that authenticity of expression is therefore less crucial than the suitability of expression to the genre, the form of theater, the acting style, the desired effect, information about the dramatic context, and so forth. Audiences have expectations about the correct degree of involvement depending on the specific theater form (3.8). Stylized expressions, which are in line with cultural expectations, will perhaps be recognized faster and will be more effective as theatrical devices than spontaneous emotional expressions. Because 'authenticity' of character-emotions appears to be unnecessary, it comes down to the command of the instrument – which is the actor himself. The impersonation of emotional behavior can in and of itself however provoke feelings, which the actor may believe to be the emotions themselves.

5.7   Imitation and Physiological Reactions

When actors portray characters believably what effect does the impersonation, mimicry, or imitation itself have? According to one psychological theory – *the peripheral feedback theory* – an emotion is aroused because imitation of its external signs relays its accompanying physical reactions back to the brain as feedback; this, in turn, causes the feeling of experiencing the emotion itself. Thus, by bringing an emotion into play, an actor would arouse the emotion in himself. If this theory is correct, all actors would have to experience emotions which concur with the portrayed character-emotions. This would include actors who deploy a style of detachment, since by mimicking or imitating behavior and expressions which are usually associated with a particular emotion, peripheral feedback will ensue.[29]

Psychological researchers, including Paul Ekman, have discovered that negative emotions make the heart beat significantly faster than positive emotions. Skin temperature was shown to

> S. Schachter and J.E. Singer (1962; 1965) did research on emotions. In their acclaimed experiments, test subjects were administered adrenaline ('epinephrine'), after which they were placed in a waiting room. There was an assistant in the waiting room who behaved either cheerfully or maliciously. The subjects who were approached cheerfully described their (adrenaline-induced) agitated feelings as positive emotions. The subjects who were treated aggressively, on the other hand, described their 'arousal' as malevolent emotions.

be higher with anger than with fear or sadness. In these studies, each of the six (basic) emotions tested showed a different pattern of physiological activation. According to the Dutch psychologist Frans Boiten, who replicated Ekman's research, the results can be attributed to the degree of difficulty of the emotion to be portrayed. It is more difficult to portray negative emotions than positive ones; this results in more and different physiological activation with negative emotions. One of the greatest problems in emotion research is how to ascertain whether someone is really experiencing a certain emotion. All in all, test results conclude that reproducing or imitating emotional expression in and of itself leads to all sorts of physiological reactions. Whether the experience of such physiological feedback is sufficient for 'feeling' an emotion, or whether this is sufficient to justify calling this emotion 'real', is impossible to say.

According to the researchers Schachter and Singer, physiological activation ('arousal') alone is not sufficient to arouse an emotion; it leads at most to feeling 'as if' there were an emotion ('as if feelings'). Physiological activation without a direct explanation motivates an individual to find an explanation in his surroundings or in his thoughts: 'He will "label" this state and describe his feelings in terms of the cognitions available to him. ... precisely the same state of physiological arousal could be labeled "joy" or "fury" or "jealousy" (Schachter and Singer 1962: 381). Their research has since become famous but also subject to criticism.[30]

Despite its problematical scientific status, the theory of Schachter and Singer provides clues as to how the emotion process works during acting. It is especially valid for the actor who has the feeling that he is experiencing the emotions of his character or imagines that he is. The presence of an audience operates as the inducing factor; it replaces the adrenaline shot in the experiment.[31] The actor subsequently looks for an explanation for this arousal either in his direct surroundings, or in the dramatic situation. In other words, the surroundings of the *character* serve as the interpretation context, which may cause the actor to attribute the portrayed character-emotions to himself.

The so-called excitation-transfer-effect provides another relevant comparison. Because physiological arousal lingers in the body as an effect of previous exertion (running, for example) emotions emerge more quickly when something (a stimulus) elicits the emotion. Theoretically, the threshold for becoming 'inflamed' with emotion would be lowered as a result of residual physical excitement.[32] This is analogous to a lowered threshold for illness with lowered resistance. In the excitation-transfer theory a person would be highly irritable (as a result of illness, lack of sleep, or exhaustion) and therefore be more susceptible to the effect of sentimental films, for example. It is conceivable that the actor's threshold could be lowered by the arousal-heightening effect of audiences, for example, and that this could make him more susceptible to 'infection' with character-emotions.

In recent research of a completely different nature – stress research – physiological activation is considered as an indicator for *mental* exertion. This further complicates the interpretation of physiological data. Even with advanced techniques it is not possible to make a distinction between physiological activation as a result of emotional or non-emotional (mental) exertion.[33] This is, coincidentally, in line with the cognitive theory of emotions, in which mental activity and emotion are indivisible. Physiological changes are therefore not automatically a valid indicator for the type of emotion, but they do appear to be useful in measuring the intensity. In particular, intense emotions and strong action tendencies will be accompanied by physiological activation and therefore signal that there is indeed something going on – something which is of importance to the person.[34]

Although the physiological emotion theories have their limitations from a theoretical point of view, this drawback plays almost no part in the 'common sense' notions about how emotions feel. Feedback of physiological change seems to be an important indicator for test subjects to determine the presence of emotion. In Shield's research, test subjects were asked how they judged whether or not they were experiencing emotion. Interviews showed that this judgment rested on the presence of one or another diffuse form of arousal as well as the nature of the cognitive state, thoughts, fantasies, memories, surroundings, and so forth. In reference to the physiological phenomena, Sartre points out that such activation is proof 'that the emotion is a serious matter. They are signs of conviction' (1971: 101), which one cannot distinguish from the behavior. However, the aforementioned studies made it clear that physiological phenomena can also accompany non-emotional states, like physical exertion, illness, chemical substances, and thought processes.

The results of the research cited on the effect of imitating emotional expressions bring me to the following conclusion: The feeling of experiencing the character-emotions oneself will mainly occur with actors who use an involvement method. When someone conveys an emotional expression with conviction, this generates a certain amount of physiological reaction. Furthermore, the behavior which accompanies the emotional representation indicates an intention of engaging in a particular relationship with the surroundings; the so-called relational activity (5.6). This relational activity is linked with an action tendency, in broad terms with the impulse to approach or to avoid. Thus, through impersonation, the feeling of an impulse can be evoked and this will also be supported by physiological changes. The feeling that accompanies an emotion portrayed with conviction can in this way seem (to an actor) deceptively like the feeling of a spontaneous, real emotion. A real emotion is accompanied by the sensed control precedence of an action tendency; an impulse to take action. The imitation of an emotional expression is accompanied by the sensed physiological changes and the invocation of an *association* with an action tendency. Hereby the actor experiences considerable arousal of the task-emotions, elicited by the acting situation. Presumably all inexperienced actors would be prey to such 'confusion', and more seasoned professionals would be able to distinguish their impersonation from their imagination.

The imitated emotional expression (the portrayed character-emotion) can via different routes lead to the semblance of a real emotion. What is missing is an actual appeal to concerns, as well as the inevitability of the dramatic situation (and with it the necessity to act based on an actual action tendency), and actual consequences of the 'emotion' for the actor, as asserted in section 5.5. Furthermore, the object of the ostensible emotion is probably different from that of a comparable real emotion. The object of the ostensible emotion, like that of a character, lies in the dramatic situation or in a corresponding imagined situation. For the actor, the object of emotion during acting will, on the other hand, lie in the task situation; in playing the intended character-emotions and in winning over and/or manipulating the audience. The above does explain why many authors solve the actor's dilemma by assuming that actors have a double consciousness.

5.8 Double Consciousness During Acting

The feeling of becoming involved with often fierce character-emotions and being in control of them simultaneously was described in chapter 3 as double consciousness. Based on the previous section, one conclusion is that the emotion process during acting contains at least four aspects which could lead to the notion of a double consciousness in the actor. Firstly, the actor has physiological reactions which create the sensation of emotion. These physiological phenomena give cause to seeking their explanation in the surroundings. The dramatic situation provides a 'willing' context.

Secondly, when the actor involves himself as much as possible in the character or the character-emotion, the fate of the character becomes part of the emotion process in the actor (5.3.1). In this sense, one may speak of double consciousness with the involvement method: Consciousness of the emotional meaning of the task situation as well as the emotional meaning of the dramatic situation. Some components of the emotion process have similar values in both situations; this became clear in section 5.4.

Thirdly, there is a perception of being removed from oneself, watching oneself act. The actor does know that he is not the character, but he does act like the character. The sensation of the difference between the feeling and the emotion is seen (in psychological research) to be a feature of double or divided consciousness. This double consciousness is sometimes also called depersonalization. The researcher Fewtrell describes depersonalization as a state in which one sees oneself acting and feels this as though from a distance, which is accompanied by the feeling that the situation is unreal. One often hears such statements from actors, and I also came across them in acting theories about double consciousness in actors (chapter 3). The theater scholar Fink talks of how an actor can experience feelings of depersonalization while acting. He refers to remarks by Stanislavsky and Chekhov: 'Stanislavski's description of the depersonalization experienced on stage is similar to examples of depersonalization drawn from the psychological research' (Fink 1980: 24).

Because the actor behaves as though he is the character and shapes his task emotions to fit, he will experience the discrepancy between feeling and behavior shown in the performance, which is characteristic of depersonalization. The ability to regulate or transform emotions is, incidentally, a capacity which all people have. It is a component of the emotion process, even though people are often not conscious of this and have difficulty describing it.[35] Likewise, Kihlstrom describes the sensation of double consciousness as the sense of dividing attention between various tasks: 'Attention is a resource that can be divided according to prevailing task demands (which is what the concept of double consciousness is all about)' (Kihlstrom 1985: 406). Paying attention, or 'existing in' the real world and the dramatic world at the same time is a central feature of the acting situation.

The fourth and final aspect is that the actor executes behavior which has become more or less automatic. The behavior of the character has first been shaped around an imaginary model and is then studied and made repeatable, without jeopardizing the believability of the expression. In as much as the actor has made the character's behavior his own, in effect becoming 'second nature', we may speak of automatic behavior in respect to the character to be played. In other words, the (literal) execution of the role in itself has become a routine activity and can be done by the actor on 'automatic pilot'. Automatic behavior is another conspicuous feature of depersonalization or double consciousness in psychological research. The sensation that the role is playing itself, as it were (compare with the 'flow' experience; 4.6.2), goes along with the feeling of the 'hidden observer' in depersonalization, or the feeling of watching oneself.[36]

This automatic character behavior is to the actor's advantage during performance. Because of it, his attention is freed for other aspects of the situation, like unexpected turns, interaction, taking cues, connecting to the audience, and fine tuning of the role. Commanding responses and transforming them becomes considerably easier if they are familiar, well rehearsed responses.[37] When the design of character-emotions becomes automatic, the actor is better able to shape or transform the spontaneous emotions of the task situation. Thus, a bridge seems to have been built between some central problems in acting: A link between required repeatability and the illusion of spontaneity. In the end, the acting theories discussed here all demand the illusion of spontaneity to be combined with a repeatable form and discipline (3.6).

5.9   Summary

I have made a connection between acting tasks (chapter 3) and aspects of the emotion process of general human emotions (chapter 4). The construction of character-emotions in drama generally contains the most important information about concerns and about aspects of the situation, which can give rise to emotions. Thus imagined emotions can be attributed to characters. Involving oneself in character-emotions is however of a different order for actors than it is for audiences. As far as one speaks of involvement, a process of identification is indicated when the relationship between actor and character is discussed, whereas a process of empathy seems more appropriate with audience members. Even if an actor evokes an emotion which is like the depicted character-emotion, the task situation during a live performance will still prevent the imagined emotion in that actor from eliciting a comparable real emotion of his own. Evoking emotions in the actor similar to character-emotions seems to be unnecessary, also for other reasons. Audiences often recognize deliberately posed emotions better than spontaneous emotions and generally do not pay attention to the right cues relevant to determine whether they observe real emotions. To determine if there is an emotion, and if so which one, information on the context in which the emotion arises is in most cases crucial. This information allows the actor the freedom and the space to actually play character-emotions.

Generally speaking, physiological changes seem to be indicators which help people judge whether or not they are experiencing emotion. Imagining an emotional expression in and of itself seems to set off something in the physiological system, but it is not yet clear exactly how this process works. Mimicking or imitating an emotional expression can give someone the feelings of experiencing the emotion itself. Together with physiological reactions linked to task-emotions, this can contribute to the illusion of spontaneity, for the actor as well as the spectator. When in addition the actor adheres to an involvement strategy, this could convince him of the authenticity or spontaneity of his acted or imagined 'emotions': The sensations resulting from auto-arousal (which may only resemble real emotions). In particular, a far-reaching degree of involvement can be considered as a twofold meaning in the situation (a twofold situational meaning structure, using Frijda's terms). This is a second aspect in the emotion process during acting, next to the physiological aspects, which might have contributed to 'solving' the actor's dilemma, in acting theories, with a so-called double consciousness. The third and fourth aspects are revealed by psychological studies as the sensation of 'the difference between feeling and behavior' and that 'automatic' behavior is characteristic of double (or plural) states of consciousness. Making the impersonation of character-emotions automatic allows the actor to free his attention for other issues relating to accomplishing the acting tasks.

From theory to practice – The current interpretation of the *Paradoxe sur le Comédien* seems, up to this point, to be in line with a psychological approach to acting. But there is something missing, namely the fact that the actor also has task emotions. From a psychological point of view, one can no longer ignore the fact that represented character-emotions are no real emotions. Character-emotions are reflections of certain kinds of behavior, with which the actor tempts or challenges the audience to interpret this behavior as pointing to the emotions of the character. In that sense, I presume on theoretical grounds, actors do not have emotions during the performance, but they *do* have emotions as far as these concern the task situation. It seems that a new 'solvable' paradox has been created: The illusion of spontaneity is an illusion to the extent that character-emotions are involved, but not an illusion to the extent that the transformation or shaping of task-emotions is concerned. Moreover, the idea that the task emotions contribute to this 'illusion of spontaneity' has now become plausible. In the next chapters, it will be seen whether the results of field research on actors in theater practice (empirical studies) support the theoretical presumptions outlined thus far. In the following, the psychological approach to acting as discussed in the foregoing chapters – like the concepts of acting tasks in acting emotions, the specific emotion process during acting, and experiencing task emotions – will be referred to with the abbreviated name 'task-emotion theory'.

6   *Actors in Practice*

A variable in a study is like a character in a play.
HARRIE VORST (December 11, 1990)

6.1   Introduction: From Theory to Practice

In this chapter I will make the transition from theoretical considerations to practical field research. To increase our understanding of acting, it is important to find support for theoretical insights about the acting of emotions in the acting profession. Field research (on emotion) with actors is still in the developmental stage; relatively little research has thus far been conducted. The research which has been published is difficult to find, poorly documented, and very sporadic. Nonetheless, I will provide an overview here. For my study it was important to review work that had already been done in this area, to see if any parallels could be found. Certainly I was interested in the results of this type of field study. Furthermore, I wanted to interpret the importance of the results in light of my theory outlined in the previous chapters. Section 6.2 will discuss research on the following subjects: Identification of actors with their characters; excitement during acting; personality traits and performance; and research on acting methods and training.

The existent literature usually takes a narrow approach to the comparison between actors' emotions and the portrayed character-emotions. This narrow focus is also true of the field research conducted to date. In general, only one category of emotions is considered: The emotions which (do or do not) coincide with emotions similar to the character's as approached from the enactment level of the character. Those emotions and feelings – such as tension, satisfaction, or challenge – linked to executing acting tasks scarcely receive any attention. I think it is important to let actors themselves talk about their experiences and the way they develop their characters. Hence the decision to develop a questionnaire and conduct a field study with professional actors (6.3). The hypotheses and assumptions I wanted to study are presented in section 6.4. The choices for this type of research as well as the considerations made in choosing the research population, developing the questionnaire, and the way the field study was conducted will also be discussed in subsequent sections.

6.2   Overview of Field Studies with Actors

In the following inventory of research on acting practices, the emphasis lies on reports which, in one way or another, relate to the emotions of actors in relation to performing their roles. Research in this area can be divided into four categories: (1) Research on the degree to which actors identify with their characters; (2) research on the excitement involved with acting and how actors deal with it; (3) research on actors' personality traits, and (4) research on acting methods and training including the interaction between directors and actors. Each category will be discussed separately in the following sections.

6.2.1 Identification of Actors with their Characters

The majority of the studies which are relevant to this study investigate the subject of the actors' identification with their characters. Although these studies have identical topics, the research methods differ. The studies will therefore be grouped according to the method used.

Questionnaires on identification. Over a century ago, the question of whether the actor himself should 'really' have the emotions of the character he portrays led Archer and Binet to conduct their research among professional actors. Their questionnaires were prompted by the revived controversy about the validity of Diderot's paradox, mainly between the theater critics Coquelin and Irving (chapter 2). As far as I know, Archer was the first to envision a systematic inquiry of Diderot's *Paradoxe sur le Comédien*. Archer sent a questionnaire containing fifteen open questions about acting out a character's emotions to a great number of primarily British leading actors and actresses. The questions all concerned phenomena which supposedly indicated the presence of emotion: Tears, sweat, blushing, and turning pale. Based on the actors' responses, supplemented by a number of (auto)biographies, Archer concluded that actors really do experience the emotions of their characters on a wide scale, because they reported shedding real tears, blushing, turning pale, and so forth. According to Archer, these symptoms indicated the actual experience of a character's emotion. His proposed explanation was that the actor becomes emotionally infected by the character, because he experiences sympathy for the character (Archer 1888).

Archer presented the results in a descriptive, almost anecdotal manner; without any quantitative data. He mentioned that there were 'many' responses; I have tried to trace the number more precisely, and suspect there were about seventy in all. However, this deduction cannot be conclusive as Archer employed some additional (auto)biographical materials of deceased actors. Further, this inquiry was not anonymous and the subjects were aware that the results were to be published. Therefore, a critique of Archer's research would propose that his results are more likely to indicate how actors of the day thought they should feel when they performed, rather than providing a representative reflection of what actually went on concerning emotions on stage.[1]

Independently of Archer, Binet surveyed nine famous French actors in 1896. According to Binet, these actors unanimously asserted that Diderot's stance in *Paradoxe* was dead wrong. Binet interpreted their responses as follows: By impersonating an emotion, it takes possession of the actor.[2] Binet explained this 'possession' by assuming a double consciousness in the actor. In his view, a portion of consciousness was subsumed by an emotion, a real emotion that coincided with the emotion of the character. A separate portion of consciousness kept the emotion under control. According to Binet this special portion also accounted for the distinction between stage emotions and emotions in daily life.

Both Archer's and Binet's studies depart from the emotions as they are portrayed as character without taking into account what other sorts of emotion the actor might have. Their point of departure is fundamentally different from my point of departure as delineated in the previous chapters. The actor himself actually disappears from view in their studies, and with him, the art of acting. General criticism of these studies includes, among other aspects, that the question of authenticity of emotions in the actor is not clearly separated from the question of the relationship between actor-emotions and character-emotions.

More recent research on the identification of actors with their characters, using questionnaires, has been conducted by Hammond and Edelman, Kepke, and Wayne-Smith. They defined identification as unity or similarity between the character and the actor. The researchers established this presumed similarity by comparing the self-image (self-perception) of the actors with the image they have of their characters. In general, the actor's self-image was not found to be similar to the actor's image of the character. Kepke studied the degree of similarity between the image three professional actors had formed of their character's and their self-image (using Tennessee Williams A *Streetcar Named Desire*). These were measured at different points in the rehearsal process using a structured questionnaire. The expectation was that the degree of similarity would increase as the rehearsal process progressed. The self-image of the actress however, did not at any point overlap with the character of Blanche. With the other actor and actress there was only a very slight degree of similarity in the perception of themselves with the character of Stanley and Stella. The changes measured as the rehearsal process progressed did not show an increased degree of similarity. Kepke, incidentally, had not intended to study identification, but according to Wayne-Smith, resemblance between the perception of oneself and the character could be interpreted as identification. According to Wayne-Smith's interpretation, Kepke failed to find identification.

Wayne-Smith himself studied identification with characters using twelve actors in a student theater company. He concluded that there was no identification of actors with their characters, but that there was a tendency to 'superimpose' the role on themselves. In another study, Schälzky also failed to establish similarity between the actors' self-image and their image of the character. According to Schälzky, the discrepancies found between the actors' self-image in tests before and after the performance were mainly related to the emotional aspects linked with the performing profession, and not with having to play, or just having played, the character.[3] In their research on identification, Hammond and Edelman studied two professional actors at various moments in the course of over a year. They found an increasing degree of similarity between the actor and character in one actor, and none in the other.

Mossman's study of the degree to which students adapted their attitudes to the opinions of the character they portrayed can be viewed as an extension of the above studies on identification. Various students were asked to play a role which went against their own points of view. They were promised payment and were assured that no one would confuse the character in the pretend situation with the student involved. The study showed that the more the students' role play was 'justified' by financial compensation, the less the students adapted their attitudes to the characters' attitudes. One could consider 'conforming to the role' in Mossman's theory as the role-player's own way of justifying playing the role. This study apparently concerned roles people play in daily life. In my view, a professional actor needs no other justification than that it is his *profession* to play roles, whether or not his attitudes are similar to the character's. However, the research results are relevant in that attitudes are apparently not adapted to the role when there is external justification or permission.

Physiology and identification. Bloch also conducted research on the identification of actors with their characters. Her study focussed on a psychophysiological acting method she had developed herself. Bloch not only concluded that the experience of an emotion could be elicited by impersonating the external features of the emotion, but also that this experience could be avoided (which she considered preferable for actors). She called her remedy the 'step-out procedure': The moment the actor feels an emotion welling up he must regain control through deep breathing. This research was based on the outmoded idea that physiological sensation was identical with the emotion itself (the peripheral feedback theory). Apart from being based on an outdated premise, the study failed to consider that physiological phenomena measured in actors might be related to things other than the presumed arousal of character related emotions. For example, Boiten's recent studies on emotion demonstrated that the effort it takes to evoke certain emotional expressions varies per emotion. He also thought that this effort influenced measurable physiological phenomena: Deep breathing in particular could in turn influence other reactions such as the heartbeat and blood pressure.

Sloman hypothesized that it would be difficult for actors to completely conceal their own feelings behind their role. Personal feelings would become visible in micro-momentary facial expressions (MMEs): Tiny facial ticks. During performances, many more MMEs were measured than during rehearsal or at home during a relaxed conversation. The increase of MMEs during performance was, according to Sloman, predominantly an expression of taking pleasure in the success of performance. Sloman did not draw any conclusion about a possible connection with impersonating the emotions of a character, and he only studied a single actor.

To test Diderot's *Paradoxe*, Villiers measured physiological reactions (pulse rate, leukocytes and blood pressure) in twelve professional actors. He did this before and during the performance. He thought this method would establish whether an actor identified with his character. Villiers found an increased level of excitement in actors prior to, during the intermission, and after playing in a performance, but no increase during the performance itself. He then concluded that there was no correlation between the actor's excitement and the acted emotions of characters. He did not report anything about the characters or the acting. Villiers saw the results as supporting Diderot's anti-involvement viewpoint; he also questioned the notion of double consciousness in actors.[4] Villiers further concluded that the results supported his idea that there was no such thing as 'stage fright', but rather a constant form of tension which he entitled 'les sentiments scèniques'. This effect was marked by heightened physiological reactions (activation) not only before but between and after performing scenes as well. Villiers' interpretation is very much in line with my own: Increased excitement in the actor is not so much associated with the portrayed character-emotions as with acting per se. Villiers, in passing, suggested that actors might exploit this tension to supply the technical presentation of their role with the warmth of authentic emotions (1942: 152).

Of the studies discussed, those of Schälzky, Sloman, and Villiers appear to lend some support to the psychological approach to acting developed in my study.[5] Each came to the conclusion that the actor's emotional state during or after a performance was not so much determined by the emotional condition of the impersonated character, but by the degree to which the actor had succeeded in his aims. The relationship between the emotions of the actor himself and those of the character during performance was not always presented clearly in the studies discussed. At any rate, these components were not measured within the same study. Schälzky talked about the actor's emotional state after the performance; Sloman limited himself to registering indications for emotions other than those of the characters portrayed; and Villiers concluded from his results that the actor's physiological activation did not coincide with the impersonated character-emotions, although he did not study the latter.

The results of these studies cannot indisputably be seen as a refutation of the involvement hypothesis, nor can they be seen as supporting it (for professional actors). For the time being, I conclude that these field studies in theater practice do not lead to the conclusion that actors identify with their characters (in the sense that the actor's emotions are similar to the presumed emotions of the character). All three of these aforementioned studies consider the emotions of the actors themselves, apart from those of their characters. I deem these emotions to be task-emotions. The tension actors experience during stage performance has been studied recently with more modern research techniques. This will be discussed in the next section.

6.2.2 **Excitement During Acting** Research on the amount of tension, stress, excitement, and anxiety present in actors while acting has been conducted from various angles by Jackson and Latané, Pritner and Lamb, Weisweiler, and myself. Such research is relevant and important because it acknowledges the emotions of the actors themselves, regardless of the specific impersonations of character-emotions.

Jackson and Latané studied a number of actors in student acting groups during a talent search on campus. They used a short questionnaire to measure tension, that is, they just asked how nervous subjects felt. They discovered that tension in the student actors increased proportionately given the number of audience members and the audience's expertise. Tension decreased when there were more fellow actors present in the performance; the assumed quality of the co-actors had no influence on the tension felt. Through a simple questionnaire, Pritner and Lamb found an increasing level of excitement among theater school students in the time period prior to an audition which peaked just after the audition.

Weisweiler and I, separately, conducted independent studies using physiological data (such as heart rate) in Munich (South Germany) and Groningen (North Netherlands), respectively. Tests were done both during rehearsals and during public performances. Both studies found that changes in physiological activity in the actor did not reflect the portrayal of character-emotions, but were linked with aspects of the task performance, like 'having to go on'. Weisweiler found a faster heart beat and a higher secretion of catecholamines (a hormone) during performances than during rehearsals. Additionally, during monologues the physiological reactions were stronger than during dialogues. She concluded that the job of acting involved a great deal of pressure. She found no correspondence with the portrayed emotions. The heartbeat was measured with modern apparatuses, but the data was assimilated 'manually': Students counted each of the separately measured heart rates and carried out analyses on them.[6]

Likewise, I found a considerable increase in the heart rate and the subjective experience of stress in amateur actors by comparing rehearsals, a mid-term 'check up' and performances. The *pattern* of heart rate was the same during rehearsals and performances: Peaking when they appeared onstage and dropping to low levels when the actor exited the stage (average levels being much higher during performances, see figure in section 4.8). During monologues the heart rate reached extremes of 180 beats per minute. By comparison, a person at rest has an average pulse of 60 beats per minute and a parachute jumper's pulse reaches 140 beats per minute just prior to jumping. The continuous monitoring of the actors' heart rates made it possible to draw parallels between video-takes of rehearsals and performances. The changes in heart beats per minute did not seem to be linked with a specific portrayal of character-emotions. Moreover, experienced judges rated the quality of the acting to be superior during the exciting (for the actors) performances than during the rehearsals. This is an indication that tension has a positive effect on acting.[7]

For my purposes it is important that the research cited has its starting point in the work of the actor, and not in the character-emotions. The researchers named in this section link the tension actors experience with the acting itself. This makes it possible to see the tension measured as an indication of the presence of task-emotions.

6.2.3   **Personality Traits and Performance**   Analysis of different personality traits in actors is central to the work of the following researchers: Clevinger and Powers, Collum, Csikszentmihalyi and Getzels, Hammond and Edelman, Koenig and Seamon, Natadze and Powers, Jorns and Glenn. These studies will be handled in general terms as it will quickly become clear that they have no direct bearing on this study.

Clevinger and Powers, Koenig and Seamon, and Powers, Jorns and Glenn exclusively studied the relationship between cognitive complexity as a personality trait, and the quality of acting achievements. They defined cognitive complexity as the degree to which someone is capable of having a subtle and shaded perception of another person. A high level of cognitive complexity was demonstrated by perceiving a high degree of nuances in the image of the other, who in this case was a character. According to Koenig and Seamon, someone with a higher level of cognitive complexity would be more precise in predicting the behavior of another person. Their explanation for this was that people with high cognitive complexity would project their own responses onto others to a lesser degree. They could easily put themselves into another person's shoes.[8] A high degree of cognitive complexity would therefore improve the quality of acting, according to Koenig and Seamon. They themselves however found no connection whatsoever between cognitive complexity and the quality of acting and drew no further conclusions. Clevinger and Powers, and before them Powers, Jorns and Glenn, did find a positive correlation between cognitive complexity and the quality of acting. Actors with a higher cognitive complexity, as was predicted, were able to act better. However, by what measure this 'quality' was judged remains unclear. Clevinger and Powers did not mention the matter; Powers, Jorns and Glenn made only vague references to 'expert opinions'.

Clevinger and Tolch showed a greater concern for more objective or reliable measures of quality in performance, as did Richardson and Waal. To maximize the reliability of quality measurements, they developed a questionnaire in which seventeen aspects of acting were judged separately. Independent of the rest, Perkey also researched qualitative judgments of performances. They 'manipulated' the audience by 'seeding' it with assistants who either applauded enthusiastically or not. To measure the different reactions of actors, they developed a quality-rating list. The results show that a 'positive' audience had a positive effect on the acting achievement. The questionnaire was translated and adapted for use with (amateur) actors in the Netherlands.[9]

Other studies of the personality traits of actors have tried to find features peculiar to actors, or features that might be less prominent in amateur or non-actors. The results of these studies can be generally summed up as follows: Firstly, actors (including amateurs, students, and professionals) were shown to be more empathetic than non-actors, but their social insight was no greater.[10] Secondly, actors were less afraid and shy, more socialized, more sensitive to expressive behavior in others, and more self-assured than non-actors, which might or might not be a result of their experience or training as actors.[11] Thirdly, the (factual) perceptions of actors seemed to be more 'upset' by their imagination or fantasy than the perceptions of non-actors.[12] One study on personality traits of artists in general was conducted by Csikszentmihalyi and Getzels. They concluded that artists, as compared to non-artists, were anti-social, introverted, maladjusted, subjective (imaginative), critical, and independent (autonomous). According to Csikszentmihalyi and Getzels these features were not a result of experience or education, but were part of the artists' personalities. These findings seem to disagree with previous conclusions that actors were more social, as discovered by Hammond and Edelman. The question is whether the sub-category 'actors' can be compared to the general category 'artists'. Moreover, this type of study needs a theoretical context which would, for example, help clarify what conclusions can be drawn from differences in the personality traits of actors versus non-actors. Without a theoretical context, the research seems to be limited to the characteristics of a single professional group.

6.2.4   Acting Methods and Acting Training Most research on acting methods and training, as well as that on the communication between directors and actors, looks at the effects of a particular aspect of training (for example the speed of memorizing text). These are far removed from this study. However, two studies do bear some relationship to portraying emotions on the stage.

Stern and Lewis found that *method*-actors, as compared to non-*method*-actors, had a higher degree of control over their galvanic skin reactions (sweating). The emotional expressions in the first group were not judged (by three directors) as superior to those of the other group. Stern and Lewis concluded that the results were due to practice, not creativity.

Wallbott studied the skills of professional actors in conveying emotions to observers by portraying emotional expressions without providing context information. Differences were found in, among other variables, expressive versus non-expressive actors, positive versus negative emotions, and between male versus female subjects. Actresses seemed better at conveying anxiety and despair, while men were better at conveying anger. Little research has been conducted on the rehearsal process, or different aspects of it. A general – and relevant – conclusion of the studies mentioned here is that specific acting skills can apparently be trained effectively. I did not find any evidence that a process of identification is required to acquire these skills.

6.3   The Questionnaire Mixed Feelings

Based on the research discussed, I concluded that there was apparently no scientific support in the actual practice of acting for the idea that actors do identify with their characters. Likewise, I found no support for the involvement theory in acting; indeed, support for the detachment theory was more readily found. The results also indicated that there were emotions at play in actors other than just the character-emotions. The tension actors feel, for example, seems to relate to their work or rather to executing acting tasks in front of an audience.

Various factors compelled me to conduct my own research among professional actors. Although there were indications that support for the involvement theory in the practice of theater was lacking, it still seemed worthwhile to test these indications yet again, but more precisely and on a larger scale. It seemed worthwhile to study various categories of emotions, including the nature of the task-emotions, by more systematically applying methods and techniques congruent with accepted research on emotions in the field of psychology. Further, it seemed important to study current theater practice. My aim was to achieve the most representative sample of professional actors possible, instead of a few amateurs or students, as was the case in most earlier studies. It was also important to base the study on the emotional experiences during actual performances with live audiences; and then perhaps later make comparisons with emotional experiences during rehearsal periods. Finally, it seemed important to pay attention to the relationship between the actors' emotional experiences and the acting styles they use. This included studying, for example, the actors' general perceptions about what their contemporaries believed 'good acting' to be. Presumably this would influence the way actors would answer questions about acting.

6.4   Hypotheses and General Expectations

Generally speaking, the main questions of this field study with professional actors covered two areas of inquiry. First, the various onstage emotions, with actors as well as with characters, and second, the acting styles applied. The first major question of the study was: When actors portray character-emotions, can it be said that the actors themselves have similar emotions? The second major question was: Does the acting style used (in the performance) have any influence on the degree of similarity between character-emotions and the emotions of the actors?

Based on the theoretical considerations in the previous chapters, it was possible to formulate different expectations for three different views on acting emotions. The involvement theory, the detachment theory, and the task-emotion theory are each distinct in their assertions about the degree of similarity between character-emotions and actors' emotions during the performance. According to the involvement theory, the actor himself has the emotions which he impersonates in his character. According to the detachment theory, the actor himself does *not* have the emotions he impersonates in his character. The *result* in the style of self-expression is the same as with the involvement theory: The emotions of actor and character overlap (chapter 3). The style of self-expression was therefore not included with its own hypothesis in the field study. The above resulted in two main hypotheses:

1. The portrayed character-emotions coincide with the emotions actors experience while acting in a performance. When support for this hypothesis is found, it would support the involvement theory (and to some extent validate the style of self-expression). If actors indicate that their emotional experiences onstage had *not* resembled the portrayed character-emotions, this would support the detachment theory. A possible similarity between character-emotions and actors' emotions could be the result of a specific acting style the actors applied in their performance. Hence the second hypothesis:

2. If actors adhere to a *style of involvement*, the portrayed character-emotions and actors' emotions coincide to a relatively greater degree than if actors adhere to a *style of detachment*. The theories of involvement and detachment make no distinction between different layers of emotions; they are mainly oriented to the enactment level of the character. These theories are principally concerned with portraying the emotions which most frequently occur in characters in dramatic situations. Such 'emotions' are mainly prototypical emotions or basic emotions (chapter 5). With the *task-emotion theory*, it is important to distinguish the prototypical emotions from the so-called task-emotions. Within the task-emotion theory, the expected results for the degree of similarity between character-emotions and actors' emotions should be different depending on whether prototypical emotions or task-emotions are measured. According to this theory, actors themselves would not have the character-emotions they impersonate (prototypical emotions), but would experience task-emotions. Furthermore, if the task-emotion theory is correct, the results for actors using a style of involvement should be similar to the results of actors using a detachment style.

Because the task-emotion theory holds that the actors' emotions primarily concern the acting tasks to be accomplished, it was expected that the actors' emotions prior to performance would be similar to those during performance. It could be expected that, in particular, the task-emotions of the actors would already be present before the performance and linger after the performance. Moreover, characterizations have not yet realized before the performance, when one would expect the emotions of the actor-craftsman to be in the foreground. The impersonated character-emotions should have no connection with the emotions the actors indicated prior to the performance.

Subsequently, a consistent application of the general emotion theory (chapter 4) prompts an inquiry concerning the relationship between onstage emotions and action tendencies or physical reactions. A defining feature of an emotion is the action tendency or impulse, and an emotion is often accompanied by physical agitation.[13] According to the involvement theory, character-tendencies and action tendencies in actors should then overlap with each other. According to the detachment theory and the task-emotion theory they will not. The task-emotion theory proposes that the 'action tendencies' in characters occupy a special place and differ somewhat from these impulses in general human behavior. Whereas in normal life, negative emotions tend to result in avoidance behavior, in a character portrayal, negative prototypical character-emotions are associated with character-tendencies leading to approach behavior. Moreover, the actors' action tendencies leading to approach behavior – associated with positive emotions – are an extension of the character-tendencies leading to approach behavior, and vice versa (5.4). With respect to onstage emotions it would then be true, based on the task-emotion theory, that positive emotions in actors will be accompanied by physiological activation, usually reflected in 'excited' physical reactions.

Concerning the second main question, I not only considered which of the acting styles was actually applied in a specific performance, but also which view was generally preferred or accepted as the norm in contemporary practice among professional actors; how do professional actors generally think one 'should' act and how does this general opinion relate to the acting style they use themselves. Finally, a few assumptions arose in the previous chapter for which I could not yet formulate explicit hypotheses. These included the general assumption that the acting style during performances would differ from the acting style during rehearsals. Further, I also aimed to gather information about applying certain emotions to support believability in acting and to achieve a certain (emotional) response from the audience.

Two preconditions needed to be met to research the above questions. The first condition was that the roles studied have emotional content. Here it was important that the response included answers for different sorts of emotions, i.e., anger as well as tenderness. To assess whether the emotions that actors attributed to their characters actually were the emotions they intended to portray in performance, the next question was: Do the emotions portrayed in characters during performance match the intended emotions? It could be expected that professional actors succeed in playing their characters as planned and that they would indicate several prototypical emotions, which match the character-emotions they impersonated in performance. A second condition was that the actors participating in this study be professionals. In addition, it was necessary to check whether answers were systematically influenced by specific demographic features (sex, age, years of experience, etc.) or specific performance situations (had the house been full or not).

In summary, the theoretical assumptions about emotions in actors and characters discussed here are based on three different views on acting: The involvement theory (which includes the self-expression theory), the detachment theory, and the task-emotion theory. There are four 'entities' to be compared: The emotions intended in the scene; the character-emotions impersonated in performance; the emotions of actors while acting; and the emotions of actors prior to the performance. The emotions can be of two categories: The prototypical emotions and the task-emotions; each category can contain both 'positive' and 'negative' emotions (see 6.7). Finally, emotions can be expressed in action tendencies and eventually in physiological sensations.

The results of the field study will be discussed in chapter seven. The next sections will discuss how the questions were designed to get the desired answers and how the hypotheses were tested.

6.5 Research Method

A questionnaire sent by mail was chosen to meet the aims of this inquiry. This choice was based on several factors pertaining to the subject of this research (6.5.1) and the research population (6.5.2). The research was in part a test of theories and in part exploratory, while the subject can be termed 'difficult to study'. Considering these factors, a personal interview would be the preferred method for gathering information.[14] However, there were other factors to consider, such as the difficulty in reaching the research population, the scarcity of financial and human resources and anticipation of a low response. The lack of resources would not have permitted a responsible use of individual interviews: Structuring such a process and organizing the resulting data for statistical analysis would have been too time-consuming and costly. Using a questionnaire sent by mail also had some advantages for this study; these will be explained below. In the Netherlands, the survey was taken in 1991 and in the United States in 1995.

6.5.1 **Difficulty of the Subject Matter** The difficulty of this study was due to various factors. The most important include: 1) The inability to establish the presence of emotions unambiguously and reliably, 2) recently altered views and developments in the field of emotion research[15], 3) the relative paucity of field studies among actors, and 4) the lack of suitable methods or questionnaires for measuring aspects of acting.

Moreover, the difficulty was increased because information proved difficult to access. In general, people are not accustomed to reporting their feelings and emotions; they find this difficult. Perhaps, it might have been an advantage that actors are relatively more accustomed to analyzing human behavior and emotion than average respondents.

Having insight into, being conscious of, and being able to report details of one's work process is also not a daily activity. Some of this

> While I appreciate the effort in collecting this data, I fail to see how an objective survey like this can provide true insights into the creative process of an actor/artist. Many questions cannot be answered by multiple choice, but need detailed, subjective responses since creativity/acting-moments are incredibly complex and not subject to pinning down like a captured butterfly. They are fleeting, layered, highly transitory – wrapped up in the wholeness of one's being. Good luck!
>
> (An American actor's reaction to the questionnaire)

unfamiliarity could, in part, be overcome by the way information was elicited from respondents. This had to be unambiguous.[16] It would be even more difficult to distinguish different layers of feeling or 'entities' and momentary sensations within a single person, as needed for this study. After all, the goal was to gain insight into the personal emotions of professional actors before, during, and after the performance, as well as into their character-emotions.

6.5.2 Composition of the Research Population

The questionnaire was directed toward professional actors; the Dutch (and Flemish) language population and American stage professionals. The size of the total actor-population is not known in the Netherlands. One way to create a good sub-population is by establishing criteria.[17]

Criterion for the target population. The proposed criterion was that the actor be active professionally. This could be established in advance by, among other things, seeing if an actor was employed by a professional company, was a member of a professional union or was registered as an actor in the *Yellow Pages*.[18] Then, it was stipulated that an actor needed to have at least three years of professional experience. This was included as a control question. Professional experience was described in the questionnaire as the number of years an actor had earned a living through professional acting (or his main activities were directed at that).[19]

Address databases and quantities. The yearbook of the trade magazine *Toneel Theatraal* 1990 included a list of theater, dance, mime, and other companies in the Netherlands and Flanders who presented productions in the 1989-1990 season. The 'theater' category was selected from this list, with the exception of 'amusement', 'cabaret', etc. Next, an expert (from the professional trade union *FNV Kunstenbond*, actors' section) helped suggest which companies on the list should be included in this research (i.e., which companies had a certain level of professionality and recognition). This resulted in 42 companies incorporating a total of 404 actors. They included companies in the Netherlands and Belgium, such as Toneelgroep Amsterdam, Het Nationale Toneel, Koninklijke Vlaamse Schouwburg, and Kaaitheater.

Afterwards actors and actresses were selected in the same way from the membership list of the trade organization and the *Yellow Pages*. This was to insure that professional actors who were not currently employed would also be included. Double listings with company address lists were carefully avoided. This round resulted in locating another 122 actors and actresses at their private addresses. All in all, the target group in the Netherlands (and Flanders) included 526 individuals. This does not suggest that the entire population of professional actors was covered; that number is an unknown quantity and undoubtedly much larger. However, it can be said that the utmost was done to achieve the best possible representation for the target group.

The size of the professional acting population in America is more or less a known quantity; in this regard the situation there was much simpler. The address base of the actors' organization *Actors' Equity* covers about 95% of the professional (stage) actors in the entire United States (over 35,000). Most of this union's members are stage actors, and to a lesser degree, film actors, who are (also) members of another union.[20] *Actors' Equity* has strict membership requirements, including evidence of a number of years of paid, professional experience. Actors must audition for membership or be offered a union contract by a producer or professional theater. Without membership in this union it is almost impossible to get work in professional theaters. The questionnaire was mailed to a random sample of 2000 addresses drawn from the membership list of *Actors' Equity*. The union made an exception to their usual practice and provided me with the private addresses of (the agents of) the actors (including for example Al Pacino, Jocelyn Brando, Morgan Freeman, and Kathleen Turner) solely to conduct this research. *Actors' Equity* expected that the readiness of members to complete and return the questionnaire would be extremely low, so they also placed an appeal to participate in the study in their member magazine.

6.6   From Theory to Questionnaire

The data gathered from the questionnaire had to provide information covering different areas and levels. Given the aim of the inquiry, the information had to concern acting emotions onstage in a role (as a character) during a live performance. Linking the questions to a recent role seemed the most appropriate and also provided respondents with a concrete focus to base their answers on. Asking questions about the memory of an emotional event is moreover a common method in emotion research.[21] To insure that the responses of different actors would be comparable with one another, the questionnaire contained guidelines about the conditions the remembered scene needed to meet.

The research questions required that information regarding onstage emotions would be obtained from different angles; for instance, information about the types of emotions such as sadness or love on the one hand, and information about emotions related to various levels of enactment on the other. The latter involved asking about (1) which emotions were intended to be portrayed in the role (on the enactment level of the inner model; section 2.4), (2) which emotions were realized as the character during performance and which ones the actor experienced, including (3) just prior to start of the performance as well as (4) during and (5) immediately after the performance. It was important to be able to check the answers about the impersonated *character-emotions* afterwards with the *emotions intended* in the scene; it is conceivable that the intended emotions were not actually conveyed in the scene. In other words, this was a check to see whether the emotions intended to be played would match the emotions attributed to the character in the performance, as planned. A comparison of the *actor's* emotions *during* and *immediately before* the performance provides information about the nature of task-emotions. Questions about emotions *immediately after* the performance were included for additional information: To what extent do the emotions relate to the character-emotions just played or to the emotions of the actor himself. This relates to the fact that authentic emotions linger longer than feigned emotions.

An emotion was measured on two levels: (1) A subjective judgment of the *degree* to which a specific named emotion had occurred, its intensity; and (2) a subjective judgment about the degree to which a specific action tendency had occurred or the sensed or acted impulse to take action. The actor was also asked to indicate which physical phenomena he had experienced while acting. On each level of questioning, different response possibilities were offered. Questions not only asked which emotions, action tendencies, and physical reactions had occurred, if any, but also what the intensity of each item had been. The research topic also required information regarding the acting style the actor had applied. Using descriptions in acting theories as well as experiences in acting practice, twenty statements were formulated. Each of these statements indicated preference for either the involvement or detachment style of acting. See also section 6.7 for more detail.

Information about the general preference for an acting style could be obtained indirectly by asking the actors how they thought other qualified actors achieved their results. To do this, each actor was asked to respond to his own personal choice of 'the best contemporary actor'. These responses, about general preference, could be cross-checked with that actor's responses on acting emotions, and on the acting style he had applied. Finally, personal data of the responding actors and actresses was collected. The data was limited to the most relevant features like sex and age, as well as whether respondents had completed training at an acting school, and their number of years of professional experience. This data could show to what extent the sample is representative of the total population. These variables could also be used to check for possible interference between these variables, for instance to check for male-female differences. For the same reason, some control questions were introduced about the specific features of the chosen performance and the performing conditions.

6.7   Structure of the Questionnaire

The questions were compiled in a small twenty-page booklet.[22] There was a short explanatory text on the cover of the booklet. The most important instruction concerned the notion of separating the emotions of the character from those of the actor:

> ...Actors speak of different types of feelings they experience when playing a role, e.g., the feelings related to practicing their craft and the feelings of the character portrayed. In the questions below these two types will be addressed separately in relation to a specific scene.

The questions were organized into seven sections in an effort to make the presentation neat and orderly. Each section has a title and begins with a short explanation. To simplify answering, I worked to the greatest extent possible with structured questions and prescribed multiple choice answer categories. Each possible answer was numbered. Most questions asked to indicate the degree to which the answer was appropriate which could be indicated on a four point scale including: 'Not at all' (=0), 'to a limited extent' (=1), 'to a great extent' (=2) and 'to a very great extent' (=3).[23] A four point scale allows for some nuance in the responses regarding the intensity of the emotion.[24] In order to be able to compare the responses, the same set of response scales were offered in each successive section (the answer range). This simplified the response process as well as the computations in the statistical analyses. A very few open (essay) questions were included, for example, one on a description of the scene in question. The structure of the questionnaire is shown in figure 6.1.[25] A short description of content of each section follows.

In the first section (I. *Remembering a Scene*) the main point was to recall the scene. Most of the questions focus on this one scene. The instructions contained some criteria for the scene chosen to allow answers to be compared. One of those conditions was that the scene had to be played during one of the last performances in a series, so that the position of the chosen scene within the run was more or less the same for all respondents. A scene recalled in a premiere, for example, would be less suitable since the special circumstances would bring special memories to mind. This was not my intention here as it could cause unnecessary confusion in the results.

Questions about the specific circumstances of the performance were posed to arrive at as precise a recollection as possible of the scene in question. Altogether there were seventeen questions in the first section. A sample question:

How many people were involved in the scene?
(possible answers: None; one other; two or more others).

In this section on 'remembering', the respondent was also asked how he felt just before the performance. There were 26 emotion-words presented (see figure 6.2). The idea was to indicate to what degree each emotion applied to the actor's experiences; the intensity of each emotion was to be given on four-point scales. Subsequently, questions inquired into what emotions the actor had *intended* to play in the chosen scene. In other words, what was the actor's assignment? Here fifteen words describing prototypical emotions were listed, to which the respondents could add two other emotions. Again, each emotion was followed by a four-point scale to indicate the intensity.

The second section of the questionnaire (II. *Two Types of Feelings*) also included a short introduction. The most important instruction here was that there would be separate questions about the actor's emotions next to the character's emotions. First, fifteen physical reactions were presented, like blushing or a dry throat. The idea was that the actor indicated to what extent he had experienced any of these reactions while playing the scene. Next the actor was introduced to reporting the emotions he himself experienced during the performance. The intensity for each of 26 possible emotion-words was asked (see figure 6.2).

This was followed by a short explanation of specific impulses, urges, and tendencies (the action tendencies) that the actor or actress felt during the scene – for instance the impulse to laugh or to hug someone (approach tendencies) as well as impulses such as crying or wanting to run away (avoidance tendencies). The idea was to indicate to what degree each of the fifteen impulses applied to the actor while playing the chosen scene. The same procedure was followed for questions regarding the portrayed character-

Figure 6.2a: Theoretical Distinctions of Emotion Designations

	Category Prototypical Emotions	Category Task-Emotions
Negative:	disgusted	ashamed
	anxious	listless
	revengeful	tired
	hatred	nervous
	angry	tense
	startled	
	guilty	
	jealous	
	sad	
Neutral:	neutral	
Positive:	erotic	excited
	in love	gutsy
	tender	strong
	pleased	concentrated
	cheerful	challenged
		certain

Figure 6.2b: Theoretical Distinctions of Action Tendencies

Negative:	Neutral:	Positive:
to attack	to do something, but what?	to hug
to hurt	to move	to caress
to cry		to go for it
to burst out		to overcome difficulties
to sink through the floor		to sing, dance, etc.
to run away		to approach
		to laugh

emotions and character-tendencies. Naturally, I did not ask whether the character had had his own physical reactions. The same 26 emotion-words and the same fifteen action tendency designations were presented for the character as in reference to the actors themselves.

In the third section of the questionnaire (III. *Expressing Emotions*) twenty statements about actors were presented. The statements concern two styles of acting: 'Involvement' and 'detachment'. The introduction stated that all the responses concern the expression of emotions as the character. The idea was that the respondent reacted based on what he had done or had experienced during the remembered scene. Examples of an involvement oriented-statement and a detachment-oriented statement follow in the box.

| Statement indicating style of involvement:
Since I forgot that I was acting, the expression of
my character's emotions came almost naturally. | 0 | 1 | 2 | 3 |

| Statement indicating style of detachment:
When expressing the emotions of the character
I had a sense of looking at myself from outside. | 0 | 1 | 2 | 3 |

This section of the questionnaire ended with statements about eliciting responses from the audience. The idea was for the actor to indicate what effect the scene had on the audience. Finally, questions were posed about what the actor had done to make his character more believable. Three statements were offered, which successively concerned the degree to which the private emotions, the task-emotions,[26] and individual charisma had been used in the scene.

In the fourth section (IV. *Afterwards*) respondents were asked about the emotions and experiences they had immediately after the *scene* ended. After a short introduction, the actor was first asked if he had been able to leave the stage after the scene or at least had been able to escape the audiences' attention. Next, seven emotion-words and a category called 'other, namely...' were presented. The seven emotions were divided into three pleasant, three unpleasant, and the word 'neutral'. In addition, three statements were presented about the experiences of the actor after the performed scene.

The introduction to the fifth section (V. *Preparation*) contained the following information:

Preparations for playing the role and the scenes during rehearsals are different from performing before an audience or acting during actual shooting. Below you will find some statements related to the rehearsal period preceding the scene you have in mind.

Here too, statements were presented which indicated a more involved or a more detached manner of acting, three of each.

In the introduction to the sixth section (VI. *Star Actors*), the questions were introduced as follows:

The questions below are about the actors and/or actresses you regard as the most capable at the present moment, especially with respect to how they practice their profession as actors.

The Dutch and Flemish actors were asked to name three top actors on an international level and also three on a national level. The American actors and actresses were asked to name their favorite stage actor or actress and their favorite film actor or actress. Next they were asked how they thought that these top actors, for each of them separately, achieved their expression of character-emotions. These were, again, statements indicating a preference toward either involvement or detachment styles.

In the last section (VII. *In Conclusion*), some personal data was gathered, such as the actor training they had, their professional experience, sex, age.

I was expected to express ...	not at all	to a limited extent	to a great extent	to a very great extent
pleasure	0	①	2	3
startledness	0	1	②	3
guilt	0	1	2	③
tenderness	0	1	2	③
sadness	0	1	2	③
cheerfulness	⓪	1	2	3
in love	0	1	②	3
anger	0	1	2	③
neutral	⓪	1	2	3
other, viz.	⓪	1	2	3

16. How difficult was this scene for you?

    0   1   2   ③

17. Did you feel warm?

    0   1   2   ③

18. To what extent was the acting style in the scene determined by the director or the company?

    0   1   ②   3

19. Can you briefly describe what happened in the scene?
(e.g. 'strong argument with a man or a woman' or 'monologue interieur about lost lover'.)

Your description of the scene: JUST Found out that Girlfriend had been killed by the NAZis

20. Did your acting produce the effect you wished to achieve?

  yes   more or less   no
  ●   O   O

Additional comments:

Very intense emotional scene for me. Very difficult when I had trouble feeling the pain. Sometimes I just didn't want to hurt. But that was my job.

Actors' mixed feelings   6

The different responses were compared to gain insight into the relationship between the emotions of the actor and those of the character. Then, I also checked to see how much the personal preference for a certain acting style was related with the degree of similarity between actor and character. The results are described in the next chapter.

6.8 Summary

The premises and hypotheses of previous empirical studies with actors described in section 6.2 are generally very different from the premises and hypotheses which I have developed in the foregoing chapters. In general, little theoretical development can be detected in the studies discussed. The results of one study were often not in line with expectations raised by another; this despite the fact that the appearance of similarity was suggested by a common terminology and more or less identical research domains (theater, actors). Furthermore, the earlier research was conducted on limited numbers of subjects, usually not professional actors, and usually not during actual live performances. The research methods used in the past also raise some doubts. For example, it is remarkable that research prior to 1900 found identification between actor and character, while more recent research has not. Research on self-perception and self-image however, has not actually concerned the emotions, which makes it of only limited use for this study.

The studies previously discussed did not particularly support the involvement theory of acting. The results tended to lend more support to the detachment theory. The most important conclusion in this respect thus far, was that there are indeed indications for the presumption that for actors there are more emotions at play than the character-emotions alone. These and other reasons led me to conduct my own field research. This chapter described the way this written survey among professional actors was planned and conducted. The questions and expectations which form the core of this study concern the different views on acting emotions. More traditional views, like those reflected in the involvement and detachment theories, are compared with assumptions based on the task-emotion theory. The resulting questions and expectations to be researched are described in section 6.4.

Different considerations resulted in the choice to use a questionnaire sent by mail as the method for gathering the information. These included among other things, the subject of the inquiry, the available means, and the accessibility of professional actors. The questionnaire was sent to a representative sample of professional actors, in the Netherlands and Flanders (1991), as well as in the United States (1995). Additionally, this chapter discussed the manner in which the theoretical concepts were converted in the questionnaire. A description of the structure and the content of the extended questionnaire which was sent to the actors was also given.

7 Professional Actors, Emotions, and Performing Styles

> Sometimes, I had the feeling you had two or more people in mind,
> although you only sent the questionnaire to one.
> (Letter from a professional respondent actor)

7.1 Introduction: Assimilating the Answers

The responses of the professional actors to the questionnaire 'Actor's mixed feelings' form the basis for the results presented in this chapter. Based on the information gathered, it was first established whether the actors participating in the research indeed fulfil the criteria for professional actors and look at which performances and scenes they chose. Next, the actors' responses were assembled so that they could perhaps provide answers to the (main) questions of this study: If actors portray character-emotions in a performance, do they also experience these emotions themselves? If actors use various performing styles, such as detachment or involvement, will different effects on the emotions experienced by actors during the performance be observed? In the context of the task-emotion theory, data was also gathered concerning whether they experienced what I categorize as task-emotions. As stated, three different views on acting were to be tested against the results from theater practice: The involvement theory, the detachment theory, and the task-emotion theory.

To answer the above questions and to test theories, a distinction was made between prototypical emotions, as they are known in psychological theory, and task-emotions (6.4). Traditional acting theories limit themselves to pronouncements on emotions in general, and are mainly concerned with the character (as seen from the spectator's perspective). Consequently these theories focus on prototypical or basic emotions. According to the task-emotion theory, actors will rarely or never attribute these emotions to themselves; if they do, such emotions will not relate to the character-emotions portrayed during the performance. On the other hand, actors will indeed experience intense emotions during performance in the category of task-emotions. These emotions will also not relate to character-emotions.

The actors' responses on various aspects related to emotions, such as action tendencies and physical reactions, will be presented later in this chapter. To gain insight into current views on acting emotions among professional actors, the performing styles of the actors themselves will be compared with those of their favorite 'top actors'. The final section concerning the responses to the questionnaire will describe how actors view the acting style they applied while they were preparing their roles, and what effect their performances had on the audiences.

This chapter gives a systematic report of the assembled data, while the following chapter provides a more theoretical interpretation and discussion of the data. The empirical results from theater practice will then find a place within acting theory, forming a link with current developments.

7.2   Characteristics of Responding Actors and Performances

The questionnaire was completed and returned by 341 professional actors: 114 Actors and actresses from the Netherlands and Flanders and 227 professionals from the United States.[1] A few Dutch actors responded by letter. They could not, or refused to complete the questionnaire, but offered their opinions on 'Actor's mixed feelings'. These letters revealed that current opinions about acting emotions differ widely. In their reactions, some Dutch-speaking actors took an anti-involvement stand: 'I can not complete the survey, because I feel nothing on stage' or: 'Only the audience has feelings.' Others voiced opinions closer to involvement: 'Everything in our profession is based on emotion' or: 'You divide what I experience as a whole'.

The American actors more frequently provided extensive responses to the survey, sometimes adding letters as well. Many of the over one hundred extra commentaries were related to involvement: 'I saw no line of separation between myself and the character's emotions'; 'Can't separate the two – they are one'; 'I did begin to silently cry – tears slowly moving down my cheeks as I said my lines. I'm not sure how I feel about that happening although it was *very* effective to the audience: I heard the tears from the audience'. But among the American actors, we also naturally found some statements related to detachment: 'Acting is pretending, nothing more. All of this crap (I call it "acting class crap") merely puts layers between the actor and what he/she is supposed to be pretending. Either one can act, or one can't, period. Good acting is a superior ability to concentrate, listen, and pretend, nothing more.'

One Dutch actor responded with an interpretation of the questionnaire which contradicted my theoretical stance: 'It illustrates the idea, usually romanticized by lay people, of getting under someone else's skin. That is a pity, your initiative is so unusual, but I have the feeling that the one-sided approach will give a limited impression of the noble craft of acting.' What is important about these letters is that they reveal that the questionnaire was not biased toward one single point of view, and not considered to be intended for just one type of actor; both interpretations occur.

The actors and actresses who participated in the study (respondents) indeed appeared to belong to the category of professional actors with at least three years of career experience.[2] Among the Dutch and Flemish respondents, over 70% graduated from a recognized acting school. Two-thirds of the Dutch actors and actresses even had more than ten years of career experience and the majority were under 45 years of age. The American respondents also had professional training; nearly 60% had studied professionally at the university level, 19% had acting training at an institute and just under 40% had

> According to the actress Renee Soutendijk, 30 to 35 percent of roles (in films) are intended for women under forty; and only 8 percent for women over forty.
>
> (in *Zomergasten*, VPRO-TV, May 30, 1992)

studied at a so-called studio.[3] In terms of career experience and age, the American respondents were comparable to the Dutch-speaking respondents: Two-thirds of the American actors and actresses had more than ten years of professional experience and the majority was also under 45 years of age.

The dispersal across education, age, experience, sex, and regional indicators was such that the sample may be considered an acceptable representation of the total population of professional actors, within the Netherlands and Flanders as well as in the United States (see figures 7.1 and 7.2). The fact that about two-thirds of the respon-

Figure 7.1: Data on the Research Sample in the Netherlands and Flanders. Compiled in the spring of 1991

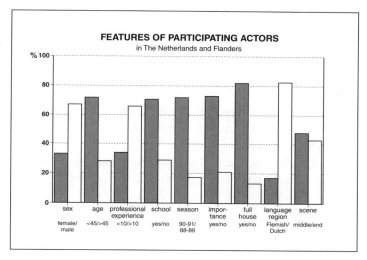

Figure 7.2: Data on the Research Sample in the United States. Compiled in the fall of 1995

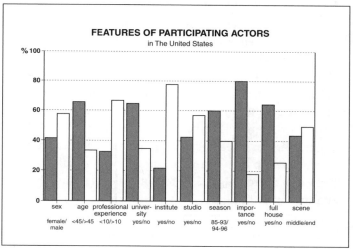

Explanation: The vertical axis indicates the respective percentage. The horizontal axis indicates the question concerned (most categories are self-explanatory: 'experience' = the number of years of professional experience (<10 = under ten years; >10 = over ten years); 'school', 'university', 'institute', 'studio' = whether or not an acting study was *completed*; 'season' = the season during which the performance recalled took place; 'important performance' = whether the scene was part of a performance which was important for the actor; and 'full house' = if the theater was filled on the night of the performance).

dents were male and one-third female corresponds to actual percentages in the theater, where there is commonly a predominance of male (leading) roles.

Statistical analysis of the information assembled did not call for further separation into subgroups based on personal characteristics or specific situations.[4] That is to say, factors like gender, age, having completed a degree, etc. did not have a differentiating impact on the response on emotions, acting styles, or other relevant data from the survey. It also appeared that age, type of training, or number of years of career experience had no connection with the specific style of acting used. In other words, a variety of acting styles was found throughout all segments of the sample population. Consequently, it was not necessary to analyze, for example, men and women separately.

Further, the data revealed that almost all of the American and Dutch actors surveyed thought the scenes they had chosen from memory were important (for them). In other words, the task situations were considered meaningful, which is a condition of a possible occurrence of task-emotions (4.5). Likewise, it is important that nearly all the actors were satisfied with their performances. Moreover, the scenes concerned had been performed recently enough so that the experiences were still fresh in their minds, plus the particular performances recalled had not taken place on an opening night but during a performance later in the run. The results concerned a variety of roles.[5] The next section will discuss which emotions were dramatized in these scenes.

Based on the documented features of the responding actors, it may be assumed that the professional actors targeted for this study were indeed found.[6] Thus it is safe to say that the results in the rest of this chapter were not distorted by respondents who did not meet the proposed professional actor criteria that were set.

7.3   Emotions Pretended on Stage

In reference to the chosen scenes, actors were asked to what degree they intended to portray certain emotions in their performance: The intended emotions. At another point in the questionnaire, they were asked to what extent the character as portrayed (during the performance of the remembered scene) had certain emotions: The character-emotions. Looking at all the responses on the intended emotions and character-emotions gave us an impression of the diverse emotions expressed in the selected scenes. See figure 7.3 for the Dutch and figure 7.4 for the American scenes.

These figures reveal the number of times an emotion was intended to be portrayed as compared to how often the emotion was actually portrayed in the character, expressed as a percentage of the total number of actors who answered the question. The information in the figures shows how many actors intended to portray a particular emotion (the darker bars) and for how many characters this emotion was realized (the lighter bars).[7] The intensity of the emotion has not been taken into account in these percentages. In the scenes chosen by Dutch actors, the emotions disgusted, anxious, sad, and angry were most frequently given as intended emotions, and were also most frequently named as the realized character-emotions: In about 70% of the scenes. These were followed by feeling erotic and tender: In about 65%. The least frequently named emotions were cheerful and in love: Intended in about 35% of the scenes. The number of characters with positive emotions was about 10% less than the number of times that these positive emotions were intended to be portrayed in the scene (see figure 7.3). Apparently it is more difficult with positive emotions to succeed in matching the actual character portrayal to the actor's intentions.

Figure 7.4 shows comparable results for the *American* actors, although negative emotions were slightly more frequent than for the Dutch (for instance, *sadness* was an intended emotion for 80% of American actors). *Eroticism* scores for the American actors were noticeably lower than those of the Dutch actors: Only 40% intended to portray *eroticism* in their characters. This was about 20% lower than for Dutch actors. Conversely, for American actors, *tenderness* was an intended emotion for over 80% of the actors, as opposed to 65% for the Dutch. This variance could possibly be caused by cultural and language differences. Scores for *being anxious* were also divergent: 90% of American actors portrayed characters with anxious feelings (*being anxious* was an intended emotion 70% of the time), while about 75% of Dutch actors portrayed anxiety in their characters (with a comparable percentage for the intended emotion of anxiety). In the

Figure 7.3: Percentages (number) of Dutch-speaking Actors per Intended Emotion and Character-emotion

Figure 7.4: Percentages (number) of American Actors per Intended Emotion and Character-emotion

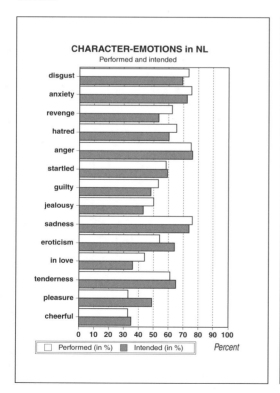 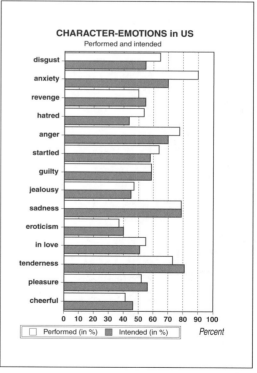

Explanation: To the left of the figure are fifteen words describing emotions. The dark gray bars indicate the percentages of actors who intended to portray the emotion. The light gray bars indicate the percentages which apply to the portrayed characters.

American idiom, 'anxious' or 'anxiety' connotes not only fearfulness but also 'tensed expectation of something to come'.

The percentage of actors indicating one of the emotions listed as one intended to be portrayed in the performance broadly matches the percentages for the same character-emotion. But, the figures among the various emotions differ widely. Certain emotions in the scenes actors recalled are applied more often than others. It is impossible to conclude from the data whether the scenes were chosen because a particular emotion was portrayed, or because of other aspects of the scene. A relatively large number of actors indicated that specific emotions were not applicable to their characters. This is obvious: All of the emotions listed could not exist within one scene. However, all of the emotions listed are well represented in the scenes recalled, especially the prototypical emotions of a negative or unpleasant nature such as *disgust, anxiety, anger,* and *sadness*. In the roles and scenes which formed the basis for responding, actors indicated many

Figure 7.5: Comparison of Character-emotions and Actors' Emotions (NL = the Netherlands, including Flanders)

Figure 7.6: Comparison of Character-emotions and Actors' Emotions (US = the United States)

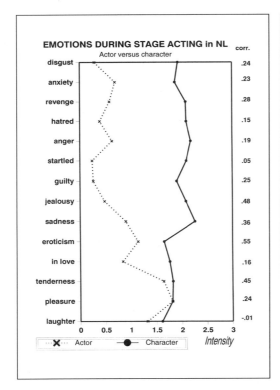

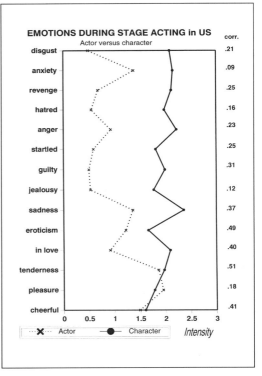

Explanation: To the left of the figure, fifteen words describing emotions are listed. The dotted line indicates the average intensity of the emotions of the actors during the performance. The solid line indicates the degree to which these emotions were portrayed in characters on stage. The lines link the average values per word describing emotion. The averages lie between 0 (not at all applicable) and 3 (applicable to a very great extent). Corr. = correlation.

different expressions of character-emotions. The results in this chapter therefore concern a wide variety of scenes and a wide variety of emotions.

7.4 Emotions of Actors and Characters

When actors portray character-emotions do they also experience similar emotions? In the questionnaire, actors indicated to what degree each emotion was expressed in the *character* during the chosen scene. Independent of this, at another point in the questionnaire, the *actors* indicated to what extent they themselves had experienced each of the emotions.[8] The answers of the Dutch respondents are shown in figure 7.5 and those of the Americans in figure 7.6.[9]

The figures clearly show that the actors' emotional experiences *did not* correspond with the portrayed character-emotions, a conclusion which is supported by statistical analysis. There is a visible distance between lines indicating the intensity of emotions for actor and character, whereby the character-emotion is always more intense than the corresponding emotion for the actor. The emotions of *disgust, anxiety, hate, anger,* etc. were all significantly weaker in the experience of the actor than they are in the characters portrayed (average of all actors).

The distance between the lines only narrows when the positive prototypical emotions of *tenderness, pleasure,* and *cheerfulness* were portrayed; it seemed at first as though actors actually experienced these emotions when portraying them in characters. This was true for both the Dutch and American surveys. However, the correlations (the numbers to the right of the figure) indicate that there is no significant connection between the *pleasure* and *cheerfulness* of the actor and that of the character. The similarity in the averages is in this case coincidental: The actors who, for example, experienced intense pleasure were not the same actors who indicated pleasure as intensely valid for their characters. Only when it came to *tenderness*, and only with the Dutch respondents, was there a significant correlation between the expression of tenderness as the character and the feelings of tenderness that the actors themselves experienced. The American actors as well, established the strongest relationship between actor and character with *tenderness*, but there was no significant and strong correlation proven with any one of the emotions (all of the correlations were under .60). The exceptional nature of tenderness will be examined more closely in a later section when task-emotions are discussed. Further, it is notable that the American actors, on average, experienced anxiety more intensely than the Dutch actors, even though as characters they did not portray a higher degree of anxiety. Could it be that American actors are more frightened of their audiences, which might include important 'casting directors'? Or should we subscribe the difference to connotations in language differences?

It is conceivable that the clear differences between portrayed character-emotions and the emotions experienced by actors themselves might be due to 'bad acting'. It is possible that the actors did not perform the way they had intended to. To test this possibility, the emotions which were intended as part of the character portrayal were compared with the emotions which were actually portrayed during the scenes chosen. The results of this comparison are shown in figure 7.7 for the Dutch actors and in figure 7.8 for the American actors.

Based on these results, it can be stated that both the Dutch and the American actors succeeded in portraying what they wanted to portray, or in any case what was intended in order to portray the character. In both figures, the lines indicating the average emotional intensities are nearly identical. There are also strong and significant correlations between the intended emotions and the portrayed character-emotions. The lack of correspondence between the actors' emotions and the characters' discussed above in fig-

Figure 7.7: Comparison of Averaged Intensity of Emotions as Intended and as Portrayed in Character (NL)

Figure 7.8: Comparison of Averaged Intensity of Emotions as Intended and as Portrayed in Character (US)

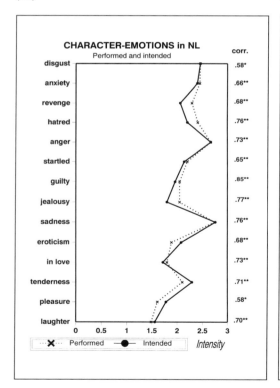

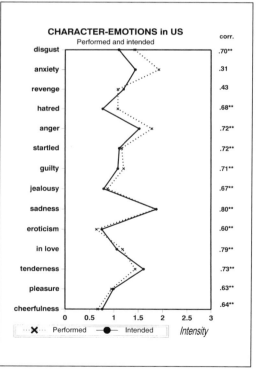

Explanation: To the left of the figure, fifteen words describing emotions are listed. The solid line indicates the degree to which each emotion was intended to be portrayed during the performance. The dotted line indicates the degree to which these emotions were portrayed as part of the character role. The lines link the average values per word describing emotion. The averages lie between 0 (not at all applicable) and 3 (applicable to a very great extent). Corr. = correlation.

ures 7.5 and 7.6, can therefore not be attributed to an inadequate performance. More-over, it appears that the nature of the data assembled is suitable for detecting this type of variation.

If the actors have indeed acted as they intended to, can we then find another explana-tion for why the emotions actors feel do not correspond to the character-emotions? Until now, all the actors have been grouped together, that is to say that actors with dif-ferent acting styles were 'added' together in the comparative analyses. The different acting styles might reveal differences in the degree to which the character-emotions and actors own emotions coincide. Therefore actors with different acting styles were separated into distinct groups and new comparisons were made.

7.5   Acting Styles and Emotions

Is there a relationship between the acting style used in a performance and the degree of correspondence between character-emotions and the emotions of the actor? To answer this question two subgroups representing the most extreme viewpoints concerning the portrayal of emotions were distinguished. The actors were classified into the acting styles on the basis of their responses to the twenty statements referring to the styles of detachment and involvement (see section 6.7). With these statements they reflected on the particular style they themselves said they had used in the chosen scene. One group of actors who predominantly used a style of detachment and another who predomi-nantly used a style of involvement were selected (for detailed information, see Konijn 1994; Konijn and Westerbeek 1997). The results for the Dutch 'detachment' actors, and the American 'detachment' actors are shown respectively in figures 7.9 and 7.10.

As expected, the 'detachment' actors showed no concurrence between the portrayed character-emotions and the emotions the actors themselves experienced during the performance. Conversely, with 'involvement' actors, one would expect to find at least a clearer correspondence between portrayed character-emotions and the emotions felt by actors than with the 'detachment' actors. In figures 7.11 and 7.12 the comparison between respectively the Dutch and the American 'involvement' actors is shown.

In general there was no clear distinction between the 'involvement' actor figures and the 'detachment' actor figures. In the United States, the 'involvement' actors (see 7.12) seemed to have slightly stronger emotions than the 'detachment' actors. But the 'in-volvement' actors also seemed to portray the character-emotions more intensely than the 'detachment' actors. Except for anger and tenderness, there was also no clear and sig-nificant relationship between American 'involvement' actors and their character-emo-tions. 'Involvement' actors' portrayal of anger in the role was matched by a weaker experience of anger in the actor. Meanwhile, tenderness in the role was matched with an evenly intense feeling of tenderness in the actor.

In general, however, there was no correspondence between character-emotions and the emotions felt by actors within the 'involvement' group. Remarkably, this was even true amongst the most adept American 'involvement' actors even though the involve-ment style or 'method-acting' in America is the foundation of much acting instruction and is viewed by many as the ideal acting style (according to the research of Brumm and Hornby, among others). If then the strongest adherents to the style of involvement according to their own statements (as opposed to the style of detachment) are selected, the results become astonishing. Overall, the results of both groups of actors, despite their opposing acting styles, do not even differ from the results of the group as a whole; compare with figures 7.5 and 7.6.

Further statistical analysis leads to the conclusion that involvement and detachment cannot be seen as two opposing styles of acting, at least not in respect to portraying emotions. This is a remarkable result because the traditional acting theories stress the antithesis of the styles precisely on the subject of emotions. On the basis of statistical analysis, four separate aspects of performing styles can be classified: (1) 'Letting oneself be carried away by the character'; (2) 'experiencing a similarity between the actor and the character'; (3) 'applying task-emotions' and (4) aspects relating to the 'technical design'.[11]

From the data assembled, it appears that there was not one single actor who thought the performing-style aspect 'applying task-emotions' was not applicable during per-

**Figure 7.9: For Detachment Actors Only –
Comparison of Character-emotions and
Actors' Emotions (NL)**

**Figure 7.10: For Detachment Actors Only –
Comparison of Character-emotions and
Actors' Emotions (US)**

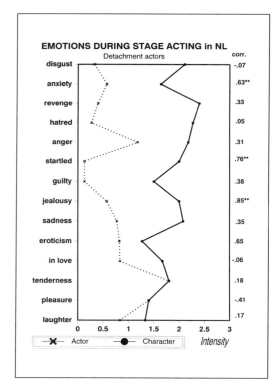

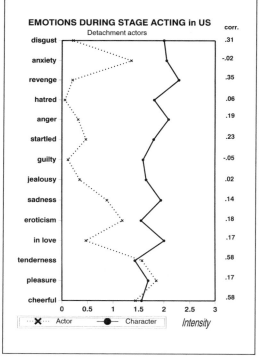

Explanation: To the left of the figure, fifteen words describing emotions are listed. The dotted line indicates the average intensity of the emotions of the detachment-actors during the performance. The solid line indicates the degree to which these emotions were portrayed as part of the character role. The lines link the average values per word describing emotion. The averages lie between 0 (not at all applicable) and 3 (applicable to a very great extent). Corr. = correlation.

formance. There were also very few actors who thought that the 'technical design' was not relevant to their acting. In other words, there was not one responding actor who exclusively applied the style of involvement during performance. Findings like these imply that involvement and detachment must be interpreted as *relative* terms. This was taken into account when determining whether an actor was oriented toward either involvement or detachment in the above comparison between actor and character. This point will be pursued in the following chapter.

In short, the traditional acting theories – specifically those of involvement and detachment – do not appear to be supported by the results gathered from actual contemporary theater practice. The task-emotion theory can thus provide an explanation of the results of this study up to this point. The actors' task-concerns, for example, the desire to execute acting tasks as well as possible before an expectant audience, will evoke task-emotions in actors.

Figure 7.11: For Involvement Actors Only – Comparison of Character-emotions and Actors' Emotions (NL)

Figure 7.12: For Involvement Actors Only – Comparison of Character-emotions and Actors' Emotions (US)

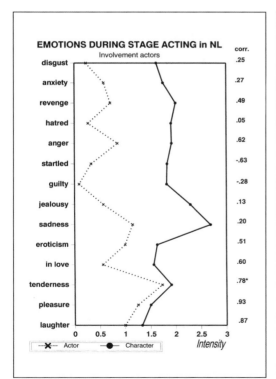

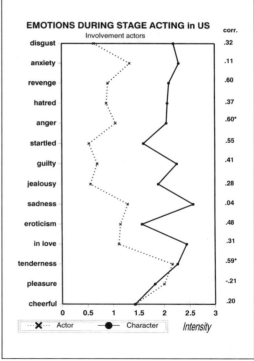

Explanation: To the left of the figure, fifteen words describing emotion are listed. The dotted line indicates the average intensity of the involvement actors' emotions during the performance. The solid line indicates the degree to which these emotions were portrayed as part of the character role. The lines link the average values per word describing emotion. The averages lie between 0 (not at all applicable) and 3 (applicable to a very great extent). Corr. = correlation.

7.6   Professional Actors and Task-Emotions

According to the task-emotion theory it is necessary to distinguish the prototypical emotions characteristic to the role, from the emotions actors may experience as a result of performing before an audience, the so-called task-emotions. In the previous chapters it was clearly delineated that from the viewpoint of the task-emotion theory, one would *not* expect actors to experience the character-emotions they portray, but *would* expect them to experience task-emotions. We have already seen that actors indeed do not have the same emotions as those they portray in characters. Do they then have task-emotions? The answer can be found in figure 7.13 for the Dutch actors and in figure 7.14 for the American actors. Just as in the previous figures, the lines indicate the average intensity of various emotions of the actors and the characters. The words describing emotion are listed vertically and were assumed beforehand to connote task-emotions (6.7).

Figure 7.13: Comparison of Character-emotions and Presumed Task-emotions (NL)

Figure 7.14: Comparison of Character-emotions and Presumed Task-emotions (US)

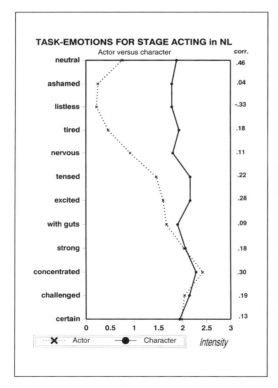

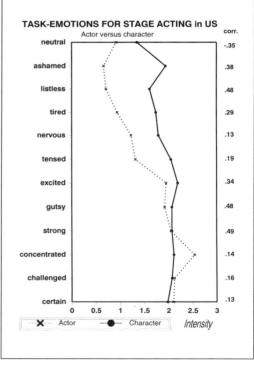

Explanation: To the left of the figure, fifteen words describing emotions are listed. The dotted line indicates the average intensity of the presumed task-emotions during the performance. The solid line indicates the degree to which these emotions were portrayed as part of the character role. The lines link the average values per word describing emotion. The averages lie between 0 (not at all applicable) and 3 (applicable to a very great extent). Corr. = correlation.

The figures clearly show that emotions appearing in the lower half of the list are more intense in a majority of the actors. In this respect, the Dutch and American actors are comparable. Although the lines almost converge at some emotions, there is no significant correlation between the emotions of actors and their character-emotions. The numbers to the right of the figures (the correlations) never reach .60. The correlations for *excitement* and *concentration* are too weak to merit a star (for significance; see box on page 129). The emotions in the lower half of the figures, from *excitement* on, are usually deemed positive, while the emotions in the upper half are usually deemed as negative. These negative task-emotions such as feeling *ashamed*, *listless*, and *tired* seldom seemed to arise in actors. They experienced, as predicted, mainly the positive task-emotions intensely, specifically *concentration*, *challenge*, and feelings of *strength* and *certainty*. These are emotions which, in a theoretical sense, can be related to challenge and 'flow' (see chapter 4).

That emotions from the category of task-emotions were attributed in comparable measures to the character (though unrelated to the actor's own emotions) ran contrary to my expectations. I thought that the portrayed character-emotions would mainly concern prototypical emotions, as explained in previous sections. Apparently prototypical emotions and task-emotions go hand in hand since characters are also intent on achieving their own goals. In order to resolve (dramatic) conflicts and overcome hurdles to reach desired results, characters – like actors – must also accomplish numerous tasks so that actors can also attribute task-emotions to their characters (although characters' 'tasks' are very different from the acting tasks). But, also with the emotions in this category, again, it cannot be stated that there is any similarity between actor and character.

To support the idea that the emotions actors have during performances mainly relate to accomplishing acting tasks, the actors' emotions just *before* the performance started should be comparable to the emotions experienced *during* the performance. In figures 7.15 and 7.16 these *task-emotions before* and *during* the performance are compared, for both the Dutch and the American actors.

The emotional experience during a live stage performance was clearly similar to the emotions the actors themselves experienced just before the performance started. This is noticeable in the overlap of the lines which depict the averages of emotional intensity, but is even more evident in the relatively strong and significant correlations. Although significant correlation cannot be claimed in all instances, there is a considerably stronger relationship between the emotions actors experience before and during the performance than between the portrayed character-emotions and the emotions of the actors themselves. This is particularly valid for the positive range of task-emotions, less so for the negative ones.

The actors' emotions which were not named as task-emotions beforehand (such as *tenderness*, *pleasure*, and *cheerfulness* in figures 7.5 and 7.6), are, I suspect, also strongly related to the emotional experiences of actors just before the performance commences. This is seen in figures 7.17 and 7.18 (on page 137), in which the prototypical emotions felt by actors just before the performance are compared with those during the performance.

The fact that here, in the category of prototypical emotions, the actors' emotional experiences *during* the performance were already present *just before* the performance, and to similar degrees, lends even stronger support to the task-emotion theory. Moreover, these *did not* relate to the character-emotions. The correspondence between the prototypical emotions reported by actors (for themselves) just before the performance with those experienced during the performance (i.e., the particular scene) supports the hypothesis that the emotions of actors relate to *acting tasks* and not to the portrayed character-emotions. Even when the actor did experience so-called prototypical emotions, these did not relate to the portrayed character-emotions. Indeed, prototypical emotions occurred in only a minority of actors.

When character-emotions portrayed by actors during the performance were compared with the emotions of actors just before the performance, it again became clear

Figure 7.15: Comparison of Actors' Emotions Before and During the Performance (NL)

Figure 7.16: Comparison of Actors' Emotions Before and During the Performance (US)

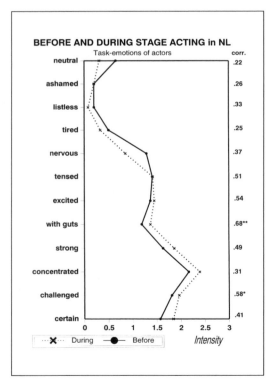

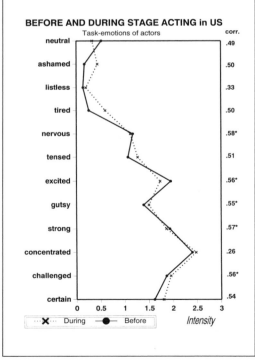

Explanation: To the left of the figure, fifteen words describing emotions are listed. The dotted line indicates the average intensity of the presumed task-emotions during the performance. The solid line indicates the degree to which these emotions were experienced by the actors just prior to the performance. The lines link the average values per word describing emotion. The averages lie between 0 (not at all applicable) and 3 (applicable to a very great extent). Corr. = correlation.

that the two have little in common.[12] The emotional experience of actors during a performance can therefore be interpreted as (mainly) related to the *acting tasks*, even when prototypical emotions are involved. I will come back to it in the next chapter.

7.7   Emotions, Impulses, and Physical Reactions

Chapter four made it clear that emotions are coupled with action tendencies. In the questionnaire these action tendencies were called tendencies, impulses or urges to do something. A list of fifteen action tendencies was presented for both the actor and the character, in the same manner as the word list describing emotions (6.4; 6.7). The tendencies can be grouped into positive and negative impulses. The positive impulses are tendencies to approach and are more likely coupled with positive emotions. The negative impulses are tendencies to avoid and are more likely coupled with negative

Figure 7.17: Comparison of Actors' Emotions Before versus During the Performance, in Reference to Prototypical Emotions (NL)

Figure 7.18: Comparison of Actors' Emotions Before versus During the Performance, in Reference to Prototypical Emotions (US)

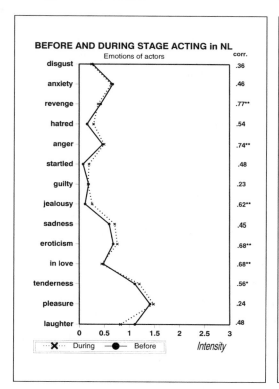

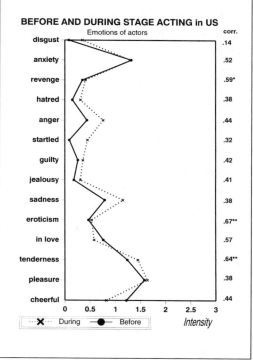

Explanation: To the left of the figure, fifteen words describing emotions are listed. The dotted line indicates the average intensity of the so-called prototypical emotions during the performance. The solid line indicates the degree to which these emotions were experienced by actors just prior to the performance. The lines link the average values per word describing emotion. The averages lie between 0 (not at all applicable) and 3 (applicable to a very great extent). Corr. = correlation.

emotions. In the following subsections, the impulses acted out as the character will be compared with the impulses experienced by the actors themselves. Subsequently the relationships found between certain emotions and their accompanying tendencies or impulses will be described. Next follows a description of the physical reactions which the actors experienced during the performance. The section will conclude with a look at the relationship between emotions, impulses, and physical reactions.

7.7.1 Comparison of Impulses of Actor and Character

The results of comparing the *impulses* in the actor and the character were much the same as the previous comparison of emotions: There was little similarity between the two. Therefore, the results presented in figures 7.19 and 7.20 have been placed in the appendix and will be handled here only briefly.[13] The lines in the figures show a clear difference in the strength of the characters' and corresponding actors' impulses. Comparing the two, the conclusion is that the actors experienced considerably less intense action tendencies. Nor was there any correspondence expected with the negative action tendencies. In fact, the actors reported very few negative impulses.

Among the actors' positive impulses, only the urge to 'go for it' showed any degree of correspondence with the characters' impulses. In the American survey, the impulse with the next 'highest' degree of correspondence between actors and characters was the urge to 'sing, dance, and move'. The American survey also showed a slight link between the characters' impulse to laugh and the actors' own urge to laugh. On the whole, then, the results indicate a lack of correspondence between the character impulses portrayed and the action tendencies experienced by actors themselves. In this respect there is thus little support for the involvement theory, but some degree of support for the detachment theory and for the task-emotion theory. The impulse to 'go for it' and to 'overcome difficulties' was experienced by 80% to 90% of the actors themselves.

Regarding this point, one would have expected that, within the task-emotion theory, emotions and their accompanying action tendencies onstage to deviate from normal emotions in daily life. According to the task-emotion theory, characters' impulses are special in that they depart somewhat from the impulses of 'real people in normal life'. *Characters* generally 'have' negative emotions, especially those in the category of prototypical emotions, which are yet expected to be accompanied by approach tendencies, rather than avoidance tendencies (4.4.3). On the other hand, it is expected that actors' positive task-emotions will be linked to tendencies to approach (as is the case 'outside the theater'). The character's tendency to approach, which is acted out in the role, would therefore be an extension of the actor's tendency to approach. Therefore, I had expected that approach tendencies, represented along with negative emotions as character, would coincide with approach tendencies and positive emotions in the actors. Yet, different levels of intensity in actor's impulses versus those of the character could be expected. At most, the slight degree of correspondence found between some tendencies for both actors and characters seemed to point in this direction. (There were four character-tendencies in both the Dutch and American surveys which were weakly linked to comparable actor's impulses; these included the tendencies 'to hug', 'to approach', 'to caress', and the neutral tendency 'to do something'). However, a closer look at the results revealed an unexpected picture, as the following subsection will clarify.

7.7.2 Correspondence Between Emotions and Impulses

What stood out while calculating the correspondence between emotions and impulses was that conspicuously high correlations in the *actor's emotions* were found chiefly between the *positive task-emotions* and the *tendencies to approach*.[14] Conversely, with *character-emotions*, in the category of positive task-emotions, there were a remarkable number of significant correlations between *negative* prototypical emotions and tendencies of *avoidance* in the character. I had expected that negative character-emotions would be accompanied by character-tendencies to approach (chapter 5), although this appeared now not to be the case. The correspondence between separate negative tendencies in the character was not accompanied by the predicted tendencies to approach, but instead, by tendencies of avoidance.

Further study of these correlations revealed that the specific character-tendencies *to attack, to hurt,* and *to burst out* actually concerned *approach* tendencies. This was contrary to the fact that these specific impulses were grouped with the negative tendencies, thus with avoidance tendencies, because it was presumed that these impulses would be linked to negative character-emotions. The character-tendencies were indeed directed toward avoiding or removing one obstacle or another, but, in hindsight, it was incorrect to call them avoidance tendencies. After all, the action required takes one closer to the obstacle to be removed. Although the action has a negative context, it must still be seen as an approach tendency. The categories created earlier (6.7) were based on general expectations about action tendencies, as belonging to either negative or positive emotions, as discussed in chapter 5. The results, however, show that this part of the task-emotion theory must be reformulated.[15] A related problem is that action tendencies can be interpreted in more than one way. The greatest ambiguity perhaps occurred with the urge 'to go for it', which with actors was linked with positive task-emotions (like *courage, feeling strong, concentration,* and *challenge*) and also, for the American actors, with the impulse *to overcome difficulties.* This was not true for the characters. *Going for it* in characters was related to *sadness, erotic feelings, tenderness,* and *cheerfulness.* With both actors and characters, the approach impulse was the most relevant impulse.

7.7.3 Connection Between Emotions, Impulses, and Physical Reactions

In addition to questions about emotions and impulses, the actors were also questioned about their physical reactions while acting. The reactions and the degree to which the actors experienced them are graphically represented in the appendix, in figure 7.21 for the Dutch and in figure 7.22 for the American actors. The physical reactions of the characters were obviously not surveyed, as this would have been implausible.

According to the task-emotion theory the positive emotions of the actor should be coupled with a specific physiological activation. In particular, excited physical reactions were expected to co-exist with task-emotions such as *tension, excitement,* and *challenge.* Excited reactions would include, for example, general *excitement, sweating, blush-*

ing, tingling, and butterflies in the stomach (see figures in the appendix). Taken on the whole, these physical reactions occurred strongly or very strongly in a large portion of the professional actors in both the Dutch and American surveys; when actors indicated having these excited types of physical sensations, then they were, on average, experienced intensely. In general, American actors reported having excited reactions more often, and more intensely, than the Dutch.

More subdued physical reactions, such as dry throat, shaking knees, trembling hands, and turning pale, occurred much less frequently, as did the negative emotions with which these reactions are coupled. The correlation between emotions and physical reactions in actors (for the entire group), was found to be moderate to weak.[16] The only strong correlation found was between excitement as an emotion felt by actors and the physical reaction of general excitement (greater than .60 and significant). Moreover, this physical sensation occurred for 85% of the Dutch and 95% of the American actors. The next highest correlation was between sadness felt by the Dutch actors and shedding tears (.50), but among the American actors this relationship was too weak to be considered (.32). The rest of the correlations between the actor's emotions and the excited type of physical reactions were too low to suggest any connection. In short, the specific expectation about the relationship between actor's positive emotions and excited physical reactions is only supported to a limited extent by the empirical results: The support holds for feeling excited, but not with the actors feeling tense, concentrated, and challenged.

When tears are perceived as indicators for 'really having' emotions, as Archer did in 1888, then the relatively strong correspondence between the selection of actors who experienced sadness and their tears could be considered as support for the idea that actors really do 'experience' sadness. The tears actors shed also corresponded to some degree with sadness acted out as a character-emotion. But section 7.5 made it clear that the sadness portrayed in a character is seldom related to sadness the actor himself feels. It was therefore remarkable that sadness occurred relatively frequently in actors onstage and that, on top of that, over half (55% of the Dutch and 60% of the American) of the actors reported tears which partially corresponded with their own sadness (though this did not stem from the character's sadness). In as much as tears are not related to experiencing sadness, the actor's tears could of course be related to a number of other emotions such as joy, tenderness, or feeling moved. It is also common that tears often flow while actors are receiving applause. Finally, things like make-up and bright lights can also affect tear glands. In chapter two we could read that some actors are able to produce tears 'on command' without any underlying emotion.

7.8   Personal Acting Styles and Acting Styles of Top Actors

To what extent are the results merely a reflection of prevailing standards in the acting profession? Which opinions about portraying emotions are most strongly asserted at this moment in time among the respondent-actors? If the actor's response was based on 'how they thought they were supposed to act' the results would be less valid than if their answers were based solely on their own experience. Therefore, it was important to find out what the prevailing views on acting emotions were among the actors surveyed.

By eliciting statements about the supposed acting style of the respondent's favorite actors, preference for a certain style of acting could indirectly be detected. Because one generally does not actually know how a certain actor performs, the ideas on the subject could be influenced by at least two factors. First, an actor's own personal preference for a style of acting; one's own 'ideal acting style' could be ascribed to his or her 'ideal actor' as 'the best'. Second, judgments about the way leading actors act could be influenced by current opinions, such as 'how people think actors should act' or what 'good acting' is.

The responding actors were therefore asked who they thought were the best actors or actresses of the present moment.[17] The Dutch and Flemish actors were asked to choose the 'best' *stage* actor among Dutch-speaking actors. They could also choose a *film* actor as the best international actor. The American respondents were also asked to name their favorite stage actor as well as the film actor they considered the best. Subsequent use of the term 'top actors' refers to the actors named by the respondent-actors.

A few of the top actors named are listed in the box. Each list shows the favorite three stage actors and the favorite three film actors, separately for the Netherlands/Flemish and the American actors. The point here is to get a general indication of 'the ideal' acting style based on the style ascribed to these top actors. Furthermore, it is important to realize that the number one actor was different for nearly every respondent. So the actors listed below were the ones most frequently named, but they were certainly not named by all. The Dutch actors chose the same 'top actor' more often than the American actors, who nearly all chose a different actor as their own favorite. There is anything but agreement on the subject.

Note that in three of the four lists of chosen top actors (in the box below), only one is a woman. This could reflect two interacting factors. First, two out of three respondent-actors, who chose the top actors, were male (7.2) and might therefore be more oriented toward male colleagues. Second, we already noted earlier that most leading roles in film and theater are written for men.[18] So, the results in this section could possibly be biased toward, or most valid for, male actors.

The Dutch and American respondents also appraised each of the top actors in how they accomplish the expression of character-emotions. From a selection of statements, they could choose to what degree each statement was applicable to their favorite actor: Three statements were more related to involvement and the other three to detachment. (In the American version there were five statements for each style, presented in a mixed order.) In general the most favored acting style was that of involvement, since this was ascribed to the top actors in significantly greater measure than the detachment style.[19]

The choice of the *Dutch* respondent-actors (spring 1991):

Top stage actors	Top screen actors
1. Pierre Bokma	1. Robert de Niro
2. Joop Admiraal	2. Meryl Streep
3. Annet Nieuwenhuizen	3. Jack Nicholson

The choice of the *American* respondent-actors (autumn 1995):

Top stage actors	Top screen actors
1. Vanessa Redgrave	1. Meryl Streep
2. Derrick Jacobi	2. Anthony Hopkins
3. Maggie Smith	3. Robert de Niro

The results of the analysis of the acting styles ascribed to top actors however, again revealed that involvement and detachment are not opposing acting styles.[20] This was also the case with the personal acting style (7.5). To answer the question about the connection between personal acting styles and the style attributed to

top actors, I compared the degree to which respondents themselves applied the acting style of involvement or detachment with the degree to which they ascribed this style to their favorite actors. The correlation was calculated separately for stage actors and screen actors.[21]

Statistical analysis revealed that, in general, personal styles were almost completely unrelated to the acting style attributed to top actors. No significant correlation was produced. Ascribing a greater orientation toward either detachment or involvement seemed unrelated to the actor's own degree of orientation toward one or the other style. In other words, when an actor himself applied a style of detachment, this does not mean that this actor thinks his favorite actors applied this style more often. The assumption is also not valid with the involvement style, even though this style was the general favorite.

Thus, it cannot be said that there is a clear connection between personal acting style and the 'ideal' or 'favorite' acting style; the prevailing standard. The personal acting style of the respondent-actors appears *not* to be a reflection of 'an ideal acting style'. The lack of correspondence between the portrayed character-emotions and the emotions of actors in this field study is evidently *not* the result of a common opinion as to 'how it ought to be done'. My interpretation of this lack of correspondence is that actors have given a realistic account of the way they portray characters during a live performance.

7.9   Preparation, Public, and Believability

I will now examine how the acting styles applied by professional actors during *the performance* compare to the styles used during *the rehearsal period*. In relation to this last part of the survey, a further description will follow of whether the application of a particular acting style relates to certain expectations among the actors about the emotional effect their performance will have on the audience. They were also asked which emotions they employed to enhance the credibility of their characters.

7.9.1   Acting Styles During Performance and Preparation   There is a general assumption that the preparation for playing a role, during rehearsals, differs from actually playing that part in a live performance before an audience. For this reason, actors and actresses were asked how they prepared their character portrayal in the scenes they chose. Three statements on the list were more related to an involvement style, while another three were more related to a detachment style (four and four in the American survey).

Most actors thought that *any* aspects of either the style of involvement or detachment could be used during the preparation of a role in rehearsal. In particular, the *detachment* statements such as 'through the rehearsal of skills for this part, acting became more and more of a challenge' and 'by acquiring a command of the technical aspects of my part, I have increased my confidence' were applied while rehearsing their parts by over 90% of the actors. These statements about technical control, and task-emotions such as challenge and security, clearly contain references to aspects of the detachment style of acting. Nevertheless, statements that referred to an involvement style during rehearsals were subscribed to more often by actors from the United States than by the Dutch actors.

Calculations of the correspondence between acting styles during preparation for a role and during performance revealed that there was no strong or significant correlation for detachment. Neither was there a correlation among the Dutch actors for involvement. With the American actors there was a moderately strong correlation (.50**) between the involvement style during rehearsals and involvement in the characters during performance. All in all, it appears that the content or significance of a more involved versus a more detached style of acting during preparation is difficult to compare with the style during performance; they seem to be relatively independent of one another. At this moment, the general assumption that acting styles during the rehearsal period differ from those during performance seems to be justifiable. There is little convincing evidence for or against either view.

7.9.2   Acting Styles, Audience, and Believability

Adherence to a particular acting style appears to be unrelated to expectations actors had about the emotional effect of their acting on the audience. (These results only pertain to the Dutch and Flemish actors, as these questions were not posed in the US survey.) A majority of the professional actors (about 80%) thought that their acting onstage would evoke in the spectator 'the same emotional experience as that which was expressed in the character'. This, despite the actors' responses that they themselves scarcely had 'the same emotional experience as the character' (it should be reminded, however, that the responses of the actors were elicited indirectly). Almost as many actors (about 80%) thought their performances would 'increase the spectator's insight'. About 70% of the actors expected their performances to provoke 'a different emotional experience' in the spectators than was expressed in the characters.

The actors apparently assumed that their performances would provoke various reactions in the spectators *at the same time*. Furthermore, it is notable that the degree to which the actors became involved in their characters is *not* related to the degree to which they thought that spectators would experience their character's emotions. Neither is there a significant correlation between the other assumed effects on spectators and the actor's own acting style. On the whole, there is no relationship between the acting style the actors used onstage and the assumed effect on the spectator.

In order to achieve the greatest degree of *believability* for the audience, actors used their private emotions as well as task-emotions on a large scale in the portrayal of character-emotions. Over 80% reported employing both categories of emotions. Apart from emotions, 'charisma' was most often reported by actors (95%) as a means to increase believability in portraying character-emotions.

It is not clear how such a widespread application of private emotions should be interpreted, since, as seen earlier, these did not become manifest as emotions through involvement in the character. On the one hand, actors indicated that the emotions they experienced did not correspond to those of the characters portrayed. On the other hand, actors indicated that they applied private emotions to their roles. There are two possible explanations. First, actors experience all sorts of private emotions which are not related to either the character or to the acting tasks (and which actually are none of our business – as spectators).

Second, the actors were probably not familiar with the term task-emotions, or professional emotions as used in the questionnaire. Since the use of the term was not explained, it might have been confusing. We cannot exclude the possibility that actors subscribed to the term private emotions to also mean task-emotions, in referring to their emotional experiences that they perceived as different from the character-emotions. This part of the questionnaire is not clarifying in this respect. However, the fact that the actors do experience a variety of emotions was discussed previously. It is clear that, although actors did not experience the emotions portrayed as a character, they did feel something. A great number of professional actors experienced emotions of a different nature than character-emotions. It is therefore not surprising that they gave different names, such as private emotions, to the variety of feelings they had.

7.10   Summary

The response of professional actors to questions about emotions and acting styles in the questionnaire 'Actor's Mixed Feelings' has been outlined in this chapter. An assessment of the respondents' personal data indicated that they form a representative sample of the profession. An assessment of the performances that respondents based their answers on revealed that these included a wide range of scenes and emotions. Of the emotions portrayed on stage, the negative prototypical emotions were portrayed more often than the positive ones. Moreover, the emotions portrayed in performance were the ones actors intended to portray.

A comparison of the emotions of actors with those of characters shows a clear divergence: Actors did not experience the character-emotions portrayed. Furthermore, after dividing the actors into one group with a distinct involvement style and another with a distinct detachment style, it appeared that the acting style applied had no effect on the comparison between the emotions of the actor with those of the character. Actors who involved themselves experienced their character's emotions *just as little* as actors who remained detached.

To support the task-emotion theory, the question of whether or not actors experience these task-emotions was explored. The survey revealed that indeed they did. The idea that these emotions are related to acting tasks and not directly to the role portrayal is further supported by the fact that the emotions the actors experienced *during* the performance strongly resembled those they felt *just before* the performance.

The relationship between emotions, impulses, and physical reactions does not appear to be as clear-cut. I had expected negative character-emotions to be linked with approach tendencies, while in daily life (and thus with the actor's emotions) I had expected them to be linked with avoidance tendencies. However, the impulses linked to the character-emotions portrayed appeared *not* of a different nature than those in daily life (in the way they are portrayed). The connection between the acting out of character-tendencies and character-emotions appears precisely to resemble the connection between approach tendencies and avoidance tendencies as these occurred in the actors. In this respect, character-tendencies do actually compare with those in daily life. Probably these provide the spectator with important information about the direction of the performed emotion: Approach toward, or avoidance of, the object of the emotion.

The personal acting style and the acting styles of top actors are, according to the results of this study, scarcely related to each other. The acting styles actors indicated (indirectly) as their own appeared not to reflect what they considered to be the ideal style (as an indicator for what the prevailing standard of acting emotions might be). Therefore, it is allowed to consider the answers of the respondent-actors to be accurate accounts of the way actors portray character-emotions onstage.

The acting style used during rehearsals while preparing a role, may or may not be related to the style used during the performance. As far as any connection could be ascertained, there was some degree of correlation between the involvement style in rehearsal and in performance among the American actors. Most actors believed that their performances would evoke emotions in their audiences parallel to the character-emotions. They also believed their performances would increase their audiences' insight. Finally, to support the believability of their roles to the audience, actors reported using private emotions as well as task-emotions, but relied mainly on 'charisma'.

8   *Actors Have Emotions and Act Emotions*

> The technique of any art is sometimes apt
> to dampen, as it were, the spark of inspiration
> in a mediocre artist;
> but the same technique in the hands of a master
> can fan that spark into an unquenchable flame.
> JOSEF JASSER (in Michael Chekhov 1953: 1)

8.1   Introduction: Development of Theory on Acting Emotions

This last chapter begins with a review of the main issues discussed thus far. The results of the field study on acting will then be related to acting theory. The heart of acting lies in giving form to emotions on stage. Emotions are central to the dramatic arts: Actors' emotions, emotional expression, character-emotions, conveying emotion, audience emotions, etc. Directors and theoreticians have postulated various notions about the relationship between how character-emotions are portrayed and the emotions actors experience.

Diderot claimed that actors themselves should not feel any emotions whatsoever in order to be able to evoke a maximum of emotion in their audiences. Various contemporary opinions on acting translate this paradoxical stance as the actor's dilemma: How much should actors become involved with the character-emotions portrayed during a performance? Within current acting theories, Diderot's standpoint in *Paradoxe sur le Comédiene* is mainly recognizable in the detachment theory, which asserts that actors should not experience the same emotions as those of their characters. Opposed to this is the involvement theory, which asserts that actors must indeed experience the emotions they portray in their characters; otherwise the performance will not be believable and will fail to move the audience. A theoretical analysis of acting emotions, based on current psychological emotion theory, has led me to develop the task-emotion theory. This theory proposes that actors experience emotions related to the actual situation of live performance. However, these task-emotions will not coincide with the character-emotions portrayed.

The theoretical insights developed in the early chapters were then tested in practice using the experience of professional actors. Professional actors in the Netherlands, Flanders, and the United States were asked to complete a questionnaire. They were asked to choose an emotional scene which they had performed recently and frequently; their answers were to be based on these scenes. They were asked about their emotional experiences, the emotions they portrayed, and also about the acting style they applied in the scene.

Based on the actors' responses, one could simply have concluded that Diderot had been right all along with his *Paradoxe*. But this would have perpetuated the same misconceptions that most accepted acting theories are based on. In particular, current acting theory underestimates or all but ignores the presence of task-emotions in actors. The *Paradoxe* and existing acting theories generalize emotions for both actor and character, concentrating on the character-emotions. Actors are viewed from an audience perspective. These factors foster the paradox. When a distinction is made between the character-emotions impersonated by actors and task-emotions experienced by actors, debating the actor's dilemma becomes pointless. This study also made a point of analyzing how emotions are acted on stage from the actors' point of view.

The results of this study revealed that professional actors, in general, did not experience the same emotions as they portrayed in their roles. However, the emotional portrayal was not completely disconnected from the emotions actors themselves experienced. It is not the case that actors were devoid of emotion when they were on stage. The actors who participated in the survey experienced quite specific sets of emotions in their 'roles' as actor-craftsmen. Professional actors experienced task-emotions of a positive nature intensely and frequently. These task-emotions appeared to be very useful in acting and in shaping emotions that were part of the character impersonation. These results from theater practice support the premise that the actors' task-emotions are more important in performing roles than the emotions evoked through involvement with their characters. The idea that actors should 'keep their cool' on stage, as suggested by the detachment theory, is also unfounded: Task-emotions are 'hot'. Actors undergo emotions that we do not recognize as such, and they display emotions that do not really exist.

In the following sections, the research method used will be evaluated (8.2), the results of this study will be tested against traditional views on acting, and the task-emotion theory will be explored. Finally, the consequences for the development of acting theory will be presented.[1]

8.2 Evaluation of the Research Method

The validity of all research is endangered by a lack of clarity in the data and possible alternative explanations for the results. Field research entails a number of factors which are difficult to control. The most important of these will be discussed below.

Due to the nature of field studies, one possible threat to the validity of conclusions is that the research population is not a representative sample of the target population as a whole. Clear insight into the size and composition of the total target population of 'professional actors' does not exist in the Netherlands because no valid system of registration yet exists. In the United States professional actors are registered as union members. I have tried to reach as wide a group of Dutch, Flemish, and American professional actors as possible (see 7.2). Although response to the questionnaire was limited (about 25% among Dutch and Flemish actors and well over 10% among American actors)[2], the more than 300 respondents did belong to the professional group targeted. Their responses can also be viewed as an acceptable representation of the target group as a whole. This claim is based, among other things, on the knowledge that the Dutch, Flemish, and American respondents all had at least three years of professional experience (a clear majority have more than ten years experience) and that over two-thirds had completed a recognized course of training. Further, they represented a wide range of ages, sex, location of acting schools, language regions, and, in the US, a wide range of states.[3]

Because the study was retrospective, the unspecified experiences or special circumstances of the respondent-actors might have had an unintended effect on the results. The recollection of emotional experiences during the chosen scenes could have easily be colored by other experiences or situations. To compensate for these unintended effects, it was important to focus the actors' choices in such a way that the scenes they chose would be comparable. Because a premiere would be considered too emotionally 'supercharged', respondents were asked that the performance selected be from among the last in a production's run. Separate analyses on (relevant) demographic data and specific circumstances of the chosen performances were also conducted to screen out unintended effects. Analyses revealed that these factors did not influence the results (for example, there was no difference between actors and actresses in relation to taking pleasure in their work). In field research it is impossible to screen out all unintended factors. It is safe to say that the most important ones have been sufficiently minimized in this study (see Konijn 1994; and Konijn and Westerbeek 1997).

Another threat to research validity is using a sample population (in this study the respondent-actors) that is too small to use as a basis for a variety of statistical analyses. Using the same relatively small sample of actors to conduct many different statistical tests could have led to inaccurate conclusions that could have been partly the result of coincidence.[4] An important reason to rule out the possibility of coincidence in this case was the consistency of the responses. The differences and similarities in results were, on the whole, comparable throughout the various forms of analysis and aspects of the study (for example, a lack of similarity between the portrayed character-emotions and the emotions experienced by actors was found among both the Dutch-speaking and the American respondents). The response was consistent on two continents, and also over a period of years: The study was repeated in the US nearly four years after the first study and the results showed strong similarities.

An important motive for repeating the survey in the United States was that American actors, in contrast to those in the Netherlands, are strongly oriented toward an involvement style through training in *method acting*. Dutch and American drama schools differ in many respects. One point of difference is that theater schools in the Netherlands are not faculties within research universities, but are part of the more practically oriented polytechnic college system. In the United States, many of the respected drama schools are part of a research university. Outside academia there are numerous private or commercial studios. The way 'acting' is taught in the US is frequently based on actors delving into their characters. Exploring personal experience to facilitate a role is widely advocated in the United States and strongly based on *method acting* (Brumm 1973; Hornby 1994). Theater practice in the Netherlands is presumed to be less passionate about character analysis, while method-acting seems to be less suited to the 'cold, sober Dutch'. The curriculum of the drama academy in Maastricht, for example, is known for its strong orientation toward technical skills. While conducting the US study (while in New York), it became clear that, although method-acting remains widely propagated, it seems less widely reflected in the attitudes of contemporary theater practitioners. For example, Lee Strasberg's famed *Actors Studio* counted 900 members in 1995. Relative to the 35,000 members of *Actors' Equity* this not a large number.

The method of disseminating the questionnaire via the postal system also involved a number of risks because it concerned a complex subject and a hard-to-reach target group. Nonetheless, this was the most efficient way to survey a relatively large number of actors. Because the questionnaire was structured, answers were gathered in the same way from all respondents. This had definite advantages in terms of compiling and interpreting data. In addition, there was no interference from the researcher, thanks to the anonymity of the method.

One problem regarding written questions about emotional experiences was that words describing an emotion are not necessarily reflections of emotional experience; naming an emotion is not the same thing as feeling it.[5] Analysis revealed that the emotion-words connoted different meanings in different instances.[6] 'Pleasure' when referring to characters was, for example, different than when referring to actors. Furthermore, the meanings of negative emotion-words seemed to be less ambiguous than positive emotion-words; negative emotion-words belonged more definitively to a single category.[7] The clear difference in the actors' responses concerning their own emotions in contrast to the emotions they impersonated, and the consistency of their responses, revealed that respondents clearly made a distinction between themselves and their roles. This difference between actor and character was underlined by the clear similarity actors noted between the intended and the portrayed emotions, as well as by their own emotional experiences before and during the performance. In this respect, the method proved surprisingly suitable for the stated purpose.

The theoretical distinction between involvement and detachment was not clearly revealed in the survey results. Does this mean that the method used was less suitable for determining a particular acting style? The responses of professional actors did seem to indicate a distinction between either involvement or detachment, but it was not true that actors who indicated a preference for involvement emphatically rejected the statements associated with detachment, or vice versa. Contrary to theoretical opinions, the acting styles in practice did not seem to clash. Thus, I am more inclined to doubt that these styles must be seen as opposing styles, than doubt that they can be identified using a questionnaire method. I must immediately add that involvement is more easily measured than detachment. Because the aspect of acting styles categorized as 'applying task-emotions' appeared to apply to almost all actors, this might have blurred the measured effects of detachment.

Finally, in hindsight, I wonder whether questions about the acting style of renowned actors was a good indicator for a norm or 'ideal' style of acting. It is conceivable that the actors' responses were influenced by publicity and the media. It is widely assumed that the majority of international film actors are trained in method-acting, an involvement-oriented style. This could be the reason that an involvement acting style was attributed to more 'name' actors, and not because of an ideal image or a prevailing standard for acting emotions.

All in all, the questionnaire method proved suitable for eliciting responses from professional actors, and thus has provided valuable insights into the way they shape characters onstage. This data provided the information needed to solve the central problem in acting. The actors' responses offered an opportunity to formulate an important and balanced supplement to the existing theories about acting emotions on the stage.

8.3   Actors Have Task-Emotions

For the development of a theory on acting emotions, it was important to show that almost all actors experienced emotions that relate to accomplishing their acting tasks. It was established that actors experienced a very specific range of emotions, including *challenge, tension,* and *excitement,* which I have called task-emotions. Positive emotions, which accompany challenge, were expected to be more in evidence during performance than negative emotions. A majority of actors indicated experiencing these emotions with a certain degree of intensity. Likewise, *pleasure* and *tenderness* were cited relatively frequently as actors' emotions during the scenes they chose (although these had previously been grouped in the category of prototypical emotions and not with task-emotions). In principle each of the emotions can apply to characters and to actors; depending on what the emotion refers to, the emotion can then be labeled a task- or prototypical-emotion.

The emotions actors had during a performance were barely, if at all, connected to the impersonated characters. This was also true of the emotions that actors experienced just prior to a performance. By contrast, the actors' emotions during performance were clearly similar to the actors' emotions just prior to the performance. This indicated that for the actor, the emotions on the enactment level of the actor-craftsman were in the foreground, and that these were connected with the task to be performed. These emotions could also have related to irrelevant personal situations, neither connected to acting tasks nor to the portrayed character-emotions.

In addition, the results established that the actors' emotions persisted after the performance, while the impersonated character-emotions did not. This after-effect, according to Frijda, indicates that the emotion was 'authentic'. In general, there was an observable tendency for negative emotions to diminish during acting. The intensity of positive emotions, by contrast, seemed to increase during performance. After playing the scene, the intensity of emotions felt decreased again.[8] This trend in the results seems to concur with the experiences actors often relate about not being 'ready' before a performance, and the changeover to a condition of 'flow' once the performance begins ('flow' meaning the feeling of performing at an optimal 'fluent' level, in top form, in other words). The individual in 'flow' is perfectly attuned to the situation, and the exertion required to do difficult tasks seems effortless, this is a peak performance situation. One condition for experiencing 'flow' is that a performance must be challenging for the actor, and that the chances of mastering the situation successfully are in balance with the risks of failure (4.6.2).[9] Conquering a challenge requires exertion (usually termed as stress or

> The training I received growing up in the sixties is often irrelevant in today's theatre. It's also alarming how few universities prepare you for the realities of everyday life. I've been in productions where actors/actresses 'live' the character. That can be terrifying if they lose a certain touch with reality.
>
> (American respondent-actor, dated November 28, 1995)

mental exertion) because concentration must not lapse.[10] For professional actors it seems important to avoid the possible negative effects of stress caused by feelings of incompetence or lack of control. Belief in one's own competence appears to be an important factor.

The negative effects of stress can generally be countered by goal-oriented activity, whether or not this is directed toward the source of the stress.[11] Portraying a character requires goal-oriented activity and the actor's task situation provides the possibility to exploit task-emotions, stress, or job tension. This provides an explanation for the positive nature of emotions experienced onstage. It also becomes clear that the notion of stage fright, as connoting anxiety or fear, is too negative and narrow. A literal translation of the Dutch term stage 'fever', in the sense of feverish excitement, would be more appropriate. Little research has been done on the positive effects of stress and challenge, but interest has increased in recent years.

Whether task-emotions are 'real' emotions is a subject for debate. Everyday notions about what emotions actually are often differ from scientific or psychological definitions. Moreover, views on what emotions actually are have changed over time, as we saw in the discussion of Diderot and Archer (in chapter two).[12] According to Kreitler and Kreitler (1972), emotions evoked through 'involvement' are less intense than 'spontaneous' feelings or emotions. Intense or passionate feelings are labeled as emotions in daily life, although the intensity of a 'feeling' is not necessarily a feature of emotion in psychological terms. The defining feature in psychological terms is an action tendency with control precedence, triggered when interests are at stake. For Frijda, control precedence is the most specific characteristic of being emotional. Control precedence interrupts other (behavioral) processes and lends extra strength to 'emotional behavior', in the sense of inevitability or tenacity.[13] In this sense, task-emotions onstage are then 'real' emotions: They are intense and are accompanied by action tendencies with control precedence. The study's findings that the task-emotions had an aftereffect, beyond the duration of the performance, support this view.

The high intensity of the positive task-emotions in actors concurs with the findings of the emotion psychologist Mesquita. According to Mesquita, situations result in intense emotions when they involve different interests and when these interests also involve social sharing. 'Social sharing' means making other people companions to one's own experiences.[14] The presence of the 'sharing' or warm feelings of tenderness, pleasure, and eroticism among actors is remarkably great. These feelings could be part of the social sharing aspects that develop in the relationships among colleagues and in conveying emotions to audiences.

The actor's task situation in performance with a live audience was analyzed using Frijda's emotion theory (chapter four). I reasoned that various interests of professional actors would be at stake, including their concerns about competence, self-image, and esthetic value. In Frijda's theory, the urgency, difficulty, and gravity of the situation are factors which give rise to intense emotions.[15] These concerns and additional factors are a fundamental part of the meaning structure of the actor's situation (3.5). In line with this, actors indicated that the scenes they remembered were ones that were important to them. The execution of tasks was therefore a source of emotion in itself. Simply carrying out acting tasks for a critical public was enough to arouse actors' emotions. Which emotions were acted out, and how this was achieved was of no apparent relevance.

The results of this study revealed that positive task-emotions in actors were coupled with action tendencies to approach (like impulses *to approach, to go for it*, and *to overcome difficulties*) which contributed to the generally positive nature of actors' emotions on stage. These approach tendencies are consistent with *challenge* and *concentration* (3.7). There was a significant correlation between the action tendencies named and the *gutsy* feeling actors experienced. As for the assumption that positive task-emotions would be accompanied by excited physical reactions, this proved especially true for the feeling of excitement with physical activation.

In situations which are unclear, or where various concerns are addressed simultaneously and the course of reaction remains uncertain, action tendencies can consist of pure excitement. This could, in part, explain why, in general, no strong correlation was found between emotions, action tendencies, and physical reactions. Frijda (1986: 239) believes that 'mere excitement' or 'sheer arousal' feels like one is being gripped by something but does not know what to do. Emotions which are primarily determined by their object are difficult or impossible to specify in terms of a particular action tendency or mode of activation. This is the case with *challenge* and *concentration*. Emotions of this kind have a marked change in action readiness, but have no characteristic facial expression and can not be recognized by expressive behavior alone.[16] This is precisely why task-emotions can have a function in designing character-emotions; by lending the external form of emotions the aspect of real emotions. I will return to this notion in section 8.5.

8.4   Actors Act Character-Emotions

No similarity was revealed between the emotions impersonated in characters and the emotions actors themselves experienced. There was no direct connection between the emotions actors portrayed and the ones they felt. The clearest discrepancy between character-emotions and actors' emotions was seen with negative or unpleasant emotions. Negative or unpleasant emotions were frequent and intense in the character roles, but were hardly present in the actors. The theoretical chapters revealed a preference for the so-called basic or prototypical emotions within character-emotions such

Cartoon by Johan Hoorn, February 22, 2000.

as *anger*, *sorrow*, and *romantic love*, which go hand in hand with the dramatic preference for conflict situations. The character-emotions impersonated in the category of prototypical emotions corresponded with the emotions intended to be conveyed in the performance. They were included in the questionnaire precisely because prototypical emotions are characteristic of dramatic roles. Negative prototypical emotions occurred in the chosen scenes more often and in greater intensity than positive prototypical emotions. Character roles contained *disgust*, *fear*, *anger*, and/or *sorrow* in 75% of the scenes.

One of actor Warre Borgmans' shortcomings or frustrations is that he is too preoccupied with task-emotions: 'While I really would like to blend completely with what has to be played, actually fuse with the character (...) I used to think, and with experience I have learned it isn't completely true, but I used to believe that great actors or actresses only experienced that intense stage reality, and nothing but that. Now, after talking to them and through my own experience, I know that is not true. And thank goodness, since I don't think you could cope if it were.

(Warre Borgmans in the documentary, *Acteurs spelen emoties* [Actors Acting Emotions], NPS 1995)

Joy was the least-frequently intended character-emotion (in only 35% of the chosen scenes) and it seemed to be more difficult for actors to impersonate happy and positive emotions successfully.[17] Each of the prototypical emotions listed in the questionnaire was cited often as an emotion to be portrayed in the recalled roles. The survey results were therefore valid for a wide range of emotions impersonated in characters and for a variety of scenes. It also appeared that emotions were not portrayed serially, but rather in all sorts of combinations. Usually negative or unpleasant emotions are dominant in character roles and dramatic situations because character-emotions are often related to threatened interests, goals, or motives.

Acting out character-impulses seems to be an important element in conveying the intended character-emotions to the audience. This is reminiscent of the emphasis Stanislavsky placed on evoking impulses which fit the character-emotions. Characters always 'want' something; they are highly motivated as they strive for specific goals. Representing action tendencies is also an important source of information for the audience. In as much as the survey revealed a connection between the portrayed character-emotions and the portrayed character-tendencies, this followed the same pattern as emotions in daily life. There was some divergence from the normal pattern however, because character-emotions were linked to approach behavior, aimed at avoiding or removing the 'obstacle' in the path of the desired goal.

Contrary to expectations, task-emotions were also consistently attributed to characters and with a good degree of intensity. *Concentration*, *challenge*, and *feeling strong* were the frequently 'felt' emotions for both the majority of characters and actors. There was, however, no question of a significant correlation between the actor and the character concerning emotions in this category (and can therefore not be interpreted as indicating 'involvement'). Furthermore, these emotions in the characters did not relate to the character-tendencies. In other words, the task-emotions the actors themselves experienced were on another level than the emotions falling into the category of task-emotions which were attributed to the character. I did not expect that characters would 'have' task-emotions when the questionnaire was designed; this still seemed implausible upon reviewing the results. It was anticipated that the category of prototypical emotions would specifically relate to the emotions intended in character portrayals.

These were indeed the emotions that are most often portrayed while performing roles. It would not be correct to conclude that the task-emotions attributed to characters were then typical character-emotions. Such a conclusion would also not be supported by dramatic literature, which seldom mentions these emotions as character-emotions.

While actors did attribute task-emotions to their characters, this might have occurred because characters typically reach their goals in dramatic situations by executing 'tasks'. This type of emotion in the character context would involve fundamentally different objects than the task-emotions of actors. The words listed as descriptions of emotions cannot as such be put into single, strict categories. The distinction between a prototypical emotion and a task-emotion is ultimately based on the object of the emotion; e.g., the pleasure impersonated in a character is of a very different nature than the pleasure an actor has in performance. As far as the intensity of 'task-emotions' of characters is similar to that of actors, this cannot be interpreted as a similarity between portrayed character-emotions and experienced actors' emotions, since the two are not correlated after all. It could be incidental or a by-product of the actor's task-emotions, independent of the dramatic, goal-oriented behavior displayed in the character. One explanation in line with task-emotion theory is that actors might have attributed emotions that fall into the category of task-emotions to their characters because the actors employed or transformed their task-emotions to portray character-emotions. The task-emotion theory assumes that actors use their task-emotions and related action tendencies, tailoring them to the particular role portrayal.

8.5   The Function of Task-Emotions

The way actors so clearly indicated experiencing and using task-emotions gives an impression of how task-emotions function in shaping character-emotions. In response to questions about the acting styles used, they indicated that the excitement and pleasure found in acting supported their portrayal of character-emotions. Assuming that task-emotions play a crucial part in impersonating character-emotions and are perhaps conditional to believable and convincing acting also does justice to the general principle of the functionality of emotions. According to current emotion psychology, emotions are now considered having a function in satisfying the individual's concerns. The actors' concerns during performance relate to the acting tasks. Actors therefore use task-emotions to flesh out character-emotions, transforming task-emotions to support their characters. Task-emotions do not have characteristic facial expressions and cannot be recognized by their appearance, but they are accompanied by increased action readiness. In this way the outwardly 'empty' behavior of characters is sustained by the actors' own relevant emotions, which creates or strengthens the illusion of spontaneous character-emotions for the audience.

The actors' task-emotions are activated during performance because the acting situation addresses concerns relevant to their profession. The threat to, or satisfaction of, at least four relevant concerns – competence, self-image, sensation seeking, and esthetic concerns – hangs in the balance (chapter four). The most important contributing components to this situation are: Objectivity, reality, demand character, difficulty, valence, urgency, controllability, and familiarity. These components come into play as a result of having to perform difficult tasks for an expectant and judgmental audience.

The actors' task-emotions are generally related to a challenging situation and are expressed in various positive or pleasant emotions. Character-emotions are generally related to situations that are threatening for the character. The hypothesis that actors use, transform, or shape their task-emotions to facilitate role play is supported by the fact that threatening and challenging situations have many features in common: Only the components control and valence differ (4.4). Variations in the levels of these two components account for the difference between threat and challenge. A low level of control over the situation and negative valence as to its expected outcome lead to feeling threatened. Challenge, on the other hand, results from a high level of control and positive valence as to the outcome of the situation. In other words, belief in being able to cope with the situation and the promise of satisfying concerns successfully will make a situation challenging instead of threatening. The action tendencies resulting from threat and challenge point in opposite directions when these emotions arise in real life situations. A feature of characters in dramatic situations, however, is that they do not avoid conflict and generally confront threats head on. Otherwise the situation would cease to be 'dramatic'. The actors' responses suggested this, since the most frequently cited impulses for both characters and actors were *to go for it* and *to overcome difficulties*. The intensity of the tendencies in actors and characters was similar, but there was no statistically strong correlation between them.

It is important for the task-emotion theory that the survey revealed a link between *negative* character-emotions and the tendency to approach in characters, just as the actors' *positive* task-emotions were, as predicted, linked to approach tendencies. The characters' tendency to approach an object or obstacle serves to remove or attack it. These results support the thought that the actors' task-emotions result in action tendencies which pull in the same direction as the characters' action tendencies; approach tendencies coincide in actors and characters and therefore add extra strength to the portrayal. It is not precisely clear how actors use task-emotions to shape character-emotions, nor how this possibly relates to audience perception of emotions or task-emotions, nor the way the audience interprets these as part of the character-emotions. Perhaps we perceive that someone has indeed become emotional. What an audience perceives of the actors' task-emotions is an increased readiness to take action, an open-eyed alertness and perhaps a keen focus on a particular goal. We notice attention fixated on the object of emotion and the intent of the impulse to act.

The broadest division in action-tendencies is between approach and avoidance, which provide a general indication of the underlying emotion. We cannot always judge what the exact emotion is without additional contextual information. When audiences try to discern whether someone really 'has' an emotion, they appear to not pay attention to the relevant signals.[18] Experiments which tested the perception of emotional facial expression, revealed that test subjects recognized pretended expressions better than spontaneously aroused emotional ex-

> While on stage I would focus my glance on a nail in the stage floor, in order not to sway from standing perpendicularly.
> (American respondent-actor, dated November 29, 1995)

pressions.[19] Moreover, audiences mainly deduce a particular emotion from contextual information: Information about the character's goals, concerns, and motives, as well as the situation they are in and the relationships between the characters. General knowledge about emotions and human behavior, and each person's own experience with emotional expressions in

> It seems to have become a fashionable phrase: 'To be' onstage. The actor is no longer seen as a professional transformer, but an acting personality. The character forms a transparent 'wall' through which the physical and spiritual autobiography of the actor shines, so to say.
> (*Toneel Theatraal*, September 1996: 12)

daily life, contribute considerably to interpreting other people's behavior. Think for example of how convincing cartoon figures or film 'creatures' like E.T. are when given a 'suitable' dramatic context; all they need are a few human features.

The indications are that most actors do not experience the emotions they act as characters – the point is that they do not actually need to. To be believable, it is important that the traits and behaviors displayed are consistent with the presented situations, goals, and motives. This implies that it is more important for the actor (and director) to insure that information conveyed through various channels is consistent, at least if the aim is to put across believable character-emotions on the stage and not to overly confuse audiences about which emotion is intended. Thus it is important that spoken text, movement direction, the created situation, and the actor's various means of expression be congruent; that his gait, for example, be just as drunken as his glance. The 'closer' the medium (for example a filmed close-up) the narrower the margin for discrepancy and the more precision and detail is desired in minute aspects of behavior (unless the discrepancy is intentional and intended to induce a degree of alienation).

The argument was made (in chapter four) that the 'radiance' of task-emotions can contribute to the actor's presence, an important ingredient for making acting believable and convincing. But one also begins to wonder precisely how actors achieve or create presence onstage. Is there a connection between 'flow' and 'presence'? This study argues that there is and that the link is formed by the right balance between the required level of skills and the risk of failure. This equilibrium forms the condition for an optimal sensation of flow, the illusion professionals give of being able to accomplish obviously difficult tasks effortlessly. We, the audience, often praise a performance precisely because we 'forget' that it is 'make believe' while we were watching. This compares to the ease with which athletes break records or musicians give great performances (3.6). For now, 'presence' can be understood as being the 'personal radiance' of an actor, supported by the 'radiance' of his task-emotions.

In the context of the theory developed in this book, further research regarding to what extent task-emotions function in the creation of the illusion of spontaneity on stage could yield important results. In addition it will be important to study the extent to which they contribute to the conviction of the performance and the presence of the performer. If task-emotions do indeed play the role I think they do in portraying characters during performance, it then becomes important to take them into account while rehearsing the role. The task-emotion theory is mainly a theory about acting emotions *during a performance*, while most accepted views on acting concentrate mainly on the *rehearsal process*. The accepted theories are mainly methods to train actors and to prepare them for their role in the performance. They are noted for their *practical* nature and for their lack of *theoretical* development. The theater critic, scholar, and actor Richard Hornby, has campaigned strongly against this situation in *The End of Acting*. To him it is high time that we begin to analyze the art of acting, and elevate stage acting (back) up to the level of a 'high art' form.

8.6   Aspects of Acting Styles

When actors indicated a preference for an involvement style, this was not necessarily an indication that they experienced character-emotions themselves, as the results of this study showed. The reverse was also not true: If actors indicated having emotions which were more or less similar to their characters', this did not necessarily indicate a preference for an involvement style. These results are actually rather surprising since it is precisely this aspect of acting which has for so long been the subject of heated debate. It renders the controversy between involvement and detachment obsolete. In theater practice involvement and detachment are probably interpreted and applied quite differently from what the respective theories advocate. This seemed particularly true for involvement, since actors with a relatively strong affinity for this style did not let themselves become so 'carried away' or 'like' the character that they themselves experienced emotions similar to the character-emotions they were portraying. The acting styles of involvement and detachment appeared not to be in opposition to each other and it was not possible to make a clear distinction between involvement and detachment.

It has become clear that there is not an either/or situation, but that ingredients of both acting styles are blended into an acting performance. Instead of involvement *versus* detachment, there seems to be a general way of acting, in the sense that there are commonly held views about how acting tasks should be executed in designing character-emotions. These views are reflected in four aspects of the acting style, which were evident in the analyses of the actors' responses. Features specific to one style could perhaps be recognized by the degree to which one of the aspects was applied, or thought to be suitable for a particular production.

The aspects of acting styles which were endorsed by a majority of professional actors were 'applying task-emotions' and 'applying technical skills' to play their characters. Involvement aspects were applied to varying degrees. In other words, actors with a predominant involvement orientation found task-emotions and technical skills just as important as the detachment actors. Within the involvement *theory*, a command of technical skills is considered to be less important than 'getting into' the emotions of the character. In practice, however, professional command of acting techniques appeared to be important for nearly all actors, regardless of their affinity for a particular acting style. Though there was some difference in the degree of importance they

> I think that it is very misleading to try to classify actors as outward and technical versus into it and emotional. In my experience the best actors work *both ways*, although they start from very different positions. A technically brilliant actor has to fill his model with emotions. An emotionally full actor will have to have the technique to repeat it when he/she's got it, and to figure out how he or she fits into the whole production. I'll bet Travolta feels his role like crazy *and* knows *exactly* how he looks at a given moment.
>
> (American respondent-actress, dated December 8, 1995)

attached to this aspect. Depending on the skills required, or the particular circumstances of the scene and the production, different aspects can be added or emphasized. Depending on the form, the genre, the text, and so on, more specific elements of detachment or involvement may be called for. Likewise, the acting style that is applied can be dependent upon the specific emotions that are to be portrayed. It is imaginable that more involvement aspects might be applied to playing pleasant emotions, because these are similar to the task-emotions actors experience. On the other hand, more sorrowful or negative emotions might call for other aspects of 'the' acting style. There are no clear indications for this possibility in the results.

The acting style applied did not seem to be specific to an individual or 'cast in stone'. Professional actors indicated that their style was determined to a great extent by the director or the company they were with. Different media might also emphasize different aspects of acting styles. An involvement style was more often ascribed to (international) film actors than to (national) stage actors, as discussed in section 8.2, though this need not be attributed exclusively to the medium. All aspects of acting styles were attributed to star actors in relatively strong numbers. Apparently, professional actors should be in command of each of the four aspects of the acting styles to meet the demands in a specific production.

Involvement as an aspect of one's acting style onstage apparently must not be construed as 'identification', in the sense that an actor would invoke emotions similar to the character-emotions in himself. Involvement aspects like 'feeling akin to the character' and 'letting oneself be carried away by the portrayed character-emotions' seemed to help a number of actors with character portrayal, but actors did not go so far as to actually experience the emotions they impersonated. It was already mentioned in chapter three that advocates of the involvement theory do not deny the involvement actors need to design the role technically, but their main goal is immersion in the character. The task-emotion theory proposes that actors will use their task-emotions regardless of their statements about more specific styles of acting. The general implication is that we should interpret involvement and detachment in *relative* terms. In determining whether an actor was oriented toward involvement or detachment, this study took this into account (7.5). Involvement and detachment have thus lost their (original) meaning in contemporary theater practice.

The same arguments for a more balanced view on acting styles during performance will also be valid for the *period of preparation*. Each of the distinct aspects of the various acting styles will be useful to actors during rehearsals. I presume that a number of aspects during the *preparation* will also be valid for all actors, regardless of specific opinions on style, because several common *acting tasks* are found within the various stylistic views. While comparing the different views on acting (chapter three) four acting tasks emerged which are necessary for playing character-emotions. The acting tasks are related to task requirements and are apparently the same for all actors. The first task is to design an inner model as a basis for building distinctive character-emotions. The second

> For me there are tremendous differences between stage and film acting. Preparations, style, and feelings while performing, are very different for me.
>
> (American respondent-actor, dated December 19, 1995)

task requires an actor to be able to re-peat these within a more or less agreed form. A third task is to make the por-trayal of a character-emotion believable and convincing. Finally, the actor's fourth task is to create an illusion of spontaneity and presence.

I suspect that different aspects of the different acting styles serve differ-ent acting tasks. In this way, involve-ment aspects such as 'feeling like the character' and 'getting carried away by the character-emotion' can help de-sign an inner model in the rehearsal phase. According to the involvement theory these aspects are also necessary for the believability and the repeatability of the portrayal of character-emotions (chapter three). Advocates of involvement find the acting style aspect 'external or technical design' subordinate for the accomplishment of the acting task 'repeatability of the portrayal' throughout many performances; with advocates of the detachment theory or the task-emotion theory, the reverse is true. The task-emotion theory proposes that making character-emotions believable and convincing is mainly a matter of sending coherent signals and information through various channels. The il-lusion of spontaneity, according to the task-emotion theory, depends less on invoking the actor's emotional experiences, and more on having presence. The 'radiance' of task-emotions probably plays an important part in this. In other words, the acting style aspect of 'applying task-emotions' seems to relate to the fourth acting task.

There will be slight differences among actors in the *degree* of importance or suit-ability they attach to each of the acting tasks or aspects of style. During preparation, differences in acting methods will become visible as shifts of accent, emphasizing a particular aspect of style. This as a result of differing opinions as to how an actor can best achieve his tasks. The general view that involvement in characters is important during rehearsal, possibly refers to designing the inner model. Involvement can pro-vide the necessary insights into emotions. One important condition for being able to evoke emotion by using the imagination is that *actual* situational components do not put relevant concerns at stake. For instance, during a performance, the actors' actual task concerns in the acting situation would prevent them from 'reliving' character-emotions. While acting in 'concern-free' situations, which can exist in a rehearsal, it is possible to evoke 'emotions' through involvement techniques. In section 4.5 it was noted that 'involving oneself in emotions' actually means 'involving oneself in emo-tional *situations*'. The question of which emotions belong to the character is thereby translated into questions about his goals, motives, and concerns; his relationship with his surroundings and co-characters; the relevant components in the dramatic situation and the possibilities the situation offers, to the character, to reach his goals.

(Dutch) director Guy Cassiers collaborates frequently with video artist, Walter Verdin, who made the slide projections for *Angels in America*. *De pijl van de tijd*, produced in 1994 by the Kaaitheatre in Brussels, used his video images as antagonists for the actors. Using advanced techniques, computer-driven projections, and sensu-sound, Cassiers developed a new theater language. He has a noticeable preference for film scenarios or novels instead of theatrical scripts. He blends art forms, renewing and enriching the theater. His new post [as artistic director of the RO theater in Rotterdam EK] will hopefully not deter him from this development.

(Marian Buijs on theatermaker Guy Cassiers, *de Volkskrant*, June 13, 1997)

Figure 8.1: A Model of the Acting Process Based on the Task-Emotion Theory

levels of enactment	acting style aspects		task demands for executing acting tasks		acting tasks
(1) private person	carried away by character-emotions	→	knowledge of everyday emotions	→	creating a model of the intended character-emotions in the imagination
(2) inner model	resemblance between actor and character	→	suitability and flexibility of the expressive instrument	→	portray believable and convincing emotional expressions
(3) character portrayal	technical design	→	making character-behavior automatic	→	repeat a more or less fixed form
(4) actor-craftsman	applying task-emotions	→	achieving presence	→	creating the illusion of spontaneity

The levels are interrelated and ordered hierarchically. The first level (1) is the most basic and this forms the basis for building the higher levels. Completing acting tasks and the skills demanded on the fourth level (4) depends on completing the tasks and skills on the previous levels. Feedback on every level influences adjustments on other levels. During a performance audiences will perceive the different levels of the acting process as an integrated whole, while the actor is more or less conscious of operating on four levels simultaneously.

Perhaps, acting styles could be better contrasted along lines other than their handling of emotion (which is not excluded by the above). Acting is, after all, not just limited to portraying character-emotions. One might even question whether this aspect is still a predominant one in contemporary theater. Many theater forms prefer conveying ideas or concepts instead of depicting specific character-emotions. Experimental theater forms, in particular, often emphasize design aspects. One also finds art forms where elements of visual arts and music are combined to form multimedia art. In this kind of experimental work, new rules govern conventions or aspects of the acting styles to achieve certain effects in the audience.

8.7   A Model of the Acting Process

The theoretical and empirical analysis of acting emotions onstage offers the chance to bridge the gap between views in diverse theories and views in theater practice. In figure 8.1 the various aspects of acting discussed in this book are brought together in a model of the acting process, based on the task-emotion theory. The levels of enactment for the actor and the emotional layers are related to the four aspects of acting styles and to the task demands or the acting tasks.

On the first level of enactment, in figure 8.1, the actor as a private person can let himself be carried away by character-emotions through involvement. Learning about emotions from daily life is a necessary task requirement in order to form a model of the intended character-emotions in the imagination. On the level of the inner model, the second level of enactment, the resemblance between actor and character supports the suitability of his expressive instrument, which must be flexible in order to portray believable and convincing emotional expressions suited to the inner model. On the third level of enactment, the level of the portrayed character, technical design helps to make character behavior constant, achieving a more or less fixed form which can be repeated throughout a series of performances. Although various approaches to acting implicitly agree on these four acting tasks, they differ in the *way* the actor reaches an optimal performance. Discussions and differences between the various acting styles become clearest when interpreting the fourth acting task and the accompanying task demands: How to create the illusion of spontaneity and achieve a quality of presence.

1. According to the involvement style of acting, the actor would have to invoke his own private emotions, which resemble those of the character-emotions to be portrayed.

2. According to the detachment style of acting, a convincing portrayal of character-emotions requires that the concerns, goals, and motives of the character are made clear to the audience, as well as the demands that the dramatic context makes on the character. The illusion of spontaneity is achieved through the technical design of the character's behavior.

3. The acting style of self-expression seeks the illusion of spontaneity in achieving presence by presenting the 'real life' experience of the actors themselves; the character is adapted to the actor to assist the expression of the actor's 'inner self'.

4. According to the task-emotion theory, the actor achieves presence by shaping (or transforming) the existing task-emotions and the 'radiance' of his task-emotions and

related action tendencies. These existing emotions support the illusion of spontaneity and 'real' character-emotions. This is the point where the task-emotion theory provides greater understanding and insight into acting.

The illusion of spontaneity. In light of the preceding arguments, how can the continued persistence of the idea that the illusion of spontaneity can only be achieved if the actor is carried away by character-emotions be explained? There are several possible explanations for why actors (and spectators) exchange or confuse the authentic emotional experiences the actor has onstage with the character-emotions he impersonates.

1. The notion of task-emotions is not a common view. For this reason, the existence of task-emotions, and their accompanying (physiological) phenomena can be interpreted, or rather misinterpreted, as experiencing character-emotions.

2. The act of imitating or impersonating emotional expressions provokes physiological activation. This 'excitement' can be attributed to, or experienced as, an effect of becoming involved in character-emotions.

3. To deduce what emotions are happening in others, we, as observers, must trust the sincerity of emotional expressions. Emotions carry information about concerns and motives for individual behavior and provide information about relationships. When an emotional expression looks real, we assume that it is real, that the emotional expression is rooted in an authentic emotion (we have to trust our feelings, since we would not otherwise know when we were being mislead). An analysis of acting is usually conducted from a spectator perspective.

4. The fourth explanation for this exchange or confusion is that accepted acting theories do not make a clear distinction between rehearsal and performance. During rehearsals it can be helpful to invoke private emotions in order to become immersed in

Spontaneous (a) facial expression of happiness (with a spark of posedness?) of actor Felix-jan Kuypers, directly after the performance *Om de liefde van Laurentia*, 1997.

character-emotions. By looking for similarities between him-/herself and the character, an actor can gain insight into real life emotions which may help him/her create an inner model of the intended character-emotions. During a *performance*, however, the demands of the actual context – acting in front of an audience – prevent the actor from losing himself in character-emotions. In studying the acting process, it is important to separate illusion from reality. Every drama school knows that illusion can actually become a dangerous reality. Beginning actors have experienced problems, even trauma, because they can no longer separate fiction from reality. In some fairly extreme cases, some actors have required psychiatric treatment.

Rehearsals also need to be distinguished from live performances. Most existing acting theory describes a rehearsal method to reach an accurate portrayal. These methods barely touch on acting in performance. To develop an acting theory it is vital to demystify acting; this book attempts to establish a point of departure for this project. Although the task-emotion theory is limited to acting *emotions* on stage, the theory is, in principle, also valid for disciplines where no emotions are portrayed. After all, the specific demands of performing for an audience are pivotal to every performing arts discipline; public performance is one of the most enervating and demanding situations for anyone – in emotional terms. Craftsmanship is fundamental to every artistic profession. The pleasure of performing is, in part, based on commanding this risky undertaking. That goes for anyone who stands in the spotlight.

Notes

Chapter 1

1. Original: 'C'est l'extrême sensibilité qui fait les acteurs médiocres; c'est la sensibilité médiocre qui fait la multitude des mauvais acteurs et c'est le manque absolu de sensibilité qui prépare les acteurs sublimes' (Diderot 1959: 313).
2. Original: '...il y a dans la langue technique du théatre une latitude, un vague assez considerable pour que des hommes sensés, des opinions diamétralement opposées, croient y reconnaitre la lumière de l'évidence' (Diderot 1959: 305).
3. All references to the actor, he, or him also apply equally to the actress, she or her.

Chapter 2

1. In 1747 R. de Saint-Albine's *Le Comédien* appeared, in which it is stated that an actor should actually experience the emotions of the character. Fr. Riccoboni takes an opposing view in *L'art du Théatre* (1750). In the same year in England, *The Actor* appears, anonymously (but likely written by John Hill); it seems to be an edited translation of *Le Comédien* with the 'emotionalist' view. The work *Garrick ou les Acteurs Anglais* by Sticotti (1769) would be a new version, translated back to the French, to which Diderot reacts (Tort 1980). For extensive bibliographical information see further the journal *Diderot Studies* (from 1949 to present) and the substantial bibliographical overview of publications about Diderot by F.A. Spear compiled in 1980 (supplement 1988). In addition one can find extensive bibliographical information with accompanying texts in, among others, Chouillet (1977) and in a completely different way in Mortier and Mat (1985). Chouillet is more akin to biography, while Mortier and Mat sketch a picture of Diderot and 231 of his contemporaries with a thematic description of their work. Wilson (1961) seems to be a well-respected source for biographical data on Diderot. In, among others, Wartofsky (1952), Wilson (1961), Hazard (1973), and Verbeek (1978; 1980) one finds descriptions of Diderot's philosophical views and also Oustinoff (1971) provides information on the work of Diderot.
2. The last round of the discussion between the speakers in *Paradoxe sur le Comédien* can be explained by these flukes. Here Diderot claims to have seen only one or two perfectly performed plays: '...a mediocre piece and mediocre actors' (1985: 114). After all, Diderot refers many times to the few sublime moments of Dumesnil and the debuting actresses (e.g., 1985: 52, 54), besides speaking repeatedly of his disgust about what he sees on stage (1985: 100, 102-104, 111). I therefore do not share Hogendoorn's interpretation (1985: 30) that Diderot

may doubt the validity of his own extreme paradoxical standpoint or that this can be considered as a 'traditionally rhetorical' finish.

3. Roach (1981, 1985), Rovit (1989), and Hogendoorn (1985) reduce the many arguments to two main ones. Binet (1896) and Villiers (1942) distinguish six and seven main arguments respectively, in Diderot's Paradoxe, whereby many arguments are more or less similar. Nearly all of these, however, can be classified under one of the two main arguments named by Roach. Hogendoorn places the separate argument for professional experience cited by Villiers under his first main argument.

4. Original: 'l'une: une actrice, toute d'étude et d'art; l'autre: une actrice, toute de tempérament' (Goncourt 1911: 1-2).

5. For a further discussion of character portraits of idealized types see Barnett (1987: 139), Rougemont (1988), Fischer-Lichte (1983), and Jomaron (1992).

6. See Dumesnil (1823: 53).

7. Discussions of French acting styles in the eighteenth century can be found in Burgund (1931), Szondi (1984), Roach (1985), Barnett (1987), Rougemont (1988), and Jomaron (1992).

8. The theater historian Barnett (1987) mainly gives examples of the declamation rules. He describes these in detail, so that contemporary actors can make the style their own.

9. Diderot's ideas about the genre serieux are first expressed in his Entretiens (Diderot 1757), according to Mortier and Mat (1985).

10. Diderot in Szondi (1984: 38).

11. See for example Hazard (1973: 1963), Kimble and Schlesinger (1985), and Pott (1922: 20).

12. As appears from the words he puts in the mouth of The Nephew of Rameau (1761), among others. See for the temperament doctrine for example Verbeek (1977) and Kouwer (1978).

13. While Diderot is radically opposed to the man-machine concept he does acknowledge the possibility of mechanical or automatic processes, but man as a mere pre-programmed machine – no: 'Diderot sees clearly that nature is a process, not a machine' (Barzun 1986: 21). In Paradoxe sur le Comédien and The Dream of d'Alembert, which are from the same period, Diderot's ideas about the unity of body and spirit are clearly expressed. For Diderot, man is definitely not a machine, there can be no doubt about that when he appeals to the reader with the words: 'Aie toujours présent à l'esprit que la Nature n'est pas Dieu, qu'un homme n'est pas une machine, qu'une hypothèse n'est pas un fait' [Have always presence of mind since Nature is not the Lord, man is not a machine, a hypothesis is not a fact] (Diderot 1753: 28). Nevertheless, the man-as-machine view, following Descartes and LaMettrie, is often ascribed to Diderot (e.g., Hogendoorn 1985: 19; Roach 1981, 1985). Roach for example writes that Diderot distances himself from Cartesian dualism, but continues to use the man-machine terminology in reference to Diderot. That Diderot rejects the man as machine idea is most sharply expressed in 'Réfutation de l'ouvrage d'Helvetius intitulé De l'Homme' (1772), a criticism of the work of Helvétius [1715-1771]: '...in his treatise De l'Homme Diderot cried out: "I am not a machine! I am a man and want causes adequate to man."' (Barzun 1986: 19). Along with Verbeek I am therefore surprised that Diderot's views are repeatedly mentioned in a single breath with Descartes' mechanism and dualism (Verbeek 1978: 112). Interesting, concise essays with various views can be found in Wartofsky (1952) and Vartanian (1983).

14. Roach says it as follows: 'Thus the diaphragm, though a principal organ of sensibility having close ties to the mind of an average man, can be isolated in the bodily system of the *genius*' (Roach 1981: 63).

15. Diderot himself: '...*la sensibilité vraie et la sensibilité jouée sont deux choses fort différentes (...) Les images des passions au théatre n'en sont donc pas les vraies images*' (Diderot 1959: 357; 1985: 58).

16. Ehrard in Chouillet (1973: 390). See for definitions of the French term '*nature*' at the end of the eighteenth and the beginning of the nineteenth century Calzolari (1984), Chouillet (1973: 390), Hazard (1973: 387), Verbeek (1977: 12) and Barzun (1986).

17. See for the meanings of the term 'sensibilité' Verbeek (1980: 117).

18. The French word '*idéal*' refers here to the imagination and not to the Dutch and English term 'ideal' or 'ideally'. I will therefore use the term 'inner model' instead of the more literal translation 'ideal model' (as in Konijn 1994).

19. Loy (in Nakagawa et. al., 1984) suggests that a translation of the terms is often impossible and that they must be recreated, but that even that results in inaccuracy and modernization. Calzolari points out the importance of positioning within a (philosophical) historical context, but I do not share the conclusion he finally makes: '*le grand comédien n'existe que dans ce jeu linguistique infini*' [*The great actor exists only in this endless linguistic game*] (1984: 126).

20. Regarding the dilemma of the actor, for example, Emmet (1975), Constantinidis (1988), Rovit (1989: 6), De Leeuwe (1981), and Worthen (1984).

21. In Brook (1968: 131). Further, Brynner in Chekhov (1953: 10), Fink (1980), Brook (1968: 113-114) and Rovit (1989).

22. The five levels which Passow (1992: 85-86) distinguishes are extensions of this. The level of the audience, which Passow adds, is not included in the study.

23. Concerning character-emotions, a distinction can also be made between the emotions which are indicated for the character, according to a specific interpretation of the text, *and* the emotions which are, in the end, portrayed in the performance. I presume that the emotions indicated as belonging to the character, according to an interpretation of the text and/or the author, will be handled during rehearsals and that the choice to present certain emotions is part of the intended emotions or the '*modèle idéal*'.

Chapter 3

1. A number of authors and practitioners are combined under a single acting style due to the context of their statements from which it can be concluded that they mean more or less the same thing, especially concerning the emotions of actor and character. Disregarding their points of difference is not to suggest that these are insignificant, but that they require a more subtle description than the aim of this study demands. The many interpretations of the work of Stanislavsky illustrate this point (see Kesting 1989, Lazarowicz 1991, Flaherty 1990, and Strasberg 1988).

2. Literature on the involvement style of acting: Stanislavsky (1985; 1989; 1991), Strasberg (1988), Worthen (1984), Hogendoorn (1985), Constantinidis (1988), Kesting (1989), Flaherty (1990), Lazarowicz (1991), Lazarowicz and Balme (1991: 256-270), and Pelias (1991).

3. One can argue here that the work *An Actor Prepares* (1985; 1936) belongs to Stanislavsky's early work (and moreover has been 'Americanized' by Ms. Hapgood; Stanislavsky Congress Paris, November 1988), but in his later work as well the 'highest goal' for him remained to arouse

personal emotions analogous to those of the character (Stanislavsky 1989; 1991). Extensive study and practice are necessary, according to the later Stanislavsky, 'in order that at a later stage the emotions of the actor are automatically sincere and lifelike' (1991: 14). It is principally the tactical method to achieve this which he developed further. Moreover *An Actor Prepares* is the best known and most used work in the practice of theater.

4. Pavlov did an experiment with a dog, in which he combined feeding with the ringing of a bell. After a while, the mere ringing of the bell caused the dog to react by salivating. Roach, among others, refers to this arousal of an automatic reflex by means of conditioning (1985), after psychological use. Strasberg too refers explicitly to the conditioning of actors, following Pavlov's lead.

5. In Schechner (1964) and Barba and Savarese (1991).

6. Literature on the style of detachment: Brecht (1967-1968), Lazarowicz and Balme (1991), Hoffmeier (1992), and Savona (1991).

7. See Brecht (1967: 312).

8. See Meyerhold (1922), Rudnitsky (1981), Picon-Vallin (1990), Bogdanov (1991), Braun (1994), and Pesochinsky (1992; translated by Drannikova and edited by Konijn, forthcoming). As with Stanislavsky, there are more interpretations of Meyerhold's views on theater. Many of them are limited to his 'biomechanical exercises' (e.g., Gordon 1974), which are only a small part of his work – these are intended as tools for shaping and training the actor's instrument.

9. Constantinidis (1988: 70) also points out that potentially real personal feelings in the actor will not per se influence the reaction of the audience.

10. A comparison between dramatic roles and social roles may be found in Konijn (1985).

11. The similarity between Kirby, Hogendoorn, and Constantinidis is that character in the traditional sense disappears from view. Hogendoorn speaks in this context of the autonomy of acting (1978: 137), Kirby of 'simple acting' (1972: 9), and Constantinidis of 'hypnotic', 'bewitched' and 'ecstatic acting' (1988: 75).

12. Many forms of the style of self-expression ascribe to the opinions of Grotowski and Artaud; here we combine the various movements and nuances, because all consider 'the expression of the self' a central feature.

13. Rijnders in Freriks and Rijnders (1992: 30).

14. In Schechner and Appel (1990: 30).

15. Respectively in Hogendoorn (1985: 34), Rovit (1989: 15, 94) and Watson (1988: 310, 311).

16. Hogendoorn also states that the double consciousness is made up of different components in the different theories of acting.

17. In Villiers (1942: 195, 202-209).

18. In Grotowski (1968: 142) and also in Brook (1968). In Barba (1991) the distilled form contains 'extra daily techniques'. Villiers speaks in this context of 'the phase of clarification of the character' (1942: 144) and Constantinidis of the 'prompt-copy subsystem' (1988; 1986).

19. In Grotowski (1968: 133-224).

20. Comparable statements can be found in Roach (1985: 133, 151) and Villiers (1942: 173; 1968: 14, 36).

21. See Hoffmeier (1992) and Lazarowicz (1991).

22. In Stanislavsky (1989: 247, 252; 1991: 55).

23. In Brook (1968: 32-34, 64).

24. In Stanislavsky (1989: 209; 1991: 203).

25. Bishop (1988: 122, 123) discusses how the theories of Stanislavsky, Brecht, and Grotowski, among others, all have the concept of presence as a common foundation.

26. It is noteworthy that precisely the capacity to 'leave behind an unforgettable impression' is the most important criteria to determine the highest rank of actors in the collective (bargaining) contract for professional actors in the Netherlands (personal communication with League of Theater Company Directors, 1991).

27. For example Roach (1985).

28. Respectively in Barba and Savarese: 'direct the spectators attention' (1991: 110), Brook (1968: 108) and Grotowski (1968: 199).

29. Schoenmakers (1986) did a study of the reception process using the film *Opname*, a film by the Dutch theater group Het Werktheater about a man who becomes incurably sick. The study shows that the stronger the experience of grief in the spectator, the greater the score for appreciation of the film.

30. In Esslin (1987: 78). Also in Brook (1968: 123-124).

31. This remark requires to mention that acting has little to do with lying (see also Kirby 1987: 7, 8). The intention to lie is the insincere deception of the 'spectator' (the communication partner in a social context), who is unaware of the deception (see Ekman 1982). With acting, on the other hand, the intention is to achieve an effect in the spectator within a theatrical context, from artistic motives. In this sense the actor is sincere: Doing his best to offer the spectator what he came for (drama!). The spectator is aware of the level of illusion in the presentation (though there are some borderline cases which can be cited from theater history; see Schechner in Schechner and Appel, 1990: 23). He comes to be 'misled' and usually pays for it. No one has ever paid to watch a liar.

32. See Tan (1996: 77-81).

33. See for example Schechner and Appel (1990: 27). In a recent study the different perspectives on perceiving a character are systematically expounded (Konijn and Hoorn, 1999). Konijn (1999) shows evidence that theater spectators experienced empathy and task emotions equally, but identificatory emotions hardly played a role.

34. See the interdisciplinary studies of Hoorn and Konijn, (1999a) 'Perceiving and experiencing fictional characters: Theoretical background (part I)' and Hoorn and Konijn, (1999b) 'Perceiving and experiencing fictional characters: Building a model (part II)'.

Chapter 4

1. The elaboration of emotion theory in this chapter is largely based on Frijda (1986; 1988) and Tan (1996). Frijda (1988) develops the formulation of 'the laws of emotions', which are not yet found in *The Emotions* (1986). The emotions of spectators will only be handled summarily from the perspective of cognitive emotions. Audience emotions are handled extensively by Schoenmakers (1988; 1990; 1992), Tan (1996), and Van Vliet, although these concern mainly film viewers. Hoorn and Konijn (1999a; 1999b) present an integrated interdisciplinary model of the spectators' perception and experience of fictional characters.

2. In Baker (1919: 46) and Schoenmakers (1989: 33).

3. Freriks in Freriks and Rijnders (1992: 56). See also Hoffmeier (1992).

4. Regarding competence see Frijda (1986: 320-322), Lazarus (1980), Zajonc (1965), Zajonc and Sales (1966), and Bond & Titus (1983; also in 3.5.3). Kuypers and Bengston (1983) discussed the importance of an adequate 'role performance', 'the capacity to adapt', and 'experienced mastery' in relation to the concept of competence.

5. This concerns here the studies of Latané and Harkins (1976; 1981), Konijn (1992), Bond and Titus (1983), Jackson and Latané (1981), Bode and Brutten (1963), Weisweiler (1983), Konijn (1991), Zuckerman et al. (1980), Piët (1986), and Frijda (1986: 347 – 349).

6. For a general discussion of these concerns, see Frijda (1986: 349).

7. A discussion of the components for the general human emotions in daily life is found in Frijda (1986: 205 – 208).

8. See also Folkman, Lazarus, Dunkel-Schetter et al. (1986), Lazarus and Folkman (1984), Lazarus and Folkman (1988), Parkes (1984), McCrae (1984), Schulz (1987), and Gallagher (1990).

9. See Frijda (1986: 207) on 'demand character'.

10. See also Lazarus and Launier (1978), Lazarus, Kanner and Folkman (1980), Lazarus and Folkman (1984), and Folkman and Lazarus (1986).

11. This poses an interesting question. We often associate challenge with a situation, or use the term to describe a situation. There are however actually no 'objective' situations which are 'challenging'. Situations are only challenging in as much as the evaluation of situational components results in the situational meaning structure (thus, including individual concerns) corresponding with 'challenge'. This is, in turn, dependent upon the ability of a person to cope with the situation and the estimate of the potential reward (the satisfaction of source concerns). In most English literature, challenge is then discussed as an emotion.

12. See Larsson (1989).

13. See Vagi and Lefcourt (1988), Hammond and Edelman (1991a).

14. See Allred and Smith (1989: 257).

15. According to Csikszentmihalyi (1988).

16. See Csikszentmihalyi & Csikszentmihalyi (1988: 30), and Csikszentmihalyi (1988: 34; 1975).

17. See also Frijda (1988: 353), Tan (1996: 90, 93), and Csikszentmihalyi (1988). Also compare Piët (1986).

18. In Tan (1996: 82,83).

19. See Frijda (1986: 441).

20. See Arnold (1960), Frijda (1986: 457), and Lazarus (1984). Meanwhile, there is some empirical support for the relation between emotions, situational components, and action tendencies, though there is scarcely any research. In Frijda, Kuipers, and Ter Schure (1989: 219) a separate action tendency and a unique linear combination of situational features was established. This concerns significant relationships, though the correlation between 'appraisals' of the situational components and the action tendencies are generally not very strong (Frijda et al. 1989: 225; also Smith and Ellsworth 1985, Scherer 1988, and Mesquita 1993).

21. In Frijda (et al. 1989: 214, 215; also chapter 4 in Frijda 1986) the following action tendencies with *challenge* are found (and which have been used in the above text and sometimes slightly altered): 'Approach: I wanted to approach, to make contact'; 'Reactant: I wanted to go against an obstacle or difficulty, or to conquer it'; 'Exuberant: I wanted to move, be exuberant, sing, jump, undertake things'. Action tendencies with *threat* are: 'Don't want: I wanted

something not to be so, to not exist'; 'Avoidance: I wanted to have nothing to do with something or someone; to be bothered by it as little as possible, to stay away'; 'Disappear from view: I wanted to sink into the ground, ..., not to be noticed by anyone'. (Frijda et al. 1989: 214, 215, 222; also Smith and Ellsworth 1985; Scherer 1988). These were starting points in formulating the action tendencies in the questionnaire (6.7).

22. See Frijda (Frijda 1986: 78, 240, 459, 471-2).
23. See Frijda (1988: 354).
24. The theater maker can sometimes also be an actor himself; the word 'theater maker' is used in the broadest sense.
25. See Ekman (1982), Ekman and Friesen (1982), and Izard (1992).
26. See Konijn (1991).
27. These studies are described in Konijn (1992).

Chapter 5

1. In psychological research this is usually limited to six basic emotions: Sadness, anger, disgust, love, surprise, and happiness. About basic emotions see for example Izard (1992), Ekman (1982), Ekman et al. (1983), and Mesquita (1993: 91).
2. See Souriau (1950), Beckerman (1979), Fischer-Lichte (1983), Polti (1990), and Laffont (1960).
3. In Frijda (1988: 352; 1987).
4. See Brecht (1967-1968: 392).
5. Likewise, the rejection of the rise of bourgeois drama in the eighteenth century was due to the portrayal of morally 'bad' characters and 'bad' morals (Szondi 1984; section 2.2). See also, for example, Diderot (1758) on the representation of the (moral) goodness and good characters on stage. Likewise, Dutch audiences reacted very emotionally to the so-called Fassbinder-affair in 1988, when the performance *Dirt, the City and Death* (Fassbinder 1975 *Der Müll, die Stadt und der Tod*) was about to be presented. The performance was canceled in the end because the texts of a Jewish character and the deeds he committed were too great an attack on people's values.
6. In Schoenmakers (1989: 110-113).
7. See Frijda et al. (1989: 214-215).
8. I will continue to use the term 'involvement' when the distinction between empathy and identification is not at issue as well as in reference to the process referred to in acting theories as 'involving oneself' in the character, in the sense of 'taking over the character-emotions' (Schoenmakers 1992). The Dept. of Theater, Film, and Television Studies at Utrecht University has, during the last few years, devoted a great deal of thought to empathy and identification in audiences of 'theatrical products'. For research on 'involvement' see Schoenmakers (1988; 1990), Van Vliet (1991), Zillman (1991), Tan (1996), and Hoorn & Konijn (1999a).
9. Respectively in Frijda (1986: 215) and Tan (1996: 174).
10. Compare with self-other-distinction in Stotland (1969), Van Vliet (1991), and Tan (1996).
11. The reason for this lies in the fact that the use of film, as compared to a theater performance, simplifies research: A film can be repeated endlessly in exactly the same form.
12. See Frijda (1986: 354- 355).
13. This is the simplest conceivable form of identification (Tan 1996: 153-156, 189-190).

14. See Koriat et al. (1982). Compare also Davis, Hull, Young and Waren (1987), and Van Vliet (1991).

15. Also in Lang (1979), Lang, Kozak, Miller, et al. (1980), and Lang, Levin, Miller, and Kozak (1983).

16. In Archer (1888) and Gladfield (1983).

17. Comparable processes are described by Frijda (1986: 309) and Lange et al. (1980; 1983).

18. See Frijda (1986: 328); compare Diderot (1985: 58). An 'imagined emotion' can actually arise quite suddenly. For example, a certain scent immediately brings memory X to mind, including (the desire for) the 'feeling' associated with X. The scent is however an actual stimulus for memory and aroused emotion (which is probably of a different nature).

19. See Sonnemans (1991: 216).

20. In Frijda (1986: 53-54), Goffman (1959; 1974), and Snyder (1974).

21. The imagined emotional experiences, resembling the character-emotions, are more like 'feelings', even though they can be very intense. About distinction between feeling and emotion, see Frijda (1986: 463-466).

22. See Gombrich (1970) and Van Meel (1989).

23. Research on the recognition of emotion in facial expression is found in, among others, Richter (1957), Frijda (1958), Ekman (1982), Wallbott and Scherer (1986), Frijda (1986), Wallbott (1988), and Ekman (1989). In this kind of research, the test subjects are usually asked to choose the correct one from a restricted number of emotion words.

24. See Frijda (1986: 57).

25. Relatively little research has been done on recognizing emotions on the basis of vocal indications (voice) (Scherer 1986; Bezooijen 1988). Scherer attributes this largely to numerous methodological stumbling blocks involved in phonetic research, as well as to the lack of a systematic and consistent measure for results (Scherer 1986: 143). Listeners usually judge the intended emotional expression, of recorded 'gibberish' (read by actors) correctly. No difference was found between judging 'faked' and 'spontaneous' emotionally loaded spoken text. To date, no specific relationships between phonetic features and emotions have been established (Bezooijen 1988).

26. In Frijda (1958: 84).

27. See, among others, Hess, Kappas, McHugo et al. (1989) and Hess and Kleck (1990).

28. Research by, among others, Stern and Lewis (1968), Wallbott (1988) and Bloch et al. (1987); see chapter 6.

29. See also Ekman et al. (1983); Bloch, Orthous, and Santibañez-H (1987); Bloch (1989) and Levenson et al. (1990).

30. See for example De Jong (1981) and Frijda (1986).

31. Similar results in Weisweiler (1983) and Konijn (1991; 1992) with actors, like the self-arousal results in the placebo group of Schachter and Singer (1962).

32. See Zillman and Bryant (1974), Zillman (1988), and Reisenzein (1983).

33. Techniques such as for example Fourier's spectral analysis of a phasic heart beat response. See among others Kamphuis and Frowein (1986), Grossman and Wientjes (1986).

34. Also Frijda (1986: 239) says that the physiological feedback ('muscle twitches or autonomic upset') probably offers the most direct signals of control precedence and urgency, and thus of intensity of an emotion.

35. See Hilgard (1977), Kihlstrom (1985), and Fewtrell (1986).
36. See Hilgard (1977), Kihlstrom (1985), and Mellor (1988).
37. According to the social facilitation and inhibition theory, see Zajonc (1965), Sanders (1983), and Bond and Titus (1983).

Chapter 6

1. See, among others, Emmet (1975), Bleijswijk (1992), and Konijn (1994).
2. Binet (1896) sees here a confirmation of James' peripheral feedback theory (explanation in section 5.7).
3. See Schälzky (1980: 127).
4. In Villiers (1942: 150-170).
5. Although Schälzky and Sloman (1972) do not place their findings in a theoretical context.
6. A more detailed discussion of this can be found in Konijn (1992).
7. This concerns only an indication because the limited number of actors in the study did not allow for statistical analysis, see Konijn (1991; 1992).
8. '...that people high on cognitive complexity are low on projection of their own responses to others, (...) they can readily put themselves in the other's place (rather than put others in their own place)' (Koenig and Seamon 1973: 561).
9. See Konijn (1992). An extensive discussion of Perky's (1976) study can be found in Konijn (1988).
10. According to Collum (1977).
11. According to Hammond and Edelman (1991a).
12. In Natadze (1962).
13. According to Frijda (1986), see chapters 4 and 5.
14. Literature on the choice of research methods: Selltiz, Wrightsman, and Cook (1976) and Judd, Smith, and Kidder (1991).
15. For recent developments in emotion research see, among others, Lazarus and Folkman (1984), Frijda (1986), Cacioppo (1990), and Ekman & Davidson (1994).
16. On 'asking questions' or 'test design' see, among others, Stelltiz, Wrightsman, and Cook (1976: 291), Hoogstraten (1979: 81), Dillman (1979), Emans (1990), and Judd, Kidder & Smith (1991).
17. For target groups and sample populations see: Cook and Campbell (1979: 70).
18. The VNT (Theater League of the Netherlands) is the organization in the Netherlands concerned with employment issues concerning theater in the Netherlands, including negotiating collective contracts. But they also have some difficulty determining whether an actor can be called professional or not. Criteria are not unambiguous, but also not easily replaced by others. The criteria used in this research have been based on discussions with the VNT.
19. See Konijn (1994).
20. It must be pointed out here that it is more common in America than it is in the Netherlands for an actor to act on stage as well as in film and television (although this is changing rapidly). American actors who work mainly in film and television, and seldom onstage are usually members of another union (i.e., *Screen Actors Guild*).
21. See, among others, Davitz (1969) and Frijda, Kuipers, and Ter Schure (1989).

22. The complete Dutch version of the questionnaire is included in the appendix of *Acteurs Spelen Emoties* (Konijn 1994). In this edition, to save space, neither the American nor the Dutch questionnaires have been included; instead an overview of the questionnaire and descriptions of the questions included are summed up in section 6.7.

23. In the Dutch questionnaire the answering categories are numbered from one to four. I used the numbers zero to three in the American questionnaire because zero more clearly indicated that the option referred to 'not at all'. In chapter 7 it can be seen that, apparently, this did not matter for the results.

24. A more detailed scale would in this case cause problems with the interpretation (among others, Selltiz 1976). Moreover, a scale with an even number of answering categories (in this case four), to some extent limits the tendency of people to choose the middle or average answer.

25. The questionnaire is available on request from Boom Publishers (Amsterdam, NL) or the Dept. of Theater, Film, and Television Studies, Faculty of Arts at Utrecht University (Utrecht, NL).

26. Because actors (like most people) are unfamiliar with the concept of task-emotions, these were called professional emotions in the questionnaire.

Chapter 7

1. Twenty-seven of the American questionnaires appeared to be from actors who had chosen a scene from a film they had acted in. This group of 'film' actors was too small to use for responsible statistical analysis. In as much as I performed some statistical analyses on this group, the results did not diverge much from the rest however. In general, I refer to the research report, *Acteurs Spelen Emoties in Amerika* (Konijn and Westerbeek 1997), for detailed, numerical data on the results from the actors in the United States.

2. Actors with less than three years of professional experience were not included.

3. The sum of the percentages is more than 100% due to overlap: A number of actors attended more than one school.

4. For detailed information on the statistical analyses see Konijn (1994) for the Dutch and Flemish actors; and Konijn and Westerbeek (1997) for the American actors.

5. Although asked specifically to choose a scene from a recent performance, some of the American actors filled in the questionnaire based on a performance from (very) long ago; sometimes even as far back as the sixties. The actors who chose a performance from before 1985 were not included, because these were considered too long ago for accurate recall. This reduced the number of American respondents to 180 persons. The presentation of the results is based on this group.

6. For the Netherlands compare the data in Attema (1992).

7. For every word describing emotion the horizontal axis reveals how many actors found the emotion not applicable as a portrayed character-emotion (a score of 0), and how many actors found one of the emotions named applicable to at least a limited extent (a score of 1 or more). These figures, given in percentages, therefore do not take the intensity of the emotion into account.

8. The reported emotions, individually named, were divided into four groups corresponding to the theoretical categories conceived for the questionnaire: The main categories prototypical

emotions (proto) and task-emotions (task), were each subdivided into positive emotions (pos) and negative emotions (neg).

9. The discussion here concerns the individual emotions. For the results on grouped emotions (e.g., about the quality of these measurements as scales) see *Acteurs Spelen Emoties* (Konijn 1994) for the Dutch and Flemish results. For precise data and results of the American statistical analyses see *Acteurs spelen emoties in Amerika* by Konijn and Westerbeek (1997).

10. Because the comparison is only relevant if a particular character-emotion actually was portrayed, only the actors who portrayed that character-emotion were selected. For details see tables and statistical data in Konijn (1994) and Konijn and Westerbeek (1997).

11. For details on the analyses of the acting styles and the four aspects of acting styles, see Konijn (1994) and Konijn and Westerbeek (1997). The correlations between the (aspects of the) acting styles do not exceed .40.

12. The results of statistical tests show a very low correlation between the portrayed character-emotions and the actors' emotions just before the performance, lower than when compared *during* the performance (see Konijn 1994, and Konijn and Westerbeek 1997).

13. For the comparison of separate action tendencies, a selection procedure was also followed: Only if an actor portrayed a certain tendency in the role, was this included in the analysis (cf. note 10). For comparisons on a larger scale, see Konijn (1994) and Konijn and Westerbeek (1997).

14. The statistical data is included in Konijn (1994) and Konijn and Westerbeek (1997).

15. The principal component analysis on the action tendencies offers no foundation for an unambiguous subdivision of action tendencies for actor and character (Konijn 1993). That the relationship between emotions and action tendencies is considerably more complicated than was suggested here is confirmed by, among others, Frijda, Kuipers, and Ter Schure (1989). Certain negative emotions also provoke specific types of approach behavior which are comparable to 'moving against' impulses in Frijda et al. (1989).

16. Just as with the calculation of the correspondence between emotions and impulses, here too only the results of the comparison of the separate items are presented. For the information per group we refer to Konijn (1994) and Konijn and Westerbeek (1997).

17. Note that 'at the present moment' for the Dutch actors was the spring of 1991, while for the American actors, it was the winter of 1995.

18. It is odd that the majority of students attending drama schools are female, while in the professional theater men predominate, among characters as well as among actors.

19. The significant difference is determined by comparing the average on the involvement scale (combining two aspects) with the average on the detachment scale (combining two aspects). Although the difference is significant, and thus meaningful, the difference is relatively small in absolute terms. Involvement in the US is subscribed to somewhat more strongly than in the Netherlands and Flanders. For detailed information see Konijn (1994) and Konijn and Westerbeek (1997).

20. In the assessment of the acting styles of top actors this means that the analyses were limited to separate statements (thus, not with a measurement scale) (see subsection 8.4.3 in Konijn 1994). This reduces the reliability of the tests, which means that the results have to be interpreted cautiously.

21. For the results of this comparison for the Dutch situation, refer to table 8.9 in *Acteurs Spelen Emoties* (Konijn 1994). The corresponding table for the American situation is included in *Acteurs Spelen Emoties in Amerika* (Konijn and Westerbeek 1997). A complicating factor in the analyses of top actors is that the respondent-actors did not answer the question in reference to the same top actor, but everyone chose their own favorites, which in all but a few cases were different.

Chapter 8

1. The empirical data is partly at odds with accepted theoretical views and this provides a supplement. In the following sections the suitability of the analytical concepts for developing more subtle acting theories will be discussed. The results obtained will be described and explained within the context of the task-emotion theory and adjustments made to that theory.

2. The relatively low response in the US can be explained by a series of circumstantial coincidences. Due to serious printer delays in New York, the mailing was greatly delayed. The questionnaire was finally mailed just before the Thanksgiving holidays and Christmas season when the postal service is especially slow. Due to financial limits I also used bulk mailing rate to cut costs. I only realized later that bulk mail has no priority and gets held up along the way. A postal strike also added to the delay. Questionnaires were still being delivered mid-January. The cover letter said the questionnaire should be returned before Christmas! In February questionnaires were still coming in with excuses for the delay and a comment that the survey had just been received by some of the participants. Add to that the fact that at least 10% no longer lived at their registered addresses. So, considering all the circumstances, I may not complain.

3. This data is comparable to the data on actors with at least three years of professional experience in Attema's study (1992).

4. This is particularly true with the great number of comparative statistical analyses for the average differences and correlation of two variables. Some specific features of the results moreover contribute to the risk of distortion in the statistical analyses and conclusions. One of these elements is the obliqueness or skewness of the responses. For example, not every emotion was present in each role, thus there were a relatively high number of zero-values in the response.

5. See Frijda (1988a: 246). Separate emotion-words appear to be ambiguous indicators for one specific emotion.

6. See *Acteurs Spelen Emoties* (1994) for the data on Dutch and Flemish actors, as well as the research report *Acteurs Spelen Emoties in Amerika* by Konijn and Westerbeek (1997) for the data on the American respondents.

7. The reactions to negative emotion-words are easier to group into coherent categories for different instances than the positive ones.

8. See *Acteurs Spelen Emoties* (Konijn 1994) and *Acteurs Spelen Emoties in Amerika* (Konijn and Westerbeek 1997).

9. About 'flow' see Csikszentmihalyi (1988; 1975).

10. Lazarus proposes that challenge is distinct from threat in the area of the person's ability to conquer the potential threat or risk of the situation (Lazarus and Folkman 1984). The feeling of control appears to be one of the determining factors in being able to cope with stress factors in daily life (Kobasa 1979; Gal and Lazarus 1975).

11. See Gal and Lazarus (1975).

12. See also Pott (1992).

13. See Frijda (1986: 459, 472; and section 2.8).

14. See Mesquita (1993: 147).

15. 'Emotional intensity may be assumed to be a function of stimulus intensity or of the gravity of the eliciting events' (Frijda 1986: 290). The gravity also depends, in part, on the temporal or spatial proximity of the meaningful events, the urgency, and because different concerns are involved.

16. In Frijda (1986: 73)

17. Because the correspondence here with intentions, the intended emotions, is weakest.

18. This was studied by the psychologists Hess and Kleck (1990; 1994) and Shields (1984).

19. When the dynamics of an emotional expression became visible in a film, audience recognition increased considerably as compared to static photographic images (see also section 4.6).

References

Allred, K.D., and T.W. Smith (1989) The hardy personality: Cognitive and physiological responses to evaluative threat. *Journal of Personality and Social Psychology*, 6, 257-266

Archer, W. (1888) *Masks or faces? A study in the psychology of acting*. Londen: Longmans, Green and Co.

Arnold, M.B. (1960) *Emotion and personality* (I). New York: Columbia University Press

Attema, J. (1992) *Loon en werken van de acteur: Een onderzoek naar de beroepsgroep en praktijk van de professionele acteur*. [Pay and work of the actor: A study into the professional group and practices of professional actors]. Utrecht, NL: Wetenschapswinkel Letteren Universiteit Utrecht (also available at Theater, Film, and Television Studies U.U.)

Baker, G.P. (1919; 2nd ed. 1947) *Dramatic technique*. Boston: Houghton Mifflin

Barba, E., and R. Fowler (1989) The fiction of duality. *New Theater Quarterly*, 5, 311-314

Barba E., and N. Savarese (1991) *The secret art of the performer: A dictionary of theater anthropology*. New York/Londen: Routledge

Barnett, D. (1987) *The art of gesture: The practices and principles of 18th. century acting*. Heidelberg: Winter

Barzun, J. (1986) Diderot as philosopher. *Diderot Studies*, 22, 17-27

Beckerman, B. (1979, 2nd ed. [1st 1970]) *Dynamics of drama: Theory and method of analysis*. New York: Drama Book Specialists

Bezooijen, R. van (1988) Het is niet wat ze zei!!! Spraak, emotie en persoonlijkheid. [It's not what she said!!! Speech, emotion, and personality.] In: M.P.R. van den Broecke (ed.) *Ter sprake: Spraak als betekenisvol geluid in 36 thematische hoofdstukken* [On speech: Speech as meaningful sound in 36 thematic chapters.] (ch. 12). Dordrecht, NL: Floris Publications

Binet, A. (1896) Réflexions sur le paradoxe de Diderot. [Reflections on Diderot's paradox.] *L'Année Psychologique*, 3, 279-295

Bishop, C. A. (1988) *The deconstructed actor: Towards a postmodern acting theory*. Ann Arbor, Michigan: University of Colorado (diss.)

Bleijswijk, J.M. (1992) *Gespeelde emotie: Acteursonderzoek naar emoties op het toneel*. [Played emotion: Actors study into emotions on stage.] Amsterdam: Dept. of Theater Studies, University of Amsterdam (MA thesis)

Bloch, S., P. Orthous, H.-G. Santibañez (1987) Effector patterns of basic emotions: A psychophysiological method for training actors. *Journal of Social Biological Structures*, 10, 1-19

Bloch, S. (1989) Effector patterns of basic human emotions: An experimental model for emotional induction. *Behavioral Brain Research*, 33, 330

Bloch, S., M. Lemeignan, T.N. Aguilera (1991) Specific respiratory patterns distinguish among human basic emotions. *International Journal of Psychophysiology*, 8, 109-132

Bode, D.L., and E. Brutten (1963) A palmer sweat investigation of the effect of audience variation upon stage fright. *Speech Monographs*, 30, 92-96

Boer, D.J. den, Bouwman H., Frissen V., and Houben M. (1994) *Methodologie and statistiek voor communicatie-onderzoek.* [*Methodology and statistics for communication studies.*] Houten/Zaventum, NL: Bohn Stafleu and Van Loghum Publ.

Boiten, F.A. (1993) *Emotional breathing patterns.* Amsterdam: Universiteit van Amsterdam, Dept. of Psychology (diss.)

Boiten, F.A., N.H. Frijda, and C.J.E. Wientjes (1994) Emotions and respiratory patterns: Review and critical analysis. *International Journal of Psychophysiology*, vol. 17(2), 103-128

Bond Jr., C.F., and L.J. Titus (1983) Social facilitation: A meta-analysis of 241 studies. *Psychological Bulletin*, 94, 265-292

Bogdanov, G. (1991, July, personal communication) 'Workshop and training in Meyerhold's Biomechanics', Amsterdam: Mime Institute, Theater Institute the Netherlands (TIN)

Bower, G.H. (1981) Mood and memory. *American Psychologist*, 36, 129-148

Boysen, K. (1988a) Machen Sie Platz für den Ausdruck: Der Beruf des Schauspielers (Views concerning the acting profession). *Theater Heute*, 9, 24-27

Boysen, K. (1988b) Machen Sie Platz für den Ausdruck: Der Beruf des Schauspielers (Views concerning the acting profession). *Theater Heute*, 10, 14-17

Boysen, K. (1988c) Machen Sie Platz für den Ausdruck: Der Beruf des Schauspielers (Views concerning the acting profession). *Theater Heute*, 11, 9-11

Braun, E. (ed.,1969) *Meyerhold on theater.* Londen: Methuen

Braun, E. (1994) *Meyerhold, a revolution in theater.* Iowa: University of Iowa Press (an updated version of the 1969 edition)

Brecht, B. (1967-1968) *Gesammelte Werke.* [*Complete works.*] Vol. 15: *Schriften zum Theater 1.* [*Contributions to theater 1.*] Werkausgabe edition Suhrkamp (edited by Werner Hecht), Frankfurt am Main, Germany: Suhrkamp Verlag

Brook P. (1968) *The empty space.* Harmondsworth, Middlesex, UK: Pelican, Penguin Books

Brook P. (1987) *The shifting point.* New York: Theater Communications Group

Burgund, E. (1931) *Die Entwicklung der Theorie der französischen Schauspielkunst im 18. Jahrhundert bis zur Revolution.* [*Development of theory on the French art of acting in the 18th C. until the revolution.*] Breslau: Sprache und Kultur der germanisch-romanischen Völker: C. Romanistische Reihe (8)

Brumm, B.M. (1973) *A survey of professional acting schools in New York City: 1870 – 1970.* New York: New York University (diss.)

Cacioppo, J.T., and L.G. Tassinary (eds., 1990) *Principles of psychophysiology: Physical, social and inferential elements.* Cambridge: Cambridge University Press

Calzolari, A. (1984) Les interprétations du Paradoxe et les paradoxes de l'interprétations. [*Interpretations of the Paradox and paradoxes in the interpretations.*] In: E. de Fontenay and J. Proust (eds.), *Interpréter Diderot aujourd'hui.* [*Interpreting Diderot today.*] Paris, Fr.: Centre Culturel International de Cérisy-la-Salle, Le Sycomore, Colloque de Cérisy S.F.I.E.D.

Carlson, M. (1993; extended edition) *Theories of the theater; a historical and critical survey, from the Greeks to the present.* London/Ithaca: Cornell University Press

Cartwright, M.T. (1969) Diderot, critique d'art et le problème de l'expression. [Diderot, critic on art and the problem of expression.] *Diderot Studies* (thematic issue), 13, 13-267

Chekhov, M. (1985) *Lessen voor acteurs.* [*Lessons on acting.*] Amsterdam: International Theater & Film Books (Transl. of M. Chekhov (1953) *To the actor: On the technique of acting.* New York: Harper & Row)

Chouillet, J. (1973) *La formation des idées esthétiques de Diderot.* [*Development of the aesthetic ideas of Diderot.*] Paris, Fr.: Librairie Armand Colin

Chouillet, J. (1977) *Diderot.* Paris, Fr.: CDU and SEDES Réunies (book review in *Diderot Studies*, 20 (1981), 381-383, by Robert Loy.)

Clevenger Jr., Th., and J.Ch. Tolch (1962) The reliability of judgments of acting performance. *Educational Theater Journal*, 14, 318-323

Clevinger, D.L., and W.G. Powers (1983) Cognitive complexity and cast performance: A research note. *Empirical Research in Theater*, 9, 3-9

Clift-Howard, P., and A. Holbrook (1974) Manipulation and measurement of vocal frequency of student actors. *Empirical Research in Theater*, 4, 21-35

Cole, Toby, and Helen Krich Chinoy (eds., 1970 [rev. ed.]; 1st ed. 1949) *Actors on acting: The theories, techniques and practices of the great actors of all times as told in their own words.* New York: Crown Publ.

Collum, Dovard K. (1977) The empathic ability of actors: A behavioral study, *Dissertation Abstracts International*, 38 (4-A), 1741, Florida State University, Dept. of Literature and Art

Constantinidis, S.E. (1988) Rehearsal as a subsystem: Transactional analysis and role research. *New Theater Quarterly*, 4, 64-76

Cook, T.D., and D.T. Campbell (1979) *Quasi experimentation: Design and analysis issues for field settings.* Chicago: Rand McNally

Coquelin, B.C. (1887) Acting and Actors (L'art et le Comédien, by C. Coquelin, 1880). *Harper's New Monthly Magazine*, may, 891-909

Cox, T. (1978) *Stress.* Londen: Macmillan Education

Cronbach, J. (1990, 5th ed.) *Essentials of psychological testing.* New York: Harper & Row

Csikszentmihalyi, M. (1975) *Beyond boredom and anxiety: The experience of play in work and games.* San Francisco: Jossy-Bass

Csikszentmihalyi, M., and I.S. Csikszentmihalyi (eds., 1988) *Optimal experience: Psychological studies of flow in consciousness.* Cambridge: Cambridge University Press

Csikszentmihalyi, M., and J.W. Getzels (1973) The personality of young artists: An empirical and theoretical exploration. *British Journal of Psychology*, 64, 91-104

Davis, M.H., J.G. Hull, R.D. Young, and G.G. Warren (1987) Emotional reactions to dramatic film stimuli: The influence of cognitive and emotional empathy. *Journal of Personality and Social Psychology*, 52, 126-133

Davitz, J.R. (1969) *The language of emotion.* New York [etc.]: Academic Press

Dennett, D.C. (1987) *The intentional stance.* Cambridge [etc.]: MIT Press

Diderot, D. (1753) Pensées sur l'interprétation de la nature. [Thoughts on the interpretation of nature.] In: *Diderot: Oeuvres complètes*, Vol. 9, pp. 1-1?? (critical and annotated edition by Jean Verloot (ed. 1981), Paris, Fr.: Hermann

Diderot, D. (1758) De la poésie dramatique. [On theatrical poetry.] In: Barrett H. Clark (ed.) (rev. ed. 1973, 1st 1947) *European theories of the drama; with a supplement on the American drama* (ed. by H. Popkin). New York: Crown Publ.

Diderot, D. (1959; [1773; 1st. ed. 1830]) *Paradoxe sur le comédien*. In: Paul Vernière (ed., 1959) *Diderot: Oeuvres Esthétique*. Paris, Fr.: Éditions Garnier

Diderot, D. (1980; [1769, 1st ed. 1820]) *De droom van d'Alembert. [The dream of d'Alembert.]* (transl. by J.D. Hubert-Reerink in Dutch of *Le rêve de d'Alembert*, 1962; 1st. 1769, (edited by J. Verloot after a copy from the St. Petersburg archive). Paris, Fr.: Éditions sociales

Diderot, D. (1984 [1770]) Observations de M. Diderot sur une brochure intitulée Garrick, ou les acteurs anglais. [Observations of Mr. Diderot about a brochure entitled Garrick, or the English actors.] In: J. Starobinski, J. Chouillet, G.E. Lessing, c.s. (eds., 1984) *Diderot (écrits sur le théâtre). [Diderot (writings on the theater).]*, pp. 281-293. Paris, Fr.: Grands Dramaturges Sycomore, Comédie-Française (Langres: Guéniot)

Diderot, D. (1985 [1773]) *Paradox over de toneelspeler. [Paradox on the actor.]* (Transl. in Dutch based on Gallimard: *Oeuvres* (Bibliothèque de la Pléade) by Gemma Pappot; introduction by W. Hogendoorn; epilogue by J. Galard). Amsterdam: International Theater & Film Books

Dienstbier, R.A. (1989) Arousal and physiological toughness: Implications for mental and physical health. *Psychological Review*, 96, 84-100

Dillman, D.A. (1979) *Mail and telephone survey's: The total design method*. New York: A. Wiley-Interscience Publ.

Dimsdale, J.E. (1984) Generalizing from laboratory studies to field of human stress physiology. *Psychosomatic Medicine*, 46, 463-469

Dumesnil, M.-F. (1823) *Mémoires de Marie-Françoise Dumesnil, en réponse aux mémoires d'Hyppolite Clairon. Revus, corrigés et augmentés d'une notice sur cette comédienne par M. Dussault. [Memories of Marie-Françoise Dumesnil, in reply to the memories of Hyppolite Clairon. Reviewed, corrected, and additional comment on this actress by M. Dussault.]* Paris, Fr.: Tenré

Ebert, G. (1991) *Der Schauspieler: Geschichte eines Berufes. [The actor: History on a profession.]* Berlin, Germany: Henschel-Verlag

Ekman, P. (ed., 1982) *Emotion in the human face*. Cambridge: Cambridge University Press

Ekman, P. (1989) The argument and evidence about universals in facial expressions of emotion. In: H. Wagner and A. Manstead (eds.) *Handbook of psychophysiology: Emotion and social behaviour*, pp. 143-164. London: John Wiley & Sons

Ekman, P. and R.J. Davidson (eds., 1994) *The Nature of Emotion: Fundamental Questions*. New York: Oxford University Press

Ekman, P., R.J. Davidson, and W.V. Friesen (1990) The Duchenne smile: Emotional Expression and brain physiology II. *Journal of Personality and Social Psychology*, 58, 342353

Ekman, P., and W.V. Friesen (1982) Felt, false, and miserable smiles. *Journal of Nonverbal Behavior*, 6, 239-252

Ekman, P., W.V. Friesen, and M. O'Sullivan (1988) Smiles when lying. *Journal of Personality and Social Psychology*, 54, 414-420

Ekman P., R.W. Levenson, and W.V. Friesen (1983) Autonomic nervous system activity distinguishes among emotions. *Science*, 221, 1208-1210

Emans, B. (1990) *Interviewen. Theorie, techniek and training. [Interviewing. Theory, techniques, and training.]* Groningen, NL: Wolters-Noordhoff

Emmet, A. (1975) Head or heart: The actors dilemma. *Theater Quarterly*, 18, 15-21

Esslin, M. (1987) Actors acting actors. *Modern Drama*, 30, 72-79

Erenstein, R.L. (ed., 1996) *Een theatergeschiedenis der Nederlanden; tien eeuwen drama en theater in Nederland en Vlaanderen. [A theater history of the Netherlands; ten centuries of drama and theater in the Netherlands and Flanders.]* Amsterdam: Amsterdam University Press (English translation soon available)

Fellows, Otis E., and N.L. Torrey (1949) Introduction to Diderot Studies I. *Diderot Studies*, 1, VII-XIII (eds., O. Fellows and N. Torrey). Genève, Switzerland: Librairie Droz

Fewtrell, W.D. (1986) Depersonalisation: A description and suggested strategies. *British Journal of Guidance and Counseling*, 14, 263-269

Fink, J.G. (1980) *Depersonalisation and personalisation as factors in a taxonomy of acting.* Ann Arbor, Michigan: University Microfilms International (Diss. New York University)

Fischer-Lichte, E. (1983) *Semiotik des Theaters: Eine Einführung. [Semiotics of theater: An introduction.]* (3 Vols.). Tübingen, Germany: Narr Verlag

Flaherty, G. (1990) Empathy and distance: Romantic theories of acting reconsidered. *Theater Research International*, 15, 125-141

Folkman, S., and R.S. Lazarus (1988) Coping as a mediatior of emotion. *Journal of Personality and Social Psychology*, 54, 466-475

Folkman, S., R.S. Lazarus, C. Dunkel-Schetter, A. DeLongis, and R.J. Green (1986) Dynamics of a stressful encounter: Cognitive appraisal, coping, and encounter outcomes. *Journal of Personality and Social Psychology*, 50, 992-1003

Freriks, F., and G. Rijnders (1992) *Tranen op bevel, een polemiek over theater. [Tears on command, a debate on theater.]* Amsterdam: L.J. Veen

Frijda, N.H. (1958) *De betekenis van de gelaatsexpressie. [The meaning of facial expression.]* Amsterdam: G.A. van Oorschot

Frijda, N.H. (1986) *The emotions: Studies in emotion and social interaction.* Cambridge: Cambridge University Press

Frijda, N.H. (1987) *De wetten van het gevoel. [The laws of emotion.]* (Lecture in the series of Prof. Duijker, april 1987). Deventer, NL: Van Loghum & Slaterus Publ.

Frijda, N.H. (1988) The laws of emotion. *American Psychologist*, 43, 349-358

Frijda, N.H. (1989) Aesthetic emotions and reality. *American Psychologist*, 44, 1546-1547

Frijda, N.H., P. Kuipers, and E. ter Schure (1989) Relations between emotions, appraisal and emotional action readiness. *Journal of Personality and Social Psychology*, 57, 212-228

Funt, D. (1968) Diderot and the esthetics of the enlightment. *Diderot Studies*, 11, 15-191 (thematic issue; eds., O. Fellows and D. Guiragossian). Genève, Switzerland: Librairie Droz

Gabel-Krauch, S. (1982) Visualization and actor training. *Empirical Research in Theater*, 8, 115

Gal, R., and R.S. Lazarus (1975) The role of activity in anticipating and confronting stressful situations. *Journal of Human Stress*, 1, 4-20

Gallagher, D.J. (1990) Extraversion, neurotism and appraisal of stressful academic events. *Personality and Individual Differences*, 11, 1053-1057

Gladstein, G.A. (1984) The historical roots of contemporary empathy research. *Journal of the History of Behavioral Sciences*, 20, 38-59

Gladstein, G.A. (1983) Understanding empathy: Integrating counseling, developmental, and social psychology perspectives. *Journal of Counseling Psychology*, 30, 467-482

Glenn, W. (1985) *The psychology of performing arts.* New York: St. Martin's press

Goffman, E. (1959) *The presentation of self in every day life.* Middlesex/New York: Penguin

Goffman, E. (1974) *Frame analysis.* New York: Harper & Row

Gombrich, E.H. (1970) The mask and the face: The perception of physionomic likeness in life and art. In: E.H. Gombrich, J. Hochberg, and M. Black (eds.) *Art perception and reality,* pp. 1-46. Baltimore/ London: John Hopkins University Press

Goncourt, E. de (1911) *Mademoiselle Clairon, d'après ses correspondance et les rapports de police du temps.* [*Mademoiselle Clairon, according to her correspondence and the police reports of her time.*] Paris, Fr.: Bibliothèque-Charpentier

Gordon, Mel (1974) Meyerhold's Biomechanics. *Drama Review,* 18 (3), t-63.

Greimas, A.J. (1973) Les actants, les acteurs et les figures. [The performers, the actors, and the the portrayals.] In: C. Chabrol (ed.) *Sémiotique narrative et textuelle.* [*Narrative and textual semiotics.*] Paris, Fr.: Larousse

Grossman, P., and K. Wientjes (1986) Respiratory sinus arrhytmia and parasympathetic cardial control: Some basic issues concerning quantification, applications and implications. In: P. Grossman, K.H.L. Janssen, and D. Vaitl (eds.) *Cardiorespiratory and cardiosomatic psychophysiology.* New York/Londen: Plenum Press

Grotowski, J. (1968) *Towards a poor theater.* Holstebro, Denmark: Christensen & Co.

Gunkle, G. (1968) An experimental study of some vocal characteristics of spontaneity in acting. *Speech Monographs,* 35, 159-165

Günther, H. (1980) Diderot übersetzen. [Translating Diderot.] In: H. Dieckman (ed.) *Diderot und die Aufklärung.* [*Diderot and the Enlightment.*] Wolfenbütteler Forschungen Series, Vol. 10, pp. 99-113. München: Kraus

Hammond, J., and R.J. Edelman (1991a) Double identity: The effect of the acting process on the self-perception of professional actors - two case illustrations. In: G. Wilson (ed.) *Psychology and performing arts,* pp. 25-45. Lisse: Swets & Zeitlinger

Hammond, J., and R.J. Edelman (1991b) The act of being: Personality characteristics of professional actors, amateur actors and non-actors illustrations, pp. 123-133. In: G. Wilson (ed.) *Psychology and performing arts.* Lisse: Swets & Zeitlinger

Hazard, P. (1973; [1946]) *European thought in the eighteenth century: From Montesquieu to Lessing.* (Transl. of *La pensée européenne au XVIIIème siècle* by J. Lewis May, 1946, Paris: Boivin) Ohio: World Publishing Company (A Meridian Book; Gloucester, Mass. Peter Smith) Heus, P., de, R. van der Leeden, and B. Gazendam (1995) *Toegepaste data-analyse; technieken voor niet-experimenteel onderzoek in de sociale wetenschappen.* [*Applied data analysis; techniques for non-experimental research in the social sciences.*] Utrecht: Lemma Publ.

Hess, U., A. Kappas, G.J. McHugo, R.E. Kleck, and J.T. Lanzetta (1989) An analysis of the encoding and decoding of spontaneous and posed smiles: The use of facial electromyography. *Journal of Nonverbal Behavior,* vol. 13(2): 121-137

Hess, U., and R.E. Kleck (1990) Differentiating emotion-elicited and deliberate emotional facial expressions. *European Journal of Social Psychology,* 20, 369-385

Hess, U., and R.E. Kleck (1994) The cues decoders use in attempting to differentiate emotion-elicited and posed facial expressions. *European Journal of Social Psychology,* 24(3), 367-381

Hilgard, E.R. (1977 [2nd ed. 1986]) *Divided consciousness.* New York: Wiley & Sons

Hoffmeier, D. (1992) Über den Zugang Brechts zum Werk Stanislawski's. [About the access of Brecht to the work of Stanislavsky.] *Theater Zeitschrift*, (Heft) 31-32, 127-149

Hogendoorn, W. (1978) Avant gardisme en acteren. [Avant garde and acting.] In: F.F.J. Drijko-ningen, E. v.d. Starre, and H.I. Schvey (eds.) *Avant garde en traditie in het moderne toneel. [Avant garde and tradition in modern theater.]*, pp. 113-140. Muiderberg: Coutinho

Hogendoorn, W. (1985) Diderot en de paradox over de acteur. [Diderot and the paradox on the actor.] In: D. Diderot (1985 [1773]) *Paradox over de toneelspeler. [Paradox on the actor.]* (transl in Dutch by G. Pappot, based on *Oeuvres (Diderot)*, 1969, Gallimard, Fr.: Bibliothèque de la Pléia-de). Amsterdam: International Theater & Film Books

Hoogstraten, Joh. (1979) *De machteloze onderzoeker. [The helpless researcher.]* Amsterdam: Boom Publ.

Hoorn, J. F., and E.A. Konijn (1999) *Perceiving and experiencing fictional characters, I: Theoretical back-ground).* (52 pp.) Manuscript submitted for publication

Hoorn, J. F., and E.A. Konijn (1999) *Perceiving and experiencing fictional characters, II: Building a model.* (29 pp.) Manuscript submitted for publication

Hornby, R. (1992) *The end of acting; a radical view.* New York: Applause Theater Books

Hull, J.G., R.R. van Treuren, and S. Virnelli (1987) Hardiness and health: A critique and alterna-tive approach. *Journal of Personality and Social Psychology*, 53, 518-530

Irving, H. (1885 [1893]) The art of acting. *The Drama*, pp. 40-69

Izard, C.E. (1992) Basic emotions, relations among emotions, and emotion-cognition relations. *Psychological Review*, 99, 561-565

Jackson, J.M., and B. Latané (1981) All alone in front of all those people: Stage fright as a function of number and type of coperformers and audience. *Journal of Personality and Social Psychology*, 40, 73-85

Jacoby, G.A. (1975) A programmed approach to dialect training for the actor. *Empirical Research in Theater*, 5, 58-60

James, W. (1884) What is an emotion? *Mind*, 9, 188-205

Johnstone, K. (1990 [1979]) *Impro: Improvisatie en theater. [Impro: Improvisation and the theater.]* (Transl. in Dutch by P. van Tongeren, London: Faber). Amsterdam: International Theater & Film Books

Jomaron, J., De (ed., 1992) *Le théâtre en France: Du moyen âge à 1789. [Theater in France: From the middle ages to 1789.]* (Vol. 1). Paris, Fr.: Armand Colin

Jong, M.A., de (1981) *Emotie en respons: Een psychofysiologisch onderzoek. [Emotion and response: A psy-chophysiological research.]* Lisse: Swets & Zeitlinger (diss.)

Judd, Ch.M., L.H. Kidder, and E.R. Smith (1991) *Research methods in social relations.* New York: Holt, Rinehart & Winston

Kalter, J. (1979) *Actors on acting: Performing in theater and film today.* New York: Sterling/ Londen: Oak Tree Press

Kamphuis, A., and H.W. Frowein (1986) Assessment of mental effort by means of heart rate spectral analysis. In: J.F. Orlebeke, G. Mulder, and L.J.P. van Doornen (eds.) *Psychophysiology of cardiovascular control: Models, methods and data.* New York: Plenum Press

Kepke, A.N. (1963) *A study of communication of perception of character among actors, director, and audien-ce, using Q-methodology.* Michigan State University: UMI (diss.)

Kerkhoven, M., van (1991) Niet meer spelen, maar gespeeld worden. Bedenkingen omtrent het acteren vandaag. [Not to play, but to be played. Thoughts on today's acting.] In: M. van Kerkhoven (ed.) *Theaterschrift* (theme: On acting), vol. 1, 5-18

Kesting, M. (1989) Stanislawski - Meyerhold – Brecht. *Forum Modernes Theater*, vol. 4/2, 122-138

Kihlstrom, J.F. (1985) Hypnosis. *Annual Review of Psychology*, 36, 385-418

Kimble, G.A., and K. Schlesinger (1985) *Topics in the history of psychology* (part 1). Hillsdale, New Jersey: Lawrence Erlbaum

Kirby, W. (1972) On acting and not-acting. *The Drama Review*, vol. 16, 3-15

Kirby, W. (1987) *A formalist theater*. Philadelphia: University of Pennsylvania Press

Kobasa, S.C. (1979) Stressful life events, personality and health: An inquiry into hardiness. *Journal of Personality and Social Psychology*, 42, 168-177

Koenig, F., and J. Seamon (1973) Cognitive styles and dramatic acting ability. *Perceptual and Motor Skills*, 36, 561-562

Konijn, E.A. (1985) *Welke rol speelt u straks? Vergelijking van sociale rollen met theaterrollen.* [What role are you playing next? Comparison of daily life roles with theater roles.] Amsterdam: University of Amsterdam, Dept. of Psychology (MA thesis)

Konijn, E.A. (1988) Wacht maar tot het publiek er is...: Onderzoek naar de relatie tussen de mate van stress, de spelprestatie en een persoonlijkheidsvariabele van toneelspelers tijdens levensechte repetities en voorstellingen. [Waiting for the audience...: Study into the relationships between stress, acting performance, and a personality characteristic of stage actors during live rehearsals and public performances.] *Reeks voor voorstellingsanalyse en receptie-onderzoek* [Series for performance analysis and reception studies] (vol. 20). Utrecht, NL: Utrecht University, Dept. of Theater, Film, and Television Studies

Konijn, E.A. (1991) What's on between the actor and his audience? Empirical analysis of emotion processes in the theater, pp. 59-74. In: G. Wilson (ed.) *Psychology and performing arts*. Lisse: Swets & Zeitlinger

Konijn, E.A. (1992) Waiting for the audience: Empirical study of actors' stage fright and performance. In: H. Schoenmakers (ed.) *Performance theory, reception and audience studies, Tijdschrift voor Theaterwetenschap*, (thematic issue), vol. 8, nr. 31/32, 157-182

Konijn, E.A. (1993) *Gemengde gevoelens van toneelspelers; Rapportage resultaten van vragenlijstonderzoek.* [Mixed feelings of stage actors; research report of a questionnaire study.] Utrecht, NL: Utrecht University, Dept. of Theater, Film, and Television Studies (internal report)

Konijn, E.A. (1994) *Acteurs spelen emoties; vorm geven aan emoties op het toneel - een psychologische studie.* [Actors act emotions; shaping emotions on stage - a psychological study.] Amsterdam: Boom Publ.

Konijn, E.A. (1995) Actors and Emotions: A psychological perspective. *Theatre Research International*, 20 (2), 132-140

Konijn, E.A. (1999) Spotlight on spectators; emotions in the theater. *Discourse Processes*, 28 (2), 169-194

Konijn, E.A. (in press) Analyse des émotions de l'acteur: La théorie des émotions-tâches [Analysis of the emotions of the actor: A task-emotion theory], pp. 225–247. In: J. Féral (ed.). *La Formation de l'Acteur.* Montréal/Paris: Québec-Amérique

Konijn, E.A. (ed., in preparation) *Mejerchold: Een filosofie over acteren, inclusief bijdragen over het hedendaagse acteren in Rusland.* [Meyerhold: A philosophy on acting, including contributions on contemporary acting in Russia.] (working title) Amsterdam

Konijn, E.A., and A. Westerbeek (1997) *Acteurs spelen emoties in Amerika; rapportage resultaten van vragenlijstonderzoek in de V.S.* [*Actors act emotions in America; research report of a questionnaire study in the U.S.*] Utrecht, NL: Utrecht University, Dept. of Theater, Film, and Television Studies (internal report)

Koriat, A., R. Melkman, J.R. Averill, and R.S. Lazarus (1972) The self-control of emotional reactions to a stressful film. *Journal of Personality*, 40, 601-619

Kouwer, B.J. (1978 [1963]) *Het spel van de persoonlijkheid; theorieën en systemen in de psychologie van de menselijke persoon.* [*Personality play; theories and systems in the psychology of the human being.*] Utrecht: Erven J. Bijleveld

Kreitler, H., and Sh. Kreitler (1972) *Psychology of the arts.* Durham, N.C.: Duke University Press

Kuleshov, L. (1921, in R. Levaco (ed., transl. and introduction), 1974) *Kuleshov on film: Writings by Kuleshov.* Berkeley [etc.], CA.: University of California Press

Kuypers, J.A., and V.L. Bengtson (1983) Ecological issues in the aging family: Intervention implications and the family support cycle. *Canadian Journal of Community Mental Health*, 2, 7-19

Laffont, R. (1960) *Dictionnaire des personnages, de tous les temps et de tous les pays.* [*Dictionary of characters, of all times and all places.*] Paris, Fr.: S.E.D.E. et V. Bompiani

Laird, J.D. (1974) Self-attribution of emotion: The effects of expressive behavior on the quality of emotional experience. *Journal of Personality and Social Psychology*, 29, 475-486

Laird, J.D. (1984) The real role of facial response in the experience of emotion: A reply to Tourangeau and Elsworth, and others. *Journal of Personality and Social Psychology*, 47, 909-917

LaMettrie, J.O., De (1978 [1748]) *De mens een machine (L'homme machine).* [*A human, a machine.*] (Transl. in Dutch by H.W. Bakx). Amsterdam: Boom Publ.

Lang, P.J. (1979) A bio-informational theory of emotional imagery. *Psychophysiology*, 16, 495-512

Lang, P.J., M.J. Kozak, G.A. Miller, D.N. Levin, and A. McLean Jr. (1980) Emotional Imagery: Conceptual structure and pattern of somato-viceral response. *Psychophysiology*, 17, 179-192

Lang, P.J., D.N. Levin, G.A. Miller, and M. Kozak (1983) Fear behaviour, fear imagery and the psychophysiology of emotion: The problem of affective response integration. *Journal of Abnormal Psychology*, 92, 276-306

Larsson, G. (1989) Personality, appraisal and cognitive coping processes, and performance during various conditions of stress. *Military Psychology*, 1, 167-182

Larsson, G., and B. Hayward (1990) Appraisal and coping processes immediately before ejection: A study of Australian and Swedish pilots. *Military Psychology*, 2, 63-78

Latané, B., and St. Harkins (1976) Cross modality matches suggest anticipated stage fright: A multiplicative power function of audience size and status. *Perception and Psychophysics*, 20, 482-488.

Lazarowicz, K. (1991) Spontaneity or training and drill. *Forum Modernes Theater*, 6, 111-121

Lazarowicz, K., and Chr. Balme (ed., 1991) *Texte zur Theorie des Theaters.* [*Texts about theory of the theater.*] Stuttgart: Phillip Reclam

Lazarus, R.S. (1975) The self-regulation of emotion. In: L. Levi (ed.) *Emotion: Its parameters and measurement*, pp. 47-68. New York: Raven Press

Lazarus, R.S. (1980) The stress and coping paradigma. In: A.L. Bond and J.L. Rosen (eds.) *Competence and coping during adulthood.* Londen: University Press of New England

Lazarus, R.S. (1982) Thoughts on the relations between emotion and cognition. *American Psychologist*, 37, 1019-1024

Lazarus, R.S. (1984) On the primacy of cognition. *American Psychologist*, 39, 124-129

Lazarus, R.S. (1985) The psychology of stress and coping. *Mental Health Nursing*, (Special issue: *Stress and anxiety issues*), 7, 399-418

Lazarus, R.S., and S. Folkman (1984) *Stress, appraisal, and coping*. New York: Springer

Lazarus, R.S., A.D. Kanner, and S. Folkman (1980) Emotions: A cognitive-phenomenological analysis. In: R. Plutchik and H. Kellerman (eds.) *Emotion: Theory, research, and experience. Volume 1: Theories of Emotion*, pp. 189-217. New York: Academic Press

Lazarus, R.S., and R. Launier (1978) Stress-related transactions between person and environment. In: L.A. Pervin and M. Lewis (eds.) *Perspectives in interactional psychology*, pp. 287-327. New York/London: Plenum Press

Leach, R. (1989) *Vsevolod Meyerhold (Directors in perspective)*. Cambridge: Cambridge University Press

Leeuwe, H.H.J., De (1981) *Over de kunst van de toneelspeler. [On the art of the actor.]* Zutphen: De Walburg Pers

Levenson, R.W., P. Ekman, and W.V. Friesen (1990) Voluntary facial action generates emotion-specific autonomic nervous system activity. *Psychophysiology*, 27, 363-384

Lewes, G.H. (1875) *On actors and the art of acting*. New York: Grove Press

Lienden, H.J.H., Van (1924) *Psychologische beschouwing over toneelspel en toneelspeler. [A psychological reflection on acting and actor.]* Groningen: Hoitsema

Manderino, N. (1994) *Alles over Method-acting. [All about Method acting.]* Amsterdam: International Theater & Film Books

Martin, M. (1990) On the induction of mood. *Clinical Psychology Review*, 10, 669-697

Matsumoto, D. (1987) The role of facial response in the experience of emotion: More methodological problems and a meta-analysis. *Journal of Personality and Social Psychology*, 52, 769-774

McCrae, R.R. (1984) Situational determinants of coping responses: Loss, threat and challenge. *Journal of Personality and Social Psychology*, 46, 919-928

McCrae, R.R., and P.T. Costa (1986) Personality, coping and coping effectiveness in an adult sample. *Journal of Personality*, 54, 385-405

Meel, J.M., Van (1989) *De emotie verbeeld: Expressie in dans, toneel, beelden, verhaal. [The represented emotion: Expression in dance, drama, images, stories.]* Nijmegen: Dekker & Van de Vegt

Mellor, C.S. (1988) Depersonalisation and self perception. *British Journal of Psychiatry*, 153, (suppl. 2), 15 19

Menninger, W.W. (1990) Anxiety in the psychotherapist. *Bulletin of the Menninger Clinic*, 54, 232-246

Mesquita, B., Gomes de (1993) *Cultural variations in emotions: A comparative study of Dutch, Surinamese, and Turkish people in the Netherlands*. Amsterdam: University of Amsterdam, Dept. of Psychology (diss.)

Meyerhold, Vs. (1922) *De acteur van de toekomst en de biomechanika. [The future actor and biomechanics.]* (Lecture on june, 12, 1922). In Dutch translation included in: B. Dieho (ed., 1989) *Literatuurbundel Meyerhold. [Reader Meyerhold.]* Utrecht, NL: Utrecht University, Dept. of Theater Studies

Miller, K.A., and C.W. Bahs (1974) Director expectancy and actor effectiveness. *Empirical Research in Theater*, 4, 60-74

Mortier, R., and M. Mat (eds., 1985) *Diderot et son temps (catalogue établi). [Diderot and his time (Established catalogue).]* Brussels, Belgium: Bibliothèque Royale Albert 1st.

Moscu, J. (1973) Experimental study of actors' stage fright. *Revue Roumaine des Sciences Sociales*, (Psychology Series), 17, 145-158

Mossman, H.W. (1973) The psychological effect of counterattitudinal acting. *Empirical Research in Theater*, 3, 18-27

Mossman, H.W. (1975) Dissonance between an acting role and an actor's personal beliefs. *Educational Theater Journal*, 27, 535-540

Müseler, W. (1992) *Te paard! Aanschouwelijk rijonderricht.* [On the horse! Illustrative riding instruction.] Ede/Antwerpen, NL: Omer & Keuning Boeken

Nakagawa, H., H. Hinterhäuser, F. de Azua, F. Lafarga, A. Calzolari, R. Loy, and S. Ichikawa (1984) Traduire Diderot aujourd'hui. [Translating Diderot today.] In: E. de Fontenay and J. Proust (eds.) *Interpreter Diderot aujourd'hui* [Interpreting Diderot today], pp. 245-279. Paris, Fr.: Centre Culturel International de Cerisy-la-Salle, Le Sycomore, Colloque de Cerisy S.F.I.E.D.

Natadze, R. (1962) On the psychological nature of stage impersonation. *British Journal of Psychology*, 53, 421-429

New Jr., G.R. (1964) *Play production as a democratic group process.* Colombia: Columbia University, Dept. of Speech-Theater (diss.)

Olivier, L. (1986) *On acting.* London: Wheelshare, Sceptre Books

Oman, C. (1958) *David Garrick.* London: Hodder & Stoughton

Oustinoff, P. (1971) Foreword to Arnold Miller's the annexation of a philosopher: Diderot in Soviet criticism, 1917-1960. *Diderot Studies*, 15, 15-18

Paasman, B. (1986) *Het boek der Verlichting; de 18e eeuw van A tot Z.* [The book of the Enlightment; the 18th C. from A to Z.] Amsterdam/Barneveld, NL: Bulkboeken Publ.

Parkes, K.R. (1984) Locus of control, cognitive appraisal and coping in stressful episodes. *Journal of Personality and Social Psychology*, 46, 655-668

Parkinson, B. (1985) Emotional review on effects of false autonomic feedback. *Psychological Bulletin*, 98, 471-494

Passow, W. (1992) Whom do they love? *Tijdschrift voor Theaterwetenschap*, 8, 85-92

Pelias, R.J. (1991) Empathy and the ethics of entitlement. *Theater Research International*, 16, 142-152

Perky, S.D. (1976) *Effects of positive and negative audience response on actors' nonverbal performance behavior and on their attitudes.* Ohio: Bowling Green State University (diss.)

Pesochinsky, N.V. (1992; translated from Russian into Dutch by S. Drannikova and edited by E.A. Konijn, forthcoming). The Actor in Vsevolod Meyerhold's Theater. In: Svetlana K. Bushueva (ed.) *Russian Acting Art in the Twentieth Century*, pp. 65-258. St. Petersburg, Russia: The Russian Institute of History of the Arts

Pfister, M. (1982) *Das Drama: Theorie und Analyse.* [Drama: Theory and analysis.] München: Wilhelm Fink Verlag

Picon-Vallin, B. (1990) *Meyerhold; les voies de la création théatrale.* [Meyerhold; the voices of theatrical creation.] (vol. 17) Parijs: Éditions du Centre National de la Recherche Scientifique (CNRS)

Piët, S. (1986) *Het loon van de angst.* [The wage of fear.] Amsterdam: University of Amsterdam, Dept. of Psychology (diss.)

Pirandello, L. (1921) Zes personages op zoek naar een auteur. [Six characters in search for an author.] (Transl. in Dutch by M. Nord.) In: J. Sternheim and H. Thiescheffer (eds., 1990) *Luigi Pirandello, tekst & context* [Luigi Pirandello, text & context], pp. 135-203. Amsterdam: Frascati Theater Productions / International Theater & Film Books

Pollock, S.E. (1989) The hardiness characteristic: A motivating factor in adaptation. *Advances in Nursing Sciences*, 11, 53-62

Polti G. (1990 [1921]) *The thirty-six dramatic situations*. (Transl. by. L. Ray) Boston: The Writer Inc.

Porter, R.E. (1975) Analyzing rehearsal interaction. *Empirical Research in Theater*, 5, 1-32

Pott, H. (1992) *De liefde van Alcibiades: Over de rationaliteit van emoties. [The love of Alcibiades: On the rationality of emotions.]* Amsterdam: Boom Publ.

Powers, W.G., D.L. Jorns, and R.B. Glenn (1980) The effects of cognitive complexity on characterization depth and performance. *Empirical Research in Theater*, 7, 8-22

Pritner, J.A., and D.H. Lamb (1981) Actor anxiety and coping styles. *Empirical Research in Theater*, 7, 8-22

Proust, J. (1984) Interpreter Diderot aujourd'hui. [Interpreting Diderot today.] In: E. de Fontenay and J. Proust (eds.) *Interpreter Diderot aujourd'hui*, pp. 9-17. Parijs: Centre Culturel International de Cerisy-la-Salle, Le Sycomore, Colloque de Cerisy S.F.I.E.D.

Quinn, M.L. (1990) Celebrity and the semiotics of acting. *New Theater Quarterly*, 6, 154-161

Reisenzein, R. (1983) The Schachter theory of emotion: Two decades later. *Psychological Bulletin*, 94, 239-264

Richardson, D., and C. Waal (1966) Increasing the reliability of judgements of acting performance. *Journal of Speech*, 52, 378-382

Richter, H. (1957) Das Verstehen des Ausdrucksgehalts stehender und bewegter Bilder. [The understanding of stills and moving images of facial expressions.] *Berichte 21 Kongress Dtsch. Gesellschaft Psychologie* [Messages 21 Congress German Society of Psychology], Bonn, pp. 235-237

Roach, J.R. (1981) Diderot and the actor's machine. *Theater Survey*, 22, 51-68

Roach, J.R. (1985) *The players passion: Studies in the science of acting*. Newark: University of Delaware press / Londen and Toronto: Associated University Presses

Rougemont, M., De (1988) *La vie théâtrale en France au XVIIIème siècle. [Theatrical life in France in the 18 C.]* Paris, Fr.: Librairie Honoré Champion

Rovit, R.L. (1989) *The marionette as an ideal in acting: Dualism resolved in Craig's 'übermarionette', Meyerhold's biomechanics, and Schlemmer's stage workshop*. Ann Arbor, Michigan: UMI (diss., Florida State University)

Rudnitsky, K. (1981) *Meyerhold, the director*. (Transl. by G. Petrov). Ann Arbor, Michigan: Ardis

Russell, J.A. (1991) Culture and the categorization of emotions. *Psychological Bulletin*, 110, 426-450

Sanders, A.F. (1983) Towards a model of stress and human performance. *Acta Psychologica*, 53, 61-99

Sartre, J.P. (1971 [1936]) *Magie en emotie (Esquisse d'une théorie des émotions*. Paris: Hermann Publ., transl. in Dutch by L.M. Tas) [Outline of a theory on emotions.] Amsterdam: Boom Publ.

Savona, G. (1991) Brecht, politics, cinema. *Theater Studies*, 36, 3-17

Schachter, S. (1965) A cognitive-physiological view of emotion. In: O. Klineberg and R. Christie (eds.) *Perspectives in social psychology*, pp. 75-105. New York: Holt, Rinehart and Winston

Schachter, S., and J.E. Singer (1962) Cognitive, social, and physiological determinants of emotional state. *Psychological Review*, 69, 379-399

Schälzky, H. (1980) *Empirisch-Quantitative Methoden in der Theaterwissenschaft. [Empirical-Quantitative methods in Theater Studies.]* München, Germany: Münchener Universitätsschriften, Münchener Beitragen zur Theaterwissenschaft, Band 7, Kommissionsverlag J. Kitzinger

Schechner R. (1964) Stanislavski at school. *Tulane Drama Review*, 9, 198-211

Schechner R. (1991) Training interculturally. In: E. Barba and N. Savarese (eds.) *The secret art of the performer: A dictionary of theater anthropology*. New York/London: Routledge

Schechner R., and W. Appel (eds., 1990) *By means of performance: Intercultural studies of theater and ritual*. Cambridge: Cambridge University Press

Scherer, K.R. (1986) Vocal affect expression: A review and model for future research. *Psychological Bulletin*, 99, 143-165

Scherer, K.R. (1988) Cognitive antecedents of emotion. In: V. Hamilton, G.H. Bower, and N.H. Frijda (eds.). *Cognitive perspectives on emotion and motivation*, pp. 89-126. Dordrecht: Kluwer

Schoenmakers, H. (1986) The pleasure of sorrow / Die Freude am Kummer. In: H. Schoenmakers (ed.) *Performance theory. Advances in reception and audience research 1*, (special issue), Tijdschrift voor Theaterwetenschap, nr. 16/17, 117-150

Schoenmakers, H. (1988) To be, wanting to be, forced to be: Identification processes in theatrical situations. In: W. Sauter (ed.) *New directions in audience research. Advances in reception and audience research (2)*, (special issue), Tijdschrift voor Theaterwetenschap, nr. 24/25, 138-163

Schoenmakers, H. (1989) *Filosofie van de theaterwetenschappen*. [Philosophy of Theater Studies.] Leiden, NL: Martinus Nijhoff

Schoenmakers, H. (1990) The spectator in the leading role: Developments in reception and audience research within Theater Studies: Theory and research. In: W. Sauter (ed.). *Nordic Theater Studies: New directions in theater research*, (special international issue; proceedings of the XIth FIRT/IFTR congress), pp. 93-106. Stockholm/Kopenhagen, Sweden/Denmark: Munksgaard Int. Publ.

Schoenmakers, H. (1992) Aesthetic emotions and aestheticised emotions in theatrical situations. In: H. Schoenmakers (ed.) *Performance Theory. Advances in reception and audience research (3)*, (special issue), Tijdschrift voor Theaterwetenschap, nr. 31/32, 39-59

Schulz, P. (1987) Regulation und Fehlregulation im Verhalten: XII. Herausforderung und Bedrohung bei einer Koöperativen Tätigkeit. [Regulation and misregulation in relationship: XII. Challenge and threat in a cooperative action.] *Psychologische Beitrage*, 129, 198-220

Schyberg, F. (1961) The art of acting: What is an actor? (part 1) *Tulane Drama Review*, 5, 56-77

Selltiz, C., L.S. Wrightsman, and S.W. Cook (1976) *Research methods in social relations*. New York: Holt, Rineheart & Winston

Shields, S.A. (1984) Distinguishing between emotion and nonemotion: Judgements about experience. *Motivation and Emotion*, 8, 355-369

Sloman, C.L. (1972) Micro momentary facial expressions and the actor; an investigation. *Empirical Research in Theater*, 2, 52-60

Slotboom, A.J.J. (1991) *Statistiek in woorden. De meest voorkomende termen en technieken*. [Statistics in words. The most common concepts and techniques.] Groningen: Wolters-Noordhoff

Smith C.A., and P.C. Elsworth (1985) Patterns of cognitive appraisal in emotion. *Journal of Personality and Social Psychology*, 48, 813-838

Snyder, M. (1974) The self-monitoring of expressive behaviour. *Journal of Personality and Social Psychology*, 30, 526-537

Sonnemans, J. (1991) *Structure and determinants of emotional intensity*. Amsterdam: University of Amsterdam, Dept. of Psychology (diss.)

Souriau, E. (1950) *Les deux cent mille situations dramatiques*. [The two thousand situations in drama.] Paris, Fr.: Flammarion

Spear, F.A. (1980-1988) *Bibliographie de Diderot, répertoire analytique international*. [Bibliogaphy of Diderot, international analytic overview.] (See also: supplements to *Diderot Studies*, vols. 21 (1983); 22 (1986); 23 (rev. ed. 1988) (eds., O. Fellows, c.s.). Genève, Switzerland: Librairie Droz

Spink, J.S. (1977) Sentiment, sensible, sensibilité: Les mots, les idées, d'après les moralistes français et britanniques du début du dix-huitième siècle. [Sense, sensitive, sensibility: The words, the ideas, after the French and English moralists at the beginning of the 18th. C.]. *Zagadnienia Rodzajùw Literackick*, 22, 33-47

Stanislavsky, K. (1985; 1936) *Lessen voor acteurs* (part 1). [An actor prepares, New York: E. Hapgood, transl. in Dutch by Anja van den Tempel]. Amsterdam: International Theater & Film Books

Stanislavsky, K. (1989; 1949) *Lessen voor acteurs* (part 2). [Building a character, New York: Theater Arts Books/Methuen, transl. by J. van Omme and A. van den Tempel]. Amsterdam: International Theater & Film Books

Stanislavsky, K. (1991; 1961) *Lessen voor acteurs* (part 3). [Creating a role, New York: Theater Arts Books/ Methuen, transl. by J. van Omme]. Amsterdam: International Theater & Film Books

States B.O. (1983) The actor's presence: Three phenomenal modes. *Theater Journal*, 35, 359-375

Steptoe, A. (1983) Stress, helplessness and control: The implications of laboratory studies. *Journal of Psychosomatic Research*, 27, 361-367

Stern, R.M., and N.L. Lewis (1968) Ability of actors to control their GSR's and express emotions. *Psychophysiology*, 4, 294-299

Sticotti, A. (1769) *Garrick, ou les acteurs anglais, ouvrage contenant des observations sur l'art dramatique, sur l'art de la représentation, et le jeu des acteurs; avec des notes historiques et critiques, et des anecdotes sur les différent théâtres de Londres et de Paris*. [Garrick, or the English actors, work containing observations on the dramatic art, the art representation, and the art of acting; with historical notes, comments, and anecdotes on the different theaters in London and Paris.] Paris, Fr.: Flammarion (in-8)

Stockwell, J.C., and C.W. Bahs (1973) Body buffer zone and proxemics in blocking. *Empirical Research in Theater*, 3, 27-41

Stotland, E. (1969) Exploratory studies of empathy. In: L. Berkowitz (ed.) *Advances in experimental social psychology* (Vol. 4), pp. 271-314. New York: Academic Press

Strasberg, L. (1988; ed. by E. Morphos) *A dream of passion: The development of the Method*. London: Bloomsbury, Davada Enterprises

Strongman, K.T. (1987; 3th rev. ed.) *The psychology of emotion*. New York: John Wiley

Styan, J.L. (1975) *The dramatic experience*. Cambridge: Cambridge University Press

SUN (1972) *Bertolt Brecht, teaterexperiment en politiek*. [Bertolt Brecht, theater experiment and politics.] Nijmegen, NL: SUN Publ.

Szondi, P. (1984) Denis Diderot: Théorie et pratique dramatique. [Denis Diderot: Theory and practice of drama.] In: J. Starobinski, J. Chouillet, G.E. Lessing, c.s. (eds.) *Diderot (Diderot et le théâtre)*, pp. 3362. Paris, Fr.: Comédie-Française, Grands Dramaturges

Tan, E.S.H. (1996) *Emotion and the structure of narrative film; film as an emotion machine*. Mahwah, New Jersey: Erlbaum Ass. Publ.

Tas, L.M. (1971 [1966]) Introductory comments to J.P. Sartre's *Magie en emotie*. [Outline of a theory on emotions.] Amsterdam/Meppel: Boom Publ.

Toneel Theatraal (editorial board of the journal *Toneel Theatraal*), Jaarboek seizoen 1990. [Year book of the season 1990]. Amsterdam: Theater Institute the Netherlands (TIN)

Tort, P. (1980; 1976) *La partition intérieur: L'origine du paradoxe sur le comédien.* [*The interior partition: The origin of the Paradox on the actor.*] Paris, Fr.: Sycomore

Trauth, S.M. (1980) Effects of director's system of communication on actor inventiveness and rehearsal atmosphere. *Empirical Research in Theater*, 6, 6-17

Tucker, P. (1994) *Secrets of screen acting.* London/ New York: Routledge

Tucker, D.M., and S.L. Dawson (1984) Asymmetric EEG changes as method actors generated emotion. *Biological Psychology*, 19, 63-75

Vagi, A.B., and H.M. Lefcourt (1988) Investigativeness as a moderator of stress. *Canadian Journal of Behavioral Science*, 20, 93-108

Vartanian, A. (1983) LaMettrie and Diderot revisited: An intertextual encounter. *Diderot Studies*, 221, 155-198

Veltrusky, J. (1978) Contribution to the semiotics of acting. *Michigan Slavic Contributions*, nr. 6, 553-606

Verbeek, Th. (1977) *Inleiding tot de geschiedenis van de psychologie.* Utrecht, NL/ Antwerp, Belgium: Het Spectrum (Aula nr. 614)

Verbeek, Th. (1978-79) Diderot en de problemen van het materialisme. [Diderot and the problems of materialism.] *Wijsgerig Perspectief op Maatschappij en Wetenschap.* [*Philosophical Perspective on Society and Science.*], 19, 110-113

Verbeek, Th. (1980) Introduction and notes to *De droom van d'Alembert.* [*The dream of d'Alembert.*] Amsterdam: Boom Publ.

Vernière, P. (1959): see Diderot (1959)

Villiers, A. (1942; ps. Bonnichon) *La psychologie du comédien.* [*The psychology of the actor.*] Paris, Fr.: Odette Livetier, Mercure de France

Villiers, A. (1968) *L'art du comédien.* [*The art of the actor.*] Paris, Fr.: Presses Universitaires de France

Vliet, H., Van, (1991) *De schone schijn: Een analyse van psychologische processen in de beleving van fictionaliteit en werkelijkheid bij theatrale producten.* [*Attractive appearances: An analysis of psychological processes in the experience of fiction and reality in theatrical products.*] Utrecht, NL: Utrecht University, Dept. of Theater, Film, and Television Studies (diss.)

Völker, K. (1978) *Bertolt Brecht, eine Biografie.* [*Bertolt Brecht, a biography.*] München, Germany: Deutschen Taschenbuch Verlag

Wallbott, H.G. (1988) Aus dem Zusammenhang gerissen: Schauspielermimik ohne Kontextinformation. [Taken out of context: Facial expressions of actors without contextual information.] *Zeitschrift für Experimentelle und Angewandte Psychologie*, 35, 596-610

Wallbott, H.G., and K.R. Scherer, (1986) Cues and channels in emotion recognition. *Journal of Personality and Social Psychology*, 51, 690-699

Walters, K.S. (1989) The law of apparent reality and aesthetic emotions. *American Psychologist*, 44, 1545-1546

Wang, K. (1984) Research on the feeling mind of actors during creative performances. *Information on Psychological Sciences*, nr. 6, 30-33

Wartofsky, M.W. (1952) Diderot and the development of materialist monism. *Diderot Studies*, 2, 279-330

Watson, I. (1988) Catharsis and the actor. *New Theater Quarterly*, 4, 306-314

Wayne-Smith, R. (1971) Actor-character personality identification in a theater production. *Empirical Research in Theater*, 1, 29-38

Weisweiler, H. (1983) *Die Belastung des Schauspielers an seinem Arbeitsplatz. [The stress of the actor in his working environment.]* Munich, Germany: Munich University (Münchener Universität), Dept. of Theater Studies (diss.)

Weisweiler, H. (1985) Die Belastung des Schauspielers auf der Bühne. [The stress of the actor on the stage]. *Münchener Medizinische Wochenschrift*, 127, 723-724

White, R.W. (1959) Motivation reconsidered: The concept of competence. *Psychological Review*, 66, 297-333

Williams, J.M.G., C.M. MacLeod, A. Matthews, and F. Watts (1988) *Cognitive Psychology and emotional disorders.* London, UK: John Wiley

Wilson, A.M. (1961) The biographical implications of Diderot's 'paradoxe sur le comédien'. *Diderot Studies*, 3, 369-383

Worthen, W.B. (1983) Stanislavsky and the ethics of acting. *Theater Journal*, 35, 32-40

Worthen, W.B. (1984) *The idea of the actor: Drama and the ethics of performance.* Princeton: Princeton University Press

Wuertz, R. (1971) When actors memorize lines: An examination of three methods. *Empirical Research in Theater*, 1, 15-22

Zajonc, R.B. (1965) Social Facilitation. *Science*, 149, 269-275

Zajonc, R.B. (1984) On the primacy of affect. *American Psychologist*, 39, 117-123

Zajonc, R.B. (1985) Emotion and facial efference: A theory reclaimed. *Science*, 228, 15-21

Zajonc, R.B., S.T. Murphy, and M. Inglehart (1989) Feeling and facial efference: Implications of the vascular theory of emotion. *Psychological Review*, nr. 3/96, 395-416

Zajonc, R.B., and S.M. Sales (1966) Social facilitation of dominant and subordinate responses. *Journal of Experimental Social Psychology*, 2, 160-168

Zarrilli, Ph. (1990) What does it mean to 'become the character': Power, presence, and transcedence in Asian in-body disciplines of practice. In: R. Schechner and W. Appel (eds.). *By means of performance*, pp. 131-149. Cambridge: Cambridge University Press

Zarilli, Ph. (ed., 1995) *Acting (Re)considered.* London/New York: Routledge.

Zillman, D. (1988) Mood management: Using entertainement to full advantage. In: L. Donohew, H.E. Sypher, and E. ToryHiggins (eds.) *Communication, social cognition and affect.* Hillsdale, N.J.: Erlbaum.

Zillman, D., and J. Bryant (1974) Effect of residual excitation on the emotional response to provocation and delayed aggressive behavior. *Journal of Personality and Social Psychology*, 30, 782-791

Zuckerman, M. (1979) *Sensation seeking.* Hillsdale, N.J.: Erlbaum

Zuckerman, M. (1988) Behavior and biology: Research on sensation seeking and reactions to the media. In: L. Donohew, H.E. Sypher, and E. ToryHiggins (eds.) *Communication, social cognition and affect*, pp. 173-194. Hillsdale, N.J.: Erlbaum

Zuckerman, M., M.S. Buchsbaum, and D.L. Murphy (1980) Sensation seeking and its biological correlates. *Psychological Bulletin*, 88, 187-214

Appendix

Figure 7.19: Comparison of Character-emotions and Actors' Emotions Concerning the Accompanying Action Tendencies (NL = the Netherlands, including Flanders).

Figure 7.20: Comparison of Character-emotions and Actors' Emotions Concerning the Accompanying Action Tendencies (US = the United States).

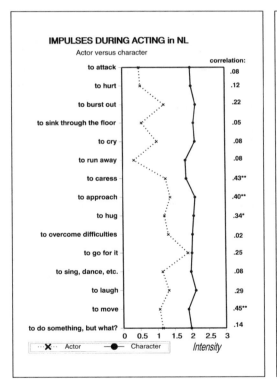

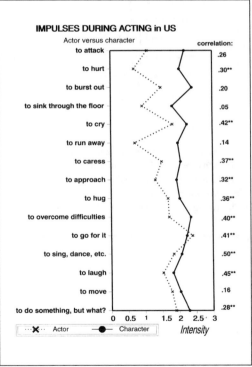

Explanation: To the left of the figure, fifteen words describing emotional impulses or action tendencies are listed. The dotted line indicates the average intensity of the impulses of the actors during the performance. The solid line indicates the degree to which these impulses were portrayed in characters on stage. The lines link the average values per line describing an action tendency. The averages lie between 0 (not at all applicable) and 3 (applicable to a very great extent).

Figure 7.21: Physical Reactions Accompanying the Actors' Emotions During Performance (NL).

Figure 7.22: Physical Reactions Accompanying the Actors' Emotions During Performance (US).

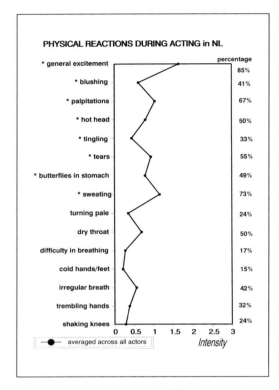

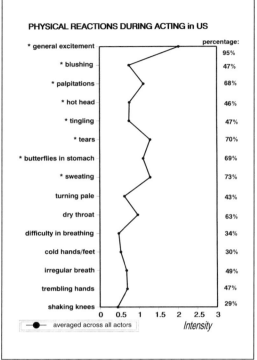

Explanation: To the left of the figure, fifteen words describing physical sensations that might accompany particular emotions are listed. The line indicates the average intensity of the physical reactions for those actors who reported to experience any of them. To the right of the figure the percentages are given for how many actors in the sample indicated that they experienced the sensation. It is only for these actors that the line links the average values of physical reactions. The averages lie between 0 (not at all applicable) and 3 (applicable to a very great extent).

An * indicates the physical sensations associated with excitement.

Glossary

Acting styles:

Style of detachment: Style of acting which rejects identification of the actor with the character. This style is most strongly associated with Brecht.

Style of involvement: Style of acting which aims to present character-emotions in such a way as to achieve the illusion of 'truth' or 'reality.' The actor himself should not be visible in the portrayal of the character. This style is associated with Stanislavsky.

Style of self-expression: Style of acting in which the expression of the inner self and of the actor's authentic emotions is of central importance.

Acting styles, aspects of: On the basis of statistical analyses, four separate aspects of acting styles were distinguished: (1) 'Letting oneself be carried away by the character'; (2) 'experiencing a similarity between the actor and the character'; (3) 'applying task-emotions' and (4) aspects relating to the 'technical design'.

Acting tasks: The tasks of an actor during a performance. These involve, among others, giving believable and convincing expression to the inner model.

Actor-craftsman: See **Levels of enactment**

Actor's dilemma, the: The question as to what degree the actor's emotions correspond to those of the character portrayed. To what extent may an actor lose his head if he acts with his heart (and vice versa)?

Action tendencies (impulses; inclinations): A change in the readiness to take action (Frijda, 1986: 69-73) a tendency, inclination, or impulse to refrain from taking action. An action tendency is directed toward a change in one's relationships with others or with one's environment with the aim of receiving specific satisfaction for a specific concern. An emotion is characterized by, among other things, a specific corresponding action tendency.

Arousal: Physiological activation, physical excitement.

Basic emotions: See **Prototypical emotions**

Character-emotions: The presentation of a character's 'emotions' as portrayed by the actor in the performance. Character-emotions are the realization of intended emotions on stage in performance.

Cognitive theory of emotion: Emotion theory as formulated by, among others, the Dutch psychologist, Nico H. Frijda (1986), in which cognitions are primary to the emotion process (as opposed to the peripheral feedback theory). In this theory, emotions are considered as functional expressions of the individual in reaction to his environment, aimed toward furthering his interests.

Concerns: Desires, needs, passions, and personality traits. The emotion process (according to Frijda) revolves around, as it were, looking after these concerns.

Contextual components: Characteristics in a situation that determine which sort of emotion will arise. In addition to the core components, contextual components determine whether it is possible to take action in a given context and how difficult it might be to do so. This action will be directed toward benefitting personal interests. The task situation of the actor on stage involves two important contextual components: Controllability or lack thereof and familiarity or lack thereof.

Context evaluation (See 'diagnoser' in the emotion process in Frijda 1986: 454): The situation or event is evaluated in order to judge whether the person can cope with the situation and, subsequently, what action he can best take. This judgment signals the main contextual components and determines which emotion will arise.

Controllability: Concerns the actor's capacity to cope with the demands of the situation. Controllability (or lack of it) is a contextual component in the emotion process.

Control precedence (in Frijda 1986: 471-2): When feelings, thoughts, impulses, or actions corresponding with emotions, which have been evoked or have arisen, take precedence over other thoughts, feelings, impulses, etc. which were intended or are being expressed. Refers 'to general control of action in the organism: interruption of other activities, preoccupation and persistence of activity...' (Frijda, 1986: 472)

Core components: Determine whether the heart of a situation is potentially favorable or harmful to the concerns of a person. Of the many different features in a situation, there are only a few which are meaningful in respect to one or more concerns. Only if a situation contains some of these meaningful features, can we say that this situation has core components which cause emotions to arise. For an actor in the acting situation there are six important core components: Objectivity, reality, valence, demand character, difficulty, and urgency.

Demand character: To command attention by addressing concerns and because the event, person or situation is of interest (Frijda 1986: 207). Demand character is the core component in the emotional process which corresponds with interest, wonder, or curiosity, but also with concentration and challenge.

Detachment: see **Acting style detachment**

Difficulty: The demands made on the actor are generally great as far as the task is concerned, but the situation itself is also a difficult one in terms of realizing personal concerns. Executing a complex task such as acting emotions in a theater performance while one or more people watch generally leads to stress or tension. Difficulty is a core component in the emotion process.

Double consciousness (*dédoublement*): To get wrapped up in emotions corresponding to those of the character emotions being portrayed, while simultaneously controlling them.

Emotional layers: Emotions which can be distinguished at each level of enactment: The private emotions of the actor as private person; the task-emotions of the actor as craftsman; the intended emotions according to the inner model; and the character-emotions as portrayed in the performance.

Emotions: functional expressions of the individual's reaction to the environment. Emotions serve personal motives, needs, or concerns with respect to pleasure and pain, attraction, and rejection (according to Frijda 1986).

Empathy: refers to the source concern of 'interest in the well being of fellow men' or concerns of 'closeness and connection' and 'intimacy', or with the need to sympathize (Frijda 1986: 215; Tan 1996: 156). These concerns can in part be traced to a specific sensitivity toward the suffering or needs in others, provoking caring behavior. Unselfishness or empathetic emotions include pity, compassion, taking pleasure in the misfortune of others, sympathy, admiration, and fascination (see also **Identification and empathy**).

Familiarity: unknown-familiar is a dual (contextual) component in the actor's task situation. The professional actor is familiar with the piece, with what he has to do, with his fellow actors, and so forth. At the same time, there are significant unknown factors like audience composition during a given performance, the course of events in a particular performance time-frame, and the alertness of the actor, his colleagues, technicians, etc.

Flow: The right balance between the risk of failure and control of the situation which results in experiencing the execution of tasks as though happening by themselves, as though accomplished in a fluid movement. Flow stems from a balanced relationship between challenging (risky) elements of a situation and the required skills.

Ideal model: see **Inner model**

Identification: A process through which the observer arrives at the same emotions as those of the observed other. 'Those processes by which the subject places himself in the situation of the object and, in so doing, experiences the same emotions which he or she supposes the object to have' (Schoenmakers 1988: 142) (see also **Identification and empathy**).

Identification and empathy: Terms within the category of 'involvement' which are used interchangeably. Empathy and identification are themselves not emotions, but processes by which to arrive at qualitatively comparative emotions between individuals. Both processes have in common that the condition of another, as the object of emotion, becomes parts of the emotional experience of the observer. The most notable difference between empathy and identification is the separation (with empathy), respectively absence of separation (with identification) from oneself, as the observer, and the other. (See also **Identification** and **Empathy**).

Impulses: See **Action tendencies**

Inner model (*modèle idéal*): The (portrayal of the) character as imagined by the actor.

Intended emotions: The emotions corresponding to the inner model. These are the emotions (of characters) as the actor aims to portray them. A mental image of the way the actor wants to depict the character-emotions on stage.

Involvement: See **Acting style involvement** as well as **Identification and empathy**

Levels of enactment: Four levels of action can be distinguished from the actor's viewpoint: (1) The actor as private person; (2) the actor as actor-craftsman; (3) the inner model (*modèle idéal*) or the idea of how the character will be; and (4) the character as presented by the actor in performance. The *spectator* will, in general, perceive all four levels of enactment as one composite.

Method acting: Method to achieve a high degree of involvement of actors with character-emotions; a method within the category of the involvement style. Method acting was developed by Strasberg on the basis of Stanislavky's ideas.

Modèle idéal: See **Inner model**

Peripheral feedback theory: In this theory, physical phenomena are seen as the primary input of the emotion process; first the physical reaction occurs, then the emotion (I shiver, thus I am afraid). Also called the James-Lange theory. The peripheral feedback theory stands in opposition to the cognitive emotion theory.

Physiological feedback theory: See **Peripheral feedback theory**

Private emotions: The actor's private emotions belong to the general human emotions as they appear in daily life.

Prototypical emotions (basic emotions): The most typical character-emotions are connected with conflict situations such as despair, anger, revenge, hate, fear, jealousy, revulsion, but also with love, eroticism, tenderness, pleasure, and happiness. Such emotions which are specific to dramatic characters and are comparable to what in psychological literature are called basic or prototypical emotions.

Reality: An essential core component for the emergence of an emotion: 'The emotional involvement varies with the degree of reality. (…) A situation can be relevant in principle, but only as play, in fantasy or in the abstract' (Frijda 1988: 352). For the emergence of 'real' emotions to arise, the situation must be judged as 'real', as having a high level of reality, and concerns must really be at stake.

Regulation: The suppression or masking of emotional aspects experienced as negative or inappropriate. In daily life, regulation is often an unconscious process (according to Frijda). In the acting process, regulation involves the conscious use of aspects of task-emotions to support the portrayal of character-emotions. In acting this is called shaping.

Relevance evaluation (see 'comparator' in the emotion process in Frijda 1986: 454): The situation or event is appraised in order to determine whether concerns are at stake. This appraisal determines whether or not an emotion will arise.

Self-expression: See **Acting style self-expression**

Source concerns: Refer to general concerns and motives related to desired situations and goals (among others, safety and competency).

Stage fright (*le trac, Lampenfieber*): A kind of impatient nervousness prior to role interpretation which usually disappears quickly (Villiers 1942: 148; 209).

Surface concerns: Refer to the specific concerns related to concrete goals, persons, and objects (for example the comforts of home); often the concrete form of more general or abstract source concerns.

Task-emotions: Emotions which stem from the level of enactment of the actor as craftsman. Task-emotions are emotions connected with executing acting tasks on stage.

Task-emotion theory: Psychological approach to acting in which the actor is considered an actor-craftsman – as someone who does his work in a certain way, under specific conditions. According to the task-emotion theory, the actor does not experience the emotions of the character, but the emotions which are related to executing the acting tasks themselves, namely in the situation of a public performance.

Urgency: One of the core components which scores high for the actor. The audience wants to see the performance right now; there is a need to act immediately since later it will be too late.

Urgency assessment (see 'evaluator' in the emotion process in Frijda 1986: 454): The intensity of the emotion is determined by how serious, urgent, and difficult the situation is. The more serious, urgent, and difficult, the more intense the emotion.

Valence (a step in the emotion process in Frijda 1986: 190, 207; after Lewin 1937): Emotional value deriving from control and the expectation that source concerns can be satisfied, as well as the chance for appreciation and success, make this a positive core component in acting. When the actor can transform the risk of failure into success, then the situation takes on positive emotional value (positive valence corresponds with attraction, negative valence with aversion).

List of Illustrations

Chapter 2

page 23: The text is copied from an original page in a manuscript of the *Paradoxe* in P. Vernière (ed. 1959) *Diderot: Oeuvres Esthétique* Paris: Garnier Frères. The portrait of Denis Diderot, which is assembled through the text, is a drawing by Garand made in 1760 after a portrait that Garand painted earlier, but which has been lost (see H. Dieckman's 'Description of a portrait' in the series *Diderot Studies II*, eds. O. Fellows & N. Torrey (1952), Syracuse University Press).

page 27: Drawings of the '18th Century acting style' by G. Austin (1806) in D. Barnett (1987, appendix: pp. 543-4) *The art of gesture: The practices and principles of 18th C. acting*, Heidelberg: Winter.

page 32: Photograph of the actress Chris Nietvelt as *Lulu* in the performance of the same name of Theater Company [NL: Toneelgroep] Amsterdam in co-production with Theater Company De Tijd, directed by Ivo van Hove, season 1988-1989, from the archive of Toneelgroep Amsterdam.

page 32: Photograph of the actress Kitty Courbois as *Medea* in the performance of the same name of Theater Company [NL: Toneelgroep] Amsterdam, directed by Gerardjan Rijnders, season 1988-1989, from the archive of Toneelgroep Amsterdam.

Chapter 3

page 37: Photograph of Konstantin Stanislavsky in K. Rudnitsky (1988, p. 38) *Russian and Soviet theater 1905-1932*. London: Thames and Hudson Ltd.

page 40: Photograph of Bertolt Brecht in Zürich 1949. In: K. Völker (1976, pp. 224-225) *Bertolt Brecht, Eine Biografie*. München, Wenen: Hanser Verlag.

page 42: Photograph of Jerzy Grotowski in P. Brook (1987, p. 39) *The shifting point*. New York: Theater Communications Group.

page 44-45: The 'masks created solely by the facial muscles' are taken from J. Grotowski (1968, p. 71) *Towards a poor theater*. Holstebro, Denmark: Christensen & Co.

page 51: Photograph of Peter Brook in P. Brook (1987, p. 166) *The shifting point*. New York: Theater Communications Group.

Chapter 4

page 74: Graph of an actress's heart rate while in rehearsal and in performance, reprinted from E. A. Konijn (1994, p. 98) *Acteurs Spelen Emoties [Actors Act Emotions]*. Amsterdam: Boom.

page 78: Photograph of the actor Fred Goessens (left) and the actresss Sigrid Koetse and Catherine ten Bruggencate (right) in the performance *Andromaché* of Toneelgroep Amsterdam, directed by Gerardjan Rijnders, season 1990-1991, archive Toneelgroep Amsterdam. The acting style in the performance was grafted onto the French Classicistic style of performing.

Chapter 5

page 97: Spontaneous (a) facial expression of disgust (while smelling a vile mixture) of actor Felix-Jan Kuypers (actor at Theater Company The Amsterdam Woods). Photograph taken by E. Konijn, July 1997.

page 97: Posed (b) facial expression of disgust of actor Felix-Jan Kuypers, while being asked to act his reaction to smelling a vile mixture. Photograph taken by E. Konijn, July 1997.

Chapter 6

page 121: One page copied from a completed and returned questionnaire of one of the professional American actors who responded to the survey (anonymously).

Chapter 7

page 125-137: The figures in this chapter and in the appendix are created by the author.

Chapter 8

page 152: Cartoon by Johan Hoorn, February 22, 2000.

page 162: Spontaneous (a) facial expression of happiness (with a spark of posedness?) of actor Felix-Jan Kuypers, directly after the performance *Om de liefde van Laurentia [For the love of Laurentia]* of Theater Company The Amsterdam Woods, directed by Frances Sanders 1997. Photograph taken by E. Konijn, July 1997.

Index

About the Author

Elly A. Konijn (1959) studied several years in practically oriented acting schools to become an actress. Since 1981, she studied Psychology, Theater Studies and Social Scientific Computer Sciences at the University of Amsterdam, while working in several fields of theater practice. In June 1988 she got her Master's degree (in Dutch: Drs., 'Old Style') in Psychology Cum Laude and continued as an assistant researcher at the Department of Theater Studies at Utrecht University in the Netherlands. In collaboration with the Faculty of Psychology (University of Amsterdam) she studied acting emotions onstage, which resulted in her PhD thesis in June 1994. The thesis was published by BOOM in Amsterdam, entitled *Actors Acting Emotions, shaping emotions on stage from a psychological perspective*. In 1997 she wrote an upgraded version in collaboration with Astrid Westerbeek: *Acting and Emotions*. Since 1995 Elly Konijn also studies, as a postdoctoral researcher, the perception and emotional experiences of spectators while watching fictional characters in theater, film, or television. She published several articles and she lectures on the relationships between emotions of actor, character, and spectator. For instance, she was a keynote speaker at the FIRT/IFTR world-congress in Moscow 1994. She also lectures on psychological approaches towards the field of Theater, Film, and Television Studies, not only theoretically but about the empirical research methods as well. At present she works as a postdoctoral researcher for the Netherlands Organization for Scientific Research (NWO) in The Hague, hosted at the *Vrije* University in Amsterdam, and she is an associate professor at the department of Theater, Film, and Television Studies at Utrecht University.